Theory in an Uneven World

D1568227

This book is dedicated to Surya
With love, respect, and gratitude
For teaching me how to live in the moment
And combine the work ethic with the pleasure principle.

Theory in an Uneven World

R. Radhakrishnan

Blackwell
Publishing

© 2003 by R. Radhakrishnan

350 Main Street, Malden, MA 02148-5020, USA
108 Cowley Road, Oxford OX4 1JF, UK
550 Swanston Street, Carlton, Victoria 3053, Australia

The right of R. Radhakrishnan to be identified as the Author of this Work has been asserted in accordance with the UK Copyright, Designs, and Patents Act 1988.

All rights reserved. No part of this publication may be reproduced, stored in a retrieval system, or transmitted, in any form or by any means, electronic, mechanical, photocopying, recording or otherwise, except as permitted by the UK Copyright, Designs, and Patents Act 1988, without the prior permission of the publisher.

First published 2003 by Blackwell Publishing Ltd

Library of Congress Cataloging-in-Publication Data has been applied for.

ISBN 0-631-17537-7 (hardback); ISBN 0-631-17538-5 (paperback)

A catalogue record for this title is available from the British Library.

Set in 10/12½ pt minion
by SNP Best-set Typesetter Ltd., Hong Kong
Printed and bound in the United Kingdom
by MPG Books Ltd, Bodmin, Cornwall

For further information on
Blackwell Publishing, visit our website:
http://www.blackwellpublishing.com

B842
.R34
2003x

0 54807333

Contents

Preface

I have always thought of theory in its broadest, "universal" meaning as being both worldly (in the Saidian sense) *and* intentionally out of sync with the world. Theory can be legitimately worldly only if it states and elaborates the conditions of its non-acceptance of the world. To put it differently, theory cannot be an acquiescence in the status quo. With one foot in and one foot out, theory has to straddle the punishing and crippling givenness of the world and the utopian–transcendent urge to imagine otherwise. Historicity and facticity cannot be ends in themselves as far as theory is concerned. It is only by invoking and gesturing symptomatically and namelessly towards "the after" that theory earns its legitimacy, its ineluctable but dissenting worldliness. Between solidarity and critique, theory opens up a space that is neither captive to the "world as it is," nor naively credulous of visions of "the world as it should be."

I am aware that such a mandate on behalf of theory might sound totalizing and falsely universalistic, hence my thematic insistence on "unevenness" as a category. Paradoxical and cynical as it may sound, what makes the world "thinkable" as one, in all its relationality, is the symptomatic richness of the term "unevenness." Once we enfranchise unevenness as a fundamental semantic principle, it becomes impossible to think of, say, "prosperity" and "development" without symptomatic–diagnostic reference to "poverty" and "underdevelopment." Contrary to friction-free visions of globalization based on the motto "The Elites and the Haves of the World Unite" (in ruthless denial of injustice and inequality, and in passionate celebration of "trickle down" visions of socioeconomic justice), theory's thematization of "unevenness" achieves the following effect: "the symptomatic *immanentization* of unevenness." Let me explain. Theory here follows a deeply ethical impulse. Whereas merely historico-political blueprints of progress, development, and techno-globalization can afford to characterize "unevenness" as the hapless shibboleth of "losers," or justify it as an inevitable result of a world-historical and hence unipolar capitalism, an ethically inspired and motivated theory dares to envision cooperations and solidarities across the divide and the asymmetry. To put it simply, it is only on the basis of such a theoretical ethic that a young entrepreneurial billionaire can be persuaded to feel, perceive, and understand his or her reality as an inhabitant symptom of global unevenness – as much of a symptom as the abject and voiceless poverty of a homeless being anywhere in the world. In other words, within the etiology as well as the pathology of the disease, both the billionaire with a plutocratic lifestyle and the instant-to-instant contingency of the homeless person are co-symptomatic.

Something is "radically wrong" with the pleasurable reality of the billionaire. To invoke Herman Melville: the stories of the narrating lawyer, of Wall Street, and of Bartleby in *Bartleby, the Scrivener* are all co-symptomatic of the disease called global capitalism. The thematization of unevenness across locations and subject positions is a guarantee against the unconscionable *naïveté* or heartlessness of manifestos such as: "How can I be symptomatic of unevenness when I am a winner and not a loser?" or "As a winner I have conquered and transcended unevenness; so why can't he, she, or they?" In a way what I am suggesting is compatible with Freud's generalization and "quotidianization" of pathology. Every reality, whatever its geopolitical location, is a surface expression of an underlying unevenness; therefore, each reality is obliged in its self-presentation to include as a constitutive prolegomenon its specific and determinate relationship to the abiding subtending unevenness. Clarissa Dalloway and her high society are as much a pathological symptom of colonial London in the wake of World War I as is the suicidal, schizophrenic, posttraumatic stress-disordered Septimus Warren Smith.

Why then look to theory to do justice to "differences in identity" and "identification despite differences?" Theory, in the best sense of the term, enables the subject to see beyond his or her nose in active and proactive acknowledgment of similarities and commonalities across situations and locations. Here, I attempt to infuse into theory a sensibility or a capacity that Amitav Ghosh calls in his novel *The Shadow Lines* "imagining with precision." What is being imagined is at the same time internal and external to the imagination. "What is" is just not enough or satisfactory, and therefore reality has to be imagined otherwise. At the same time, such an imagining is neither wildly capricious nor non-referential; indeed, it has the obligation to be precise. It should be precise with respect to the way things ought to be and precise with respect to a vision whose reality is otherwise than the solidity of the world as it is. In a move that is at once both representational and post-representational, Ghosh's narrative intelligence finds a way to dwell critically in "the shadow lines" of regnant identity regimes, and thereby render the very authority of those regimes "shadowy." In the radical and vertiginous cartographic reordering of the world that Ghosh's protagonist imagines towards the end of the novel, a newness is born: a newness in and of the imagination. If only the world could be imagined that way! – new and emergent perceptions of nearness and distance; longdenied and repressed affirmations of solidarities and fellow-heartedness in transgression of dominant relationships and axes of power; new and emergent identifications and recognitions in profound alienation from canonical–dominant mystifications and fixations of identity. What is most appealing (sensuously and affectively) and persuasive (theoretically and cognitively) about this reordering is the rigor with which it attempts to align, connect, and cathect experiential impulses with a meta-level reflexivity. In other words, the critical–utopian desire of Ghosh's novel insists that the world – structurally, systemically, cartographically – cannot remain the way it is if new realities are to be ushered in and celebrated. To state it obversely, the staging of these new registers of being demands a different stage, a different performative space. This world exists *in theory, and therefore in principle and reality*. The novel resolutely refuses to surrender reality to "what is," the facticity of history. That precisely is why and how *The Shadow Lines* is theoretical and fictional within and about itself: its abiding commitment to referentiality is realized as a critical function of its disobedience of referentiality in its available and dominant manifestations.

Theory can help build connections and find common ground where they seem least likely or plausible (here again I am indebted to Edward Said), whereas a merely locational immurement in one's own history can actively militate against the capacity of the subject to generalize, or honor the historicity in an "other" history. Theory, I believe, can be invoked in much the same way "Poesie" was valorized by Philip Sidney as superior to the non-ideal and non-transformative descriptive facticity of history on the one hand, and the utterly other-worldly and esoteric complexity of philosophy on the other. The provocative argument that Sidney constructs takes the form of a post-veracious claim on behalf of the "veracity of Poesie." The poet can neither lie nor tell the truth, for he does not deal in truths and lies: that indeed is his superior truthfulness.

True, theory has been deservedly in disrepute for its complicity with a variety of dominant "isms," and for trying to anoint itself as a transhistorical form of knowledge. The cry "Always historicize" was intended as a powerful antidote to the self-indulgent excesses of "high theory." Just as I argue in chapter 5 in the case of Nadine Gordimer's *Burger's Daughter* and "dominance in deconstruction" in general, it is precisely because these sins of omission and commission have been internal to the body/history of theory, that theory is a desirable and viable site for projects of "correction," transformation, and "self-consciencization." Nowhere else has "representation" been posed both as poison and remedy, as problem and answer, as oppression and liberation, to such an extent than within the symptomatic body of "theory." Whereas in the realms of politics and history, "representation" continues to be exercised axiomatically, correctly, and virtuously, it is "in theory" that representation is besmirched, compromised, and compelled to view itself "otherwise." And that is a good thing.

What, then, about unevenness? In theory, unevenness is a symptom to be "enjoyed" in a Žižekian psychoanalytic sense of the term, and thematized intransitively even as its virulent transitive effects are to be resisted and combated transitively. I certainly do not advocate a historically truncated experience of "symptom as *jouissance*"; instead, I point to a rigorous critical sensibility that will dwell in the symptom, speak from within the symptom, and only on that basis initiate the discourse of cure and remediation. In other words, in my vocabulary, theory, unevenness, and double consciousness function together as powerful coordinates. If there is unevenness between the "West" and the "Rest" (and of course there is), the most rigorous and systemic way to dismantle this unevenness is through a critical instrumentalization of double consciousness, and not through a disavowal of it. There is indeed a qualitative difference between merely inheriting unevenness as a given world-historical condition, and making it work against itself through critical exercises of double consciousness. Unlike a few decades ago, when postmodernism enjoyed an exemplary hold over the flows and movements of "post-ality," now, on the basis of the historical realities of "double consciousness," the "post-" has traveled, and not necessarily in celebration of its metropolitan/European provenance. And just as discourses of Eurocentric modernity have been taught to understand themselves as "colonial modernity," so too, the Eurocentrically avant-gardist "post-" has been hybridized, relativized, and radically reterritorialized and deterritorialized in response to postcolonial subaltern and non-Western histories and cultural formations. As Edward Said would have it, it is through travel that theory is made to divest itself of its dominance and its hubris of avant-gardism. My only significant departure from Said is that I do not necessarily see any antagonism between "theory" and "critical consciousness." I discuss some of this in my treatment of Said and Spivak in chapter 5.

In a sense, what I am calling for is a more subtle and inflected relationship between "Always historicize" and "Always theorize." Sometimes and often enough, when history and histories become vertical traps from which the subject is unable to escape, it may not be a bad idea to combine a certain kind of strategic "over-theorizing" with a certain kind of strategic "under-historicizing." As I have tried to maintain throughout this volume, it is only through these strategies that a "common humanity" entrenched in different histories and historiographies can delineate a transcendent ethical horizon that is not reducible to the merely historico-political. The virulently overdetermined binary oppositions of self and other in a variety of macro-political contexts are in need of a double strategy: historico-political measures to rectify imbalances within the binary unevenness have to be co-thought with ethico-theoretical gestures towards alterity as such. Perhaps it is in the name of a post-political persuasion (i.e., a persuasion that will last beyond the polemicized heat and urgency of the moment), the kind that Mohandas Gandhi strove for all his life, that this book makes a big deal of the figure of the hyphen, which both conjoins and differentiates ethics and politics, history and theory. I hope my discussion of the triangulated relationship among ethics, epistemology, and politics, by way of Gayatri Chakravorty Spivak's theorization of subalternity, will reassure my readers that the ethical dimension I am trying to "ubiquitize" through theory is neither a privatized ethics nor a primordial ethics protected from historical and ideological "contamination." It is only on the basis of a deep-seated dissatisfaction with the ways in which the "relative autonomy" of each of these domains has inflated itself into a non-negotiable absolute that this book aspires to the immanence of the ethical–theoretical connection, as a corrective to the myopias of history and the inadequacies of the exclusively political.

This work, like my *Diasporic Mediations*, is a collection of essays, but "theory" resonates a lot more consistently as a theme than did "diaspora" in the earlier volume. I suspect I will never write a conventional book that is "about" a theme/period/author within the logic of a representational one-to-one correspondence. I prefer the idea of a book as a contingent collec-tivization of multiple intersections, departures, and arrivals. Chapter 1, "Postmodernism and the Rest of the World," seeks to provincialize the mighty claims of postmodernism from a postcolonial/subaltern perspective that both allows and disallows "the postmodern." My "double-conscious" point here is not that "Pomo" is or should be alien to postcoloniality. Instead, I am con-cerned with how the political and the theoretical/epistemological claims of postmodernity are in mutual contradiction, particularly when it comes to issues such as representation, nationalism, and essentialism. Postmodernism, to be deserving of global attention, has to learn to historicize itself multilater-ally and multi-historically. If postmodernism is an epistemological condition, such a condition as "universal" claim cannot be unilateral: it has to bear the burden of multiple and uneven histories before it can be legislated. Chapter 1 also argues against the thesis that the so-called "origins" of an "ism" have a privileged hold over its meaning and valence.

Chapter 2, "The Use and Abuse of Multiculturalism," finds itself in a symptomatic dangle between a resistance politics that is in response to a world structured in dominance and an "ethical surrender" to alterity as such. In this chapter the hyphen opens up between the ethical and the political, both as a problem and as an enabling condition of persuasion. The bulk of the chapter takes the form of a rigorous phenomenological and discursive critique of liberal versions of multiculturalism, including a critical reading of Charles Taylor. Its objective is to open up a space of empowerment between "recognition" and "representation": a space where profound relationalities may be imagined beyond liberal empathy and ontological binarism. The chapter ends on an ambivalent note envisioning "fusion" groundlessly, and this after a thorough problematization of the "fusion of horizons."

Chapter 3, "Globalization, Desire, and the Politics of Representation," argues for a return, not to the practice, but to critical considerations of how nationalism works differentially between the developed and the developing worlds. Deracinated and simulacral seductions of a transnational techno-capital, I argue, are attempting to mediatize the real in the here and now of techno-temporality: a move that has to be resisted ethically, politically, and epistemologically. I suggest that the way out of representation also has to be a way through and beyond representation, and that deterritorialized utopian longings need to be marked by the ethics of universal suffering, as theorized by Ashis Nandy.

Chapter 4, "Derivative Discourses and the Problem of Signification," performs a double-take on the category of "derivativeness" (developed superbly by Partha Chatterjee), viewing it as a "corrigible historical symptom" *and* as an inevitable epistemological condition experienced by hegemonic, dominant, and subaltern formations. In the space that opens up between the allegory and the history of derivativeness, and between derivativeness as an epistemological phenomenon and derivativeness as a political predicament, the postcolonial dilemma both finds and loses itself.

Chapter 5 has the same title as the book and is the *pièce de résistance* (at least on the basis of its prolixity): it is appropriately way too long and thereby symptomatic of the reluctant unevenness of closure. Starting with a critical rehearsal of the "politics of location" and the "politics of subject positionality," it takes on the problem of unevenness both micro-politically and macro-politically; that is, both from the perspective of general intellectuality and that of academic or specific intellectuality. The overall objective of the first half of the chapter is to articulate a sharable ethic between dominance in deconstruction and subalternity in emergence. Crucial in this context is my reading of Nadine Gordimer's *Burger's Daughter*. Starting with an appreciative reading of a powerful short story by the famous contemporary Tamil writer and intellectual Jayakanthan, the remainder of the chapter reads diagnostically into the politics of secularism as it functions internationally between the West and the East. Is secularism an ontology, an epistemology, or both? If it is indeed a "worldview," how did the "worlding" of such a world take place? How does the third world signify itself on the "Western" body of secularism? *Contra* Rushdie, is it even thinkable that the third world may have critical and "reasonable" options that are not reducible to "Occidental" secularism? The work of William Connolly was a tremendous inspiration in the context of my critical engagement with the claims of secular discourse. His deeply moving book, *Why I am not a Secularist*, is of great importance to non-Western critiques of secularism – not as a model, but as a "fellow venture" inaugurated from a different location.

If these five chapters do not add up to a cumulative thesis, that too is symptomatic. Fragmented and alienated by location, limited and chastened by subject positionality, and yet haunted by utopian visions of oceanic oneness, my problem has been similar to that of the storyteller who is caught without recourse between perspectivism and the impulse to get the whole picture, between the need to produce authority and a kind of empathic "negative capability" that laughs at authority. Add to this my conviction that each human subject simultaneously occupies different terrains – dominant, hegemonic, and subaltern – and what you get is not the plenitude of representation, but representation as interruption. Perhaps for me, existentially speaking, the truest and most moving moment in the book is the conclusion to chapter 2. The answer to representation is "Who knows?" intended as a question, but in the name of an answer.

R. Radhakrishnan
Cornell University, Ithaca

Acknowledgments

Acknowledgments belong to the register of "gratitude," and gratitude I think is quite indivisible. There is something necessary and Sisyphean about quantifying and enumerating one's indebtedness. There are many, many indeed to whom I owe a "thank you," both underscored and italicized. Let me begin with my generous and patient editor Andrew McNeillie, who waited for the "forthcoming" – nay, what had indeed become "the fifth and the sixth coming" – of *Theory in an Uneven World*. His abiding faith in the project has meant a lot to me all along. To all the diligent and supportive staff at Blackwell Publishing: Stephan Chambers, Alison Dunnett, Emma Bennett, Jack Messenger, and Lisa Eaton, thanks in no small measure. It has been fun working with you and exchanging constant email, often tinged with whimsy and humor.

Chapter 5 of this book was conceived, developed, and completed during the fall and winter of 2003 at the Society for the Humanities at Cornell University, where I have been a research Fellow for the entire academic year. It has been a remarkably productive and pleasurable year for me thanks to the generosity and the intellectual presence of the society's director Dominick LaCapra, and the memorable efficiency and hospitality of Mary Ahl, Lisa Patty, and Linda Allen. I owe much to all my fellow Fellows who have made the entire year such a consistent feast of thoughts and ideas and daring insights. As a collective, we have indeed alternated merrily between "food for thought" and exquisite "food" in all its sensuous literalness. Among the many friends, new and old, at Cornell, special thanks to Satya Mohanty, Biodun Jeyifo, Davydd Greenwood Natalie Melas, Peter Hohendahl, Jonathan Culler, Tim Murray, and Susan Buck-Morss for their comradeship and collegiality. I have been part of multiple conversations at Cornell, and to the organizers of all those conversations, thank you: in particular to the graduate students of English and Comparative

Literature. Also, I would be totally out of my mind if I did not make public my indebtedness to my good friend, colleague, and department chair Anne Herrington, and my dean Lee Edwards for sparing me a whole year away from U-Mass Amherst. Even as I had a blast in Ithaca (and I am not thinking of the particularly harsh winter), I have missed my colleagues in good old Bartlett Hall. Arthur Kinney's magnanimity in allowing me to use his ancestral house in Cortland as my abode during this entire year has been just amazing. Arthur knows that I have both taken good care of his home and made it my own.

My Appa and Amma have both, in one long-distance international conversation after another, kept an informal ledger of the "taking shape" of this book. She would ask as non-judgmentally as possible, "Is the book still in process?" and he, with his inimitable humor, would refer to the conception–delivery of this book as "an elephantine pregnancy." The diasporic son acknowledges and reciprocates your love and solicitude. To Ashok, Meera, Mahzu, Bhaskar, Uma, mami, and Seenu: my love and gratitude, and my unending (some might say unbearable) humor.

My intellectual–academic debts are numerous and they constitute an unmappable domain. In ways both direct and subtle, you have all influenced me (some of you I know personally and others exclusively through your thoughts in writing), and I have learned from you as I have attempted to coordinate my cognitive–affective–intellectual location in active interlocution with your worlds and ideas: Dipesh Chakrabarty, Homi Bhabha, Gayatri Spivak, Edward Said, William Spanos, Donald Pease, Jonathan Arac, Rey Chow, Lisa Lowe, Tejumola Olaniyan, Susan Stanford Friedman, Bruce Robbins, Kalpana Seshadri-Crooks, Partha Chatterjee, Ashis Nandy, S. Shankar, Amitav Ghosh, Ketu Katrak, Chandra Talpade Mohanty, David Lloyd, Tani Barlow, Asha Varadharajan, Neil Lazarus, Gauri Viswanathan, Kamala Visweswaran, Abdul JanMohamed, Akhil Gupta, and the brilliant and rigorous boundary 2 editorial collective. To my student colleagues and friends: Satish Kolluri, Ibish Hussein, Anita Mannur, Vamsee Juluri, Josna Rege, Gill Gane, Halil Nalcaoglu, Okey Ndibe, Goldie Osuri, Marian Aguiar, and Lingyan Yang, WOW! What a conversation we have been having! Let us keep it going.

I have had the pleasure and privilege of presenting these chapters, in one form or another, as invited talks and lectures at several venues: the Institute for Postcolonial Studies (Melbourne), Macquarie University (Sydney), La Trobe University (Melbourne), Australian National University (Canberra), Harvard University, Columbia, Cornell, Stanford, UC-Berkeley, University of Pittsburgh, University of Minnesota, Carnegie-Mellon University, University of Hawaii, UC-Berkeley, UCLA, University of Southern California, UC-Irvine, Queen's College (Canada), University of Toronto, University of Saarbrucken, Saarland (Germany), University of Trento (Italy), Hamilton College, SUNY-

Binghamton, Dartmouth College, Northwestern University, Syracuse University, University of Washington-Seattle, Chennai University (India), Madras Christian College and Stella Maris College (India), and the Institute for Journalistic and Media Studies (Chennai, India). I would like to thank my hosts and my audiences for their spirited participation, questions, endorsements, and vigorous disagreements. Thanks to you all for prodding my self-reflexivity.

To Asha, my comrade–friend–*humsafar*: let me begin with something specific. Thank you for letting me know ever so casually and matter-of-factly that my pages need to breathe: " Hello! Will you please break up those monolithic paragraphs?" Through ups and downs, you egged me on towards the farther side of procrastination. Yes indeed, there is the other side, and it sure feels good. Whichever side of whatever bounded space I may find myself in, I would want you there, with love and gratitude. To Surya, my main man: I think I will try and keep pace with you as you introduce me, from your point of view, to a world drenched in complexity and rhythms too deep even for pulsation. Let us hang out, chill, and share some music (rev up the volume); talk to me about globalization – its pros and cons – and we will keep driving on and on. It is time for me to ask you, "Who am I?" I know you will respond with candid humor.

1
Postmodernism and the Rest of the World

I want to begin with a gloss on my title. In yoking together "postmodernism" and "the rest of the world" my purpose is to suggest both a connection and a disjunction: in other words, an uneven relationship, or a relationship structured in asymmetry. Postmodernism is no more idiosyncratic or singular than the world is general or normal. Nor is it the case that there are two entirely hermetic worlds: the one postmodern, and the other "non-postmodern." There is lots of travel and traffic among locations and what they represent; and postmodernism, for whatever reason, has taken on the imprimatur of the avant-garde; particularly when it comes to questions of theory and epistemology. At the same time, as postmodernism travels from its metropolitan "Western" origins to other sites and occasions, or is appropriated differentially by the minorities and feminists even within the West, its truth claims get "multi-historicized" and relativized with reference to "the Rest." My title attempts to engage this overdetermined binarity between "the West" and "the Rest," and in the process think through and (if possible) beyond it. The entire book is an attempt to critically "theorize" the unevenness of the global situation from a postcolonial perspective. In other words, "postality" is a condition that has to be contested and negotiated between the elite avant-garde and the subaltern. It is all a matter for a "double-conscious" but agential and perspectival signification.

For one thing, I am interested in delineating postcoloniality as a form of double consciousness, and not as an act of secession from the metropolitan regime. Not only is postcoloniality a historiography in its own terms, but it is also a critical perspective on metropolitan goings on. Indeed, these two functions of postcoloniality are mutually constitutive. It seems to me that it is incumbent on the third world, having been coercively interpellated by colonialism and modernity, to continue to have a crucial say in the further developments, post- or otherwise, of modernity. The third world, which is often and almost always choicelessly globalized by advanced capital, cannot afford to forfeit its capacity to intervene in matters transnational and postmodern. Unlike theorists of the third world such as Aijaz Ahmad, I do not read ambivalence as a sign of postcolonial weakness or instability. Quite to the contrary, I wish to argue that postcoloniality is always already marked by ambivalence, and the task is to politicize this "given ambivalence" and produce it agentially. This taking charge of ambivalence, this polemical production of double consciousness, is intended as an act of affirmation and as a substantive intervention in the "business as usual" of metropolitan temporality.

It might be argued that there are indigenous realities of the non-West that are not necessarily related to colonialism and modernity. While this is indeed true, the brute fact that every conceivable local–native–indigenous reality has been touched by the morphology of modernism and the dominance of nationalism and the nation-state (notice that the very efficacy of countless grassroots movements and NGOs has to be mediated athwart the authority of regnant nationalisms) makes it imperative for postcoloniality to participate on more than one level, in more than one location. My purpose here is neither to realize a pure either/or relationship between West and non-West, nor to offer any one version of postcoloniality as exemplary or authentic. Rather, my assumption is that there is a place for the ethico-politics of persuasion, and within this space postcoloniality or the "rest of the world" has much to say to the postmodern West. I am aware that there are sections where I might be guilty of conflating postmodernism and poststructuralism. It is well beyond my scope here to begin to differentiate postmodernism and poststructuralism, but suffice it to say that for my present purposes postmodernism is the object of address if for no other reason than that more than poststructuralism, "pomo" has taken on the authority of a global umbrella. And besides, the travel of pomo all over the world, on the wings of capital and virtual technologies, has been more insidious than the travel of poststructuralism, which in many ways can actually be articulated sympathetically with the concerns of postcoloniality.

I would like to begin this chapter with a naive and perhaps brazen "world-historical" observation. The peoples of the world are currently unevenly situated between two historiographic discourses: discourses of the "post-" and the "trans-" whose objective seems to be to read historical meaning in terms of travel, displacement, deracination, and the transcendence of origins; and discourses motivated by the need to return to precolonial, premodern, and prenationalist traditions of indigeny. My intention here is somewhat to bridge the gap between these polar choices and to suggest that these two paths need to be historicized relationally, and not as two discrete and mutually exclusive options.

Having said this, I would like to briefly analyze three recent happenings in the context of global postmodernity and the emerging new world order. First, the NAFTA agreement. Much has been written about this deal from both sides. The debates are over, and NAFTA is for real. And yet the real implications of the treaty are far from clear. If on the one hand NAFTA represents deterritorialization, the breaking down of international economic borders, and the celebration of a seamless spatiality achieved by the spread of capital,[1] why then on the other hand did the rhetoric of NAFTA advocacy resort to assurances that *American* jobs will not be lost and that *American* identity will be intact, undeterritorialized by NAFTA? As Marx's elegant analysis of the contradictory logic of capitalism points out, the discourse of protectionism on behalf of the dominant order goes hand in hand with the dehistoricization of the periphery. The polemical focus on American jobs and American identity demonstrates that despite all claims of free trade, clearly, there is a *home* and a *not-home*, an *inside* to be protected and an *outside* that is really not our concern. And how do we distinguish between who is "us" and who is "them"? Of course, through the good old category of "nationality." Thus, the return of nationalism lies at the very heart of a despatializing postmodernity.

Secondly, the floundering of GATT on issues concerning cultural autonomy and specificity. The sticking point here was the exportation to Europe of American culture through videos and television programs. Unlike NAFTA that pits two developed countries against a third world country, here the transaction is all Western. And yet this particular instance dramatizes the disjuncture between cultural and political/economic interests. It was not just a question of taxes and tariffs. Surely we are all aware that in the age of late capitalism, culture itself is nothing but a commodity infiltrated irrevocably by exchange value? And still Europe resists American cultural commodities in the name of its own separate identity. Falling back on the notion of organic cultural interpellation, Europe resists the logic of postmodern homogenization or dedifferentiation. Clearly this confrontation is taking place on the all too familiar turf of Identity; and we had thought that Identity had been sent packing in the advanced postmodern world of simulacra and the hyperreal. Culture becomes the embattled rhetoric of home, authenticity, and "one's ownness" deployed strategically to resist the economic impulse toward "sameness." Yes, we want to be part of the borderless economic continuum, but at the same time, let us be who we are; our cultural identities are not up for sale or commercial influence. It would seem then that the economic terrain activates a pure process without a Subject,[2] whereas the cultural domain is anchored deeply in Identity.

Thirdly, in the case of the Puerto Rican referendum concerning statehood, "culture" became a fraught term. Would Puerto Rico sacrifice its cultural/historical uniqueness as a consequence of economic/political unionization? Tax issues and citizenship questions apart, the question of culture was raised in all its resistant autonomy. Not unlike a number of non-Western ex-colonized nations that assimilate the West as part of their "outer selves" and cultivate their "inner selves" in response to indigenous imperatives, the people of Puerto Rico chose to symbolize the cultural domain in opposition to a capitalist postmodernist integration with the "Nation of nations."[3]

I bring up these examples to show that the "identity question" in our own times is profoundly fissured along different and often mutually exclusive trajectories. Also, all these events are taking place in a progressively postmodern world, which is also being seen as a postnationalist world. Why is it that Identity and Nationalism are celebrating their return under the postmodern aegis? Why is it that the ideology of postmodernism is unable to chase away or exorcize the ghosts of Identity and Nationalism? Is it possible that the "identity question" and a variety of nationalisms[4] have become the political weapon of "underdeveloped" peoples in their battle against the phenomenon of "unequal global development":[5] a phenomenon that is being exacerbated by the spread of postmodernism? But before we can respond to these questions (questions that focus on the global effects of postmodernism), we need to take a closer look at postmodernism as it has developed in the West.

Historicizing Postmodernism

What are the origins of postmodernism? What is the extent of its geopolitical jurisdiction and what is its statute of limitations? Let us keep in mind that the text that gave postmodernity its undeniable cognitive–epistemic status (Jean-François Lyotard's *The Postmodern Condition*)[6] made three important and binding gestures. First of all, postmodernity was a condition. Secondly, it had to do with knowledge and epistemology. And third, it was taking place within the advanced capitalist, postindustrial computerized societies. The term "condition" (as in say, the human condition) has a strong ontological appeal. Unlike words such as "crisis," "predicament," or "dilemma," "condition" carries with it a semantics of finality and fully achieved meaning. It is in the form of a *fait accompli*. In other words, the condition is real, and it was theorized into lexical significance within the first world well before the underdeveloped world could even take a look at it, leave alone have a say in its ideological determination.

Well might one ask, why should the underdeveloped countries of the third world even be allowed a peek into what after all is exclusively a first world phenomenon? And here lies the ideological duplicity of postmodernity as an epistemic condition: its simultaneity both as a regional and a global phenomenon. The epistemic location of postmodernity, given the dominance of the West, has a *virtual* hold over the rest of the world too. If modernity functions as a structure-in-dominance that regulates and normativizes the relationship between the West and the Rest, postmodernism, despite the so-called break from modernity,[7] sustains and prolongs this relationship. Furthermore, given the avant-gardism of the West, it is only inevitable that the very regionality of Western forms will travel the world over as dominant universal forms. In other words, Western realities have the power to realize themselves as "general human conditions." The passage from a specific reality to a general condition is effected through the mediation of knowledge and epistemology.

It is the formulation of the postmodern "condition" as a matter of "knowledge" that paves the way for the uncontested spread of first world priorities across the world. It is the ability of the developed world to conceptualize and theorize its particular organic empirical reality into a cognitive–epistemic formula on behalf of the entire world that poses a dire threat to other knowledges.[8] For after all, how can knowledge be irrelevant, especially when accompanied by claims of universality? Thus a report on epistemology elaborated in the metropolis either begins to speak for the human condition the world over, or assumes a virtual reality to be devoutly wished for by the rest of the world. To put it differently, the theoretical need to take postmodernism seriously becomes an imperative even in places where postmodernity is not a lived reality (i.e., has no historical roots). The third world is then compulsorily interpellated by postmodernity even though its own realities are thoroughly out of sync with the temporality of the postmodern.[9]

To what extent and in what specific ways does postmodernism problematize and deconstruct the ideology of modernity? To what extent is postmodernism a radical critique of, and perhaps a form of secession from, the authority of modernity? If indeed postmodernism is an effective interrogation of the legitimacy of modernity within the confines of the first world, then how useful or relevant is this interrogation to other geopolitical areas in the rest of the world? Is there common cause between the interrogation of modernity within the developed world and third world critiques of modernity? Are there sharable issues, agendas, and objectives between these two constituencies, despite the fundamental asymmetry that sustains East–West relationships? In other words, why should the rest of the world pay attention to the emergence of postmodernism in politics if all it is is an intramural "occidental" antagonism?

Before I examine the relevance or otherwise of postmodernism to post-coloniality and to third world cultural politics, I would like to briefly and selectively look into the claims of postmodernism within its place of origin. I would also like to keep in mind that even within the first world, the evaluation of postmodernism is far from complete. There are great resistances and "differences within" the first world. Whether postmodernism is good or bad, whether it is a progressive development or a repressive development in complicity with the rationality of capitalist dominance, are issues that are part of an ongoing debate. My purpose here is not to rehearse the by-now many familiar attitudes to postmodernism, both supportive and antagonistic,[10] but rather to focus on a few issues that have to do with the generalization of the "post" and the implications of such a generalization in the context of first world–third world relationships.

Postmodernism within the metropolitan context is often equated with the advocacy of local, regional, and specific politics in opposition to total/global/universal politics. Western authority is over, the process of decolonization is well afoot the world over, and the dominance of Eurocentrism is viable no more. There is the reality of the other, not just the abstract Other capitalized by theory into a transhistorical form of alterity, but several determinate others with different histories, cultures, and political destinies. The postmodern choice that gets formulated in response to this crisis is quite stark: an illegitimate universalism, or relativism. But what about a universalism based not on dominance or representational violence but on relationality and a dialogism based on multiple interlocking histories?[11] Confronted by its ideological embeddedness in Eurocentrism (i.e., Eurocentrism masquerading as authentic universalism), postmodernism eschews universalism altogether in favor of a rigorous and uncompromising relativism. Given its relativist stance, postmodernism can have nothing to say about other cultures. Its narrative, used to being "grand" and totalizing, fails altogether.

If narrative in Conrad is either mystified or enraged to hatred by the darkness of the Other,[12] the postmodern withdrawal from narrative attests to the objective reality of the Other while at the same time it claims that the Other is unknowable. The Other's reality to the Self is postulated on the prior premise of the Other's unknowability by the Self. Withdrawing from its sorry history of knowing the Other through dominance, a self-critical Eurocentrism abandons the Other altogether in the name of non-interference. The epistemology of relativism justifies this denial of reciprocity and relationality among different knowledges of the world.

This failure of postmodern relativism both at the epistemological level and the political level is typically recuperated as a radical triumph through the practice of what has become a quintessential postmodernist/poststructuralist strategy: the strategy of self-reflexivity as a catch-all answer for cross-cultural crises and problems.[13] If canonical anthropology's message to premodern societies was "I think, therefore you are," postmodern orthodoxy takes the form of "I think, therefore I am not. You are 'I am not.'" The Other becomes the burden of the Self's negativity, a negativity produced by the Self through its own auto-critical deconstructive engagement with itself. As Edward Said has argued eloquently in his analysis of Albert Camus' political as well as epistemological orientation towards Algeria, the postmodern impulse furthers the modernist thesis by actively negating the other through knowledge.[14] I am not trivializing the significance of deconstructive self-reflexivity within the metropolitan theater, but the problem is that such a self-reflexivity *by itself* does not and cannot guarantee the knowability of other cultures and histories.

Perhaps a brief explanation is in order here: an explanation of how postmodernism functions predominantly as a critique[15] that is derived oppositionally from the very order that is the object of the critique.[16] The very exteriority of the postmodern critique relies on the givens of modernity, and hence postmodernism, despite vociferous claims to the contrary, enriches modernity in the very act of transgressing it. The putative "break" that is associated with postmodern rebellion in fact rests securely on the spoils of nationalism/modernism. Nowhere is this more visible than in the so-called post-identitarian, postnationalist formations. Postnationalist developments, as my opening paragraphs attempt to demonstrate, are never at the expense of nationalist securities; if anything, they *foundationalize* nation-based verities and privileges to the point of invisibility. The benefits of citizenship of developed nationalism are effectively sublated through postnational transcendence, just as the legacies of modernity are preserved in the postmodern critique. All I am saying is that postmodernism does not absolve itself of modernity, just as powerful post- and transnational developments do not forfeit the privileges of first world nationalism.

This entire discussion leads to an important question: how real and historical is the "post?" I would argue that critiques (such as the postmodern critique of modernity) that are paradigmatically homogeneous with their objects cannot be real alternatives.[17] What then is a paradigm and how are its parameters recognized? How is a paradigm identified economically, politically, culturally, philosophically? My concern here, quite Marxist in its intention, is with the self-identification of any paradigm, both in its totality and through the relative autonomy of the many levels and spheres that account for the totality. Though the historical reality of any paradigm – such as modernity – is independent of the conscious theory or the epistemology of the paradigm, it is through the latter that the paradigm achieves self-awareness *qua* paradigm. I say this to make two points: (1) that the relationship between any paradigm and its epistemology is one of *identification*, and (2) that the epistemology is not constitutive of the paradigm; rather, the paradigm as an interrelated set of practices is anterior to the epistemology. In other words, the epistemology of the paradigm is a function and a product of the paradigm even as it enjoys its relative autonomy as theory.

Given this, what does it mean to assert that postmodernism is an epistemological break from modernity in particular, and from Western thought in general? Is it possible that postmodernism functions as a "break" in matters epistemological even as it remains complicit with the West in matters political and economic? If the break is merely epistemological and not accompanied by concomitant economic and political changes, what is the status of the break, and indeed, what is the "subject" of the break? By and large, theories of postmodernity have focused exclusively and obsessively on theory and epistemology to claim that a break has actually occurred. In this sense, postmodernism has been a revolution "in theory," in both senses of the term. It is a revolution that seems quite prepared to leave history behind in search of theoretical virtual realities informed by the temporality of the "post."[18] The decapitation[19] of history by theory, the celebration of subjectlessness, and other such motifs have been the burden of epistemology's impatience with history.[20] It is significant that there exists a telling divide between Marxist postmodernists and "pure" postmodernists when it comes to the question of accounting for the political and the social. Marxist postmodernists such as Neil Smith, David Harvey, Fredric Jameson, and Nancy Fraser tend to see postmodernism as a symptom of late capitalism; the pure postmodernists, *à la* Jean Baudrillard, are happy to inhabit the world of postmodernist immanence, virtually and theoretically. Also, the former are able to raise such questions as "Is postmodernism good or bad, desirable or not?" whereas the latter are happy to thematize postmodernism intransitively (i.e., as an end in itself).[21]

The dangers of hypostatizing postmodern theory as its own autonomous content are as follows.[22] First of all, the so-called theoretical break takes the form of an "innocent" counter-memory that chooses to forget an uncomfortable and often guilty past.[23] Radical theory begins to function as a form of forgetfulness (i.e., as a way of justifying the non-accountability of theory to history). The organic and representational connectedness of postmodernity to its past is deliberately and strategically overlooked, so that gains in epistemology may be localized in all their micropolitical specificity, and then legitimated as a successful politics of secession. It is important to keep in mind that what is passed off here, through the dubious reference to the transgressive autonomy of epistemology, as an exclusively metropolitan course of events, has in fact tremendous global repercussions. The minimalization of the grand narratives into the *recit* of postmodernism is an epistemological move that in a sense attempts to "launder" the guilt of Eurocentrism. Modernity, after all, was achieved as an effect of colonialism with unequal impact on the colonizer and the colonized. Much of the capital needed for industrialization came from the colonies (one obvious example being cotton from India for the mills in Lancashire), and it was the production of surplus value from the colonies that paved the way for the universal sovereignty of modernity. And of course, in the process, other knowledges were wasted. If the dominance of modernity was the result both of the creation and the maintenance of the developed–underdeveloped divide, how come then, suddenly and by the sheer occult power of high theory, postmodernism finds itself absolved of its modernist past?

The epistemological *coupure* begins to function as an alibi. Unable to deal with the enormity of its modernist–colonialist past, postmodernism desiccates itself into a bodiless theory so that its accountability to a *global past* could just be forgotten. I am not denying the possibility that postmodernism can be, or even is, an authentic quarrel of the West with itself, but the valence of such a quarrel can hardly speak for the victims of modernity in Africa or Asia. The postmodern quarrel with modernity is much in the nature of a family squabble that takes place within a well-established domain of solidarity and shared economic and political interests. There is nothing in postmodern epistemology that disinherits the beneficial legacies of modernism, in particular, the riches of developmental progress built on piratical capital accumulation. The post-identitarian "games"[24] of postmodernism are possible precisely because identity "here" is no more at stake.[25] Postnationalist postmodernism, for example, does not cancel earlier identifications such as German, American, French, British, etc. If anything, these identifications are the rich but ideologically invisible bases from which postmodernity is deployed as the politics of heterogeneity, hybridity, and difference.[26]

This calculated suppression of macropolitical global memory results in the provincialization of the metropolitan political imaginary. The call for specific intellectuality, the insistence on an isolationist subject-positional politics, and the understanding of "location" in opposition to global relationality, the grand obituary notice regarding the death of representation and narrative voice: these themes that constitute the very essence of postmodernity highlight a certain failure, the failure of Eurocentric thought to confront with conscience[27] the history of its own Narrative.[28] Such a version of postmodernism has been severely questioned within the West by feminists who have sought to postmodernize their feminisms without at the same time conceding to postmodernity its master claims concerning knowledge and theory. (In a way we could also understand this venture as the feminization of postmodernity.)[29] In what sense could postmodernism be seen as an ally of Western feminism, and how and for what reasons does such an alliance break down?[30] For my purposes here, I wish to focus on areas where feminism has pressured post-modernism to acknowledge its shortcomings, blind spots, and internal contra-dictions. The distinction (and here I draw on the distinguished work of such feminist postmodernists as Nancy Fraser, Linda Nicholson, Iris Marian Young, and Donna Haraway, to name just a few) is between *social* postmodernisms, in the plural, and an unqualified *postmodernism as such*. In other words, the work of these intellectuals warns us that the social significance of post-modernism is not to be taken for granted. Nancy Fraser and Linda Nicholson were among the first theorists to conceptualize postmodernism as simulta-neously exciting and problematic, and to spell out a critique of postmodernism from a macropolitical perspective that is external to the epistemic space pro-vided by postmodernism itself (i.e., the agential political space of feminism). Their significant contribution was to demystify the immanence of postmod-ernism in terms of its undeclared ideology, and to insist on the accountability of the epistemics of postmodernism to its social conditions of production. It would be redundant to capture the overall direction of their well-known and much dis-cussed essay (in particular, the sophisticated way in which they turn the tables on Lyotard), so I will take their critique for granted and proceed further.

Fraser and Nicholson rightly point out that the radical valorization of post-modernism as an epistemological *coupure* in fact throws the baby out with the bathwater (i.e., unless, of course, the very denial of the *socius* by postmodern theory is to be construed perversely as the ultimate revolution, and that would indeed be a bizarre comment on the teleology that Marx had devoutly wished for). Nicholson and Fraser point out that the epistemological site is made into a pure *elsewhere* that connects neither with history nor with sociality. Hence, their diagnosis that postmodernism is very much a *philosophical* formulation authored by male theorists and thinkers. Their essay makes us see that what gets celebrated in postmodernist thought is the capacity of Eurocentric phi-losophy to master and own itself even during its periods of dark and menac-ing crisis, its genius to launch its very negativity in the form of a persuasive philosophy. Its loss of privilege thus recuperated by theory, postmodernism begins to assume the function of a non-organic, free-floating signifier with global epistemic ambitions. If the West is the home of progressive knowledge, and if the West itself has begun to question its own knowledge, then clearly, knowledge must be in universal jeopardy. And who else to the rescue but the Western subject all over again, who can convert loss of authority into a pure theory of subjectless knowledge?

The uncoupling of the "post" from postmodernity confers on the "post" a universal sanction to be exercised the world over in the guise of knowledge. It is this philosophical autonomization of the epistemology of the *post* that has facilitated the production of categories such as post-feminism, postcoloniality, post-ethnic, post-historical, post-political, etc.[31] Every other constituency is then constrained, for reasons of knowledge, to work under the "post" umbrella. Without a doubt, a strong distinction needs to be made between the indigenous claims of postmodernism and its traveling authority as a blank, generic imprimatur. For after all, why should ethnicity go "pomo," or for that matter, Islam? What if Islam and postmodernism, and ethnicity and postmodernism, are mutually exclusive and/or irrelevant? Why should these constituencies update themselves in the name of postmodern epistemology and theory? If the historical irrelevance, to these constituencies, of postmodernism is demonstrable, why should they still find room for postmodernism as theory within their internal structures? Why hitch their interests to an alien knowledge and risk their solidarity with themselves?

My purpose here is to submit postmodernism to the relevance test. How relevant and how representative is the postmodern condition, both within the first world and in global terms? In adopting the postmodernist framework as a meta-framework, isn't there the real danger of distorting and misrepresenting other realities and other histories? As Fraser and Nicholson have argued, postmodernism is real as a crisis. To Fraser and others, the denial of globality by postmodern theory indicates a dire need for imagining a politics of connections, correlations, correspondences, and common ground – and clearly postmodernism is no help at all here. How can postmodernism be socialized and politicized is a question that Fraser and Nicholson take up in their work.[32] As Western feminists they share with postmodern theory a common heritage: Eurocentrism and the history of Western dominance. But there the commonality stops, for as feminists they occupy a different ground from the one inhabited by male postmodern theorists. Though they take heed of a whole range of self-reflexive practices prescribed by postmodern theory, they articulate (Fraser in particular) quite programmatically their political difference from male, white postmodernism. As feminists of the Western world they have a relationship of difference-in-identity with postmodernism, and the difference is to be explained in terms of interests and polemical situatedness and not just in terms of pure knowledge or epistemology. It is indeed the notion of interestedness and perspectivity that separates postmodern feminists from their male counterparts. Furthermore, in sizing down postmodernism into adjectival significance (i.e., not postmodernism as its own plenary politics, but rather *postmodern* feminism), theorists like Fraser reinvent the need for a macropolitics that will not shrink into a narcissistic self-reflexivity or a technology-driven set of non-organic, specialist practices.

There is yet another important historical context that differentiates postmodern feminism from male, white postmodernism. Unlike the latter, which is obsessed with self-reflexivity, postmodern feminism sees the postmodern epistemological condition as a problem. Why is it that an increase in epistemological complexity results in the lessening of knowledge, especially of the Other? Why are knowledge and practice, knowledge and "worldliness,"[33] posited in terms of mutual incommensurability? What helps them out of this aporia is not yet another "pure" epistemological nuance but, rather, a very real historical challenge: the challenge both from women of color in the first world and from third world women.[34] Postmodern feminism is different precisely because it responds (I am not saying that the response has always been successful) to the ethico-political authority of other worlds and other knowledges and other histories. There is a real *horstexte* to the history and the discourse of postmodernism, and unless this "outside" is acknowledged in its own terms, there cannot be any meaningful coalitions or cross-cultural projects between white women and women of color. It is the reality of other knowledges (and not merely the realities of other histories, for classical anthropology flourished on the notion of "their histories" requiring "our theories") that makes postmodernism vulnerable and thus open to dialogue and cross-locational persuasion.[35]

The major issue that in some sense brings feminists together, despite fundamental differences of race, class, sexuality, and nationality, is that of identity, and to be more specific, the issue of identity politics and its relationship to the theoretical/epistemological critique of *identity as such*.[36] First world feminism found itself in critical double sessions both with male postmodernism and with the feminisms of women of color, with the two double sessions connected through a relationship of asymmetry. With postmodernism, on the one hand, there was the project of deconstructing the claims of essentialism, and the stranglehold of metaphysical thought; and on the other, spelling out assertively the difference of an agential feminist politics from a male critique of phallogocentric identity.[37] In the contexts of the feminisms of women of color, however, the double session had a different sense of historical direction. On the one hand, there was the solidarity of women the world over in their fight against an omni-historical patriarchy (with individual historical differences and variations to be worked contextually), but on the other hand, there were real race- and colonialism-based differences when it came to the identity question in its theoretical aspect. The battle against essentialism that is an integral component of postmodern feminism resonates very differently in the subaltern women's context, since "essentialism" had a different ring in the third world context.

Postmodern feminists have done an impressive job of pointing out the slippage within postmodernist and poststructuralist theory between notions of "agency" and "subjectivity." Unlike postmodern theory that glorifies this slippage as a hallmark of its "difference-from-itself," postmodern feminism wonders whether this slippage is in fact real, and if indeed it is real, whether such a condition is something to be ecstatic about or a cause for worry. The postmodern "turn" taking shape exclusively as critique would have us believe that a critique is subjectless and that identity is a bad essentialist habit to be discarded by a hardheaded theory. We have heard great claims that the epistemology of the "post" is a daring and self-consuming process of thinking that puts itself at risk, defoundationalized perennially by its own radical momentum. The "subject" of knowledge is dissolved in the "process" of knowing,[38] and what is left is the intransitive *jouissance* of epistemological play. There are at least two ways of questioning such claims. First, by way of Marxist ideology critique (interestingly, "ideology" is the neglected term in so much postmodernist critique) one could argue that postmodern pleasure is nothing but the most abject form of mystification by the commodity form; and secondly, by a form of global reasoning that tells us that the so-called "subject in peril" of postmodern epistemology is in fact a hyper-identitarian subject so secure in its dominant identity regime that it can afford to play games without in any way endangering its politico-economic base. The decentered play that the early Jacques Derrida champions[39] neither forswears Eurocentric privilege nor does it situate itself relationally *vis-à-vis* the other coeval histories and cultures of the world. In all these critical operations we find the negative ontology of Eurocentrism playing doctor to the rest of the world. This negative ontology would have us believe that narrative in general is devoid of epistemological validity, a belief with shattering consequences for narratives in the rest of the world.

The "theme of themes" in postmodern thought is the statement of a relationship: identity-knowledge-narrative. To put it broadly, postmodernism eviscerates narrative and purports to be fiercely anti-essentialist in its attitude to Identity. (Such an attitude in the final analysis turns out to be anti-Identity also, since postmodernism reads "identity" and "essentialism" as interchangeable and synonymous terms.) As we can see, these two operations are closely related. Why does postmodernism posit an adversarial relationship between narrative and radical epistemology? If narrative is seen as an act of agential–ideological production with the purpose of anchoring identities in their proper, teleological "homes," radical epistemology is understood as the celebration of the free and unbounded spatiality of *knowing* in all its verbal–processual and desubjectified flows and energies.[40] If narrative works within specific parameters, historical and political, and the constraints of solidarity that go with parameters, postmodern *knowing* is endorsed as the perennial breaking down of boundaries, barriers, and roots by the sheer will to knowledge. Knowledge is a mercurial form of restlessness that disdains the category of "home." In the choice between postmodernism as the champion of a freedom-seeking knowledge (or better still, as a border-busting knowledge)[41] and narrative as a conservative protectionist policy, postmodernism comes off as the more liberating option. After all, who in their right mind can be *against* freedom and *for* censorship and repression through narrative interpellation, particularly during times of NAFTA and a capital-centered world order where any threat to the free flow of capital is construed as an act of terrorism, a heinous crime against the cause of universal freedom?

My polemic here is not to deny the "post" its travel from the center to the periphery, or to assert that third world resistances are necessarily pure and uncontaminated by metropolitan influence.[42] Rather, my intention is to mark the meta-theory of the "post" with the historical realities of its uneven travel across contesting terrains and cultures. How differentially is the "politics of the post" received and experienced in third world locations, and in particular, how are the identity politics of those locations pressured by the epistemology of postmodernism? Let us now take a critical look at the form in which the identity question is brought to the third world on the postmodern platter.

First of all, the identity question is presented as an unfashionable and backward preoccupation. The third world, in other words, has to choose between a relevant but backward project, and a cutting-edge subjectivity that is purely virtual and devoid of an experiential base. Secondly, the identity question as it affects the third world is as urgent as it is chronic (for nowhere else does the "enjoy the symptom" syndrome find a better context than in the third world Body),[43] since the underdeveloped world has to seek an alien epistemology to understand itself better. Thirdly, "identity" is put forward as a necessary and desirable object for deconstruction. Fourthly, identity is divorced form the agential authority of specific narrative projects and their hegemonizing strategies. Fifthly, the quest for identity is separated from legitimation procedures, since all legitimation is deemed by theory to be "always already" repressive. And, finally, the discourse of subaltern identity is emptied epistemically (i.e., alienated from its prerogative to make its own truth claims, for the truth claims would come from the Self of the dominant West).

For the deconstructive attitude towards Identity to attain universal purchase, postmodernism sets up something called "essentialism" as the ideal straw enemy. In spite of prolific scholarship in the areas of "essentialism" and "strategic essentialism,"[44] it is still not clear what essentialism is precisely, or why it holds such a dominant position in contemporary debates in theory, cultural studies, postcoloniality, and gender and ethnic studies. Why is essentialism bad, why are essentialists naive/stupid and/or evil, and why has anti-essentialism secured a monopolistic hold over theoretical–moral virtue? I am not for a moment discrediting a number of poststructuralist feminists who have argued memorably on behalf of a constructed and de-essentialized notion of identity

(Judith Butler and Diana Fuss to name two prominent theorists) without sacrificing the agential power of identity politics. My point is that when it comes to questions of essence and legitimation, deconstructive theories that emanate from the metropolis egregiously misread the burden of essence as it falls on the third world and thus fail to appreciate the nuance of the "risk of essence" that Gayatri Spivak so eloquently talks about even as she advances the claims of poststructuralist epistemology.

I wish to suggest that the exaltation of the essentialism debate as the "Debate of all debates" only serves to obfuscate our understanding of the term "essentialism" and its specific underpinnings in Western thought. First, essentialism is one pole of a binary interpellation peculiar to Western epistemology: the other pole could be variously termed as "history," "existence," "the non-essential/accidental/adventitious." Secondly, essentialism has been ideologically determined as a critical bone of contention (i.e., prepared as the main battleground where the main event will be the deconstruction of Western ontology by itself). And, as Foucault would have it, this deontologizing project takes the perennial form of an anti-Platonism, so that the genus "anti-Platonic" is canonized as the permanent form of the permanent revolution in thought and theory.[45] Thirdly, the drama of essentialism is always played out with reference to the non-West, which is made to take on the dark and mysterious burden of essentialism, whereas the West is busy producing its own powerful history. The primitivism of the other (stranded forever in the quagmire of an ahistorical essence) is variously cultivated by the West either as an object of dread to be kept at bay, or as an object of exoticism to be used as a source of rejuvenation (the example of Gauguin comes to mind) to revive the fading Western spirit. Fourthly, the West, particularly during the period of high modernism, was in the habit of projecting its inner fissures, dreads, and hatreds onto the Other, so that the Other was made to appear as the Manichaean counterpart of the dominant Western self. Africa in particular became the favorite dumping ground of all those atavistic drives and terrors that conscious modernity could not account for. Africa thus became the dark continent (the ideal theater for the modern European self to encounter its primordial origins) that would absorb the detritus of the modernist process. The co-implication of the Thames and the Congo, for example, in Conrad's *Heart of Darkness*, does not so much invoke a common humanity, but rather, an unequal humanity, where the African brother is constrained forever to remain the younger brother.[46] The contemporaneity of the other is psychologized as the atavistic prehistory of the dominant self, and the way is paved for the creation of the "third world" as a necessary backdrop for the history of modernity.[47]

This little detour has been necessary to drive home the point that whatever the valences might be of the debates over essentialism within the developed world, such debates would not have been possible unless essentialism had also been deployed as a powerful weapon against the histories of other cultures. No chapter in Western modernity can really be understood unless it is located in the context of the history of colonialism in both contexts: the colonizer's as well as that of the colonized.[48] I also would like to emphasize that this cognitive–theoretical hang-up with essentialism is not a postmodern phenomenon. It is in fact a quintessential modernist theme (the modernist angst with history and origins) that has been bequeathed to postmodernism. The allegorization as well as the anthropologization of the native, the ascription of a timeless irrationality or a brute unregenerate facticity to native cultures, the attribution of a phenomenological/perceptual immediacy devoid of cognitive import to native bodies and behavior, and the dark and menacing idealization of the other's geography as primordial earth, nature, etc., have all been thoroughly constitutive of modernity's schizophrenic obsession with itself. Postmodernism's advocacy of these very themes, therefore, is if anything but a continuation of the *longue durée* of modernism, and not a break from it. Postmodernism's sensitivity to the politics of difference and heterogeneity and its seeming solicitude for the other need to be grounded in a history of mutual relationality. On the contrary, what has been happening under the postmodern aegis is that familiar phenomenon of high metropolitan theory repeatedly accusing third world identity politics of essentialism.

This is hilariously ironic when we consider that this entire obsession with essences and the deconstruction of binarity have very little to do with a number of indigenous African and Asian knowledges that do not axiomatize binarity as the founding principle of all thought.[49] It is the hubris of Western thought that accommodates the belief that the West's antinomian struggle with itself is *the* universal form of all revolution, and that other cultures should genuflect to the jurisdiction of Platonism and its *alter ego*. To vary Derrida's dictum, it is as though the world can never really step out of the pages of Western thought; the only alternative is to turn the pages in a certain way. What is even more alarming is the fact that the postmodern counter-memory quite conveniently forgets the history of essentialism as it has been foisted on the non-West. It was during the modernist regime (in collusion with colonialism) that traditions were invented by the colonizer on behalf of the colonized,[50] and as Lata Mani had demonstrated brilliantly in the context of *sati*, the so-called authority of indigenous traditions was created and constructed by the colonizer to legitimate and inferiorize indigenous traditions, all in one move. This so-called authority was really not representative of indigenous practices and worldviews. As Dipesh Chakrabarty has argued powerfully (and here I extend his insight somewhat), the native's obsession with "history" as well as with "knowledge" was produced in response to the colonizer's need to dominate and not in response to the native's need for self-knowledge and authentication.[51]

But this is not all. Even if the discussion of essentialism were restricted to the first world, there is still quite a bit of semantic fuzziness to be accounted for. Even within the discourse of Western metaphysical thought, I doubt whether "essences" were ever considered as empirically valid. In the attempt to construct and valorize the discourse of ideality, and in the effort to mediate the gap between "what is" and "what ought to be," the category (the essence-function, if you will) of the essence functioned as a kind of *telos*, as the positing of an *a priori* authority to direct and regulate the paths that history is to take on its way, not to any random resolution, but rather to a desired and willed denouement. Essences therefore belonged to the level of abstract, transhistorical categoriality, whereas the historical world of narrative was subject to error and misdirection. How to theorize ideality with reference to history is by no means an easy task, and nor is it an unnecessary one. My point here is that both "the real/the historical" and "the ideal" are products of human imagination, and are therefore historical through and through. As in Saussurean linguistics, where the signified itself is understood as a function of the linguistic sign and signifying practices, here too, "the ideal" itself should be comprehended as a discursive effect. Ideality and the notion of "essences" that direct history towards a desirable and ideal resolution are themselves (for "essence" connotes completion and an ideal completion) historically motivated categories. Essences have no significance whatsoever except in relationship to the changing world of history and circumstance.

The next step in my argument is to state that the term "strategic essentialism" is redundant, for essentialism has been nothing but strategic. To restate my earlier point, the recourse to essences is a matter of strategy to gain control over processes of history along agential lines. In this day and age, I find it difficult to believe that a Hindu, Muslim, or Jewish person subscribes to Hinduness,[52] or Muslimness, or Jewishness except as a form of authority to live by and realize one's already given objectives as a group. The important issues here are the extent to which the anterior givenness of teleological objectives are open to historical modifications and reversions; and the political process of representation through which the teleological blueprint is endorsed (from the grassroots and not as top-down authority) and "hegemonized" in authentic response to the will of the members that constitute the group.

There is yet another deployment of strategic essentialism: the recourse by one group, in the context of multiple contradictory and competing historical claims, to the notion of "ontological essence," with the purpose of elevating and prioritizing their claims over and above the "merely historical" claims of other competing groups.

To transfer this philosophic discussion of essence and ideality to the realm of identity, identity politics, and the role played by narrative in the construction of identity: how are narratives interpellated, and how are narratives adjudged as failures or as successes? Before I undertake this analysis, I would like to make it very clear that my position on these issues is historical to the core, and I have undertaken this polemical excursion into essentialism only to show that essentialism itself has been an interested practice undertaken by human beings in search of specific goals, and not a disembodied and disinterested body of knowledge separated form the world of historical praxis.

Why do human communities have recourse to the rhetoric of essences? Any community has a given identity that is sedimented by the imbrication of many histories. There is also the desire to produce from the given identity an ideal community which one can call one's own, and "narrative" as a socially symbolic act is the way from *here* to *there*.[53] Can narrative function as pure process (i.e., without the authority of some form of ideological apriorism)?[54] Which prescripts does and should narrative follow? If narrative is an act of self-fashioning, which prescripts are liberating and which are repressive? Can the narrative function be divorced from the need for identity? Is narrative owned and operated by any agency, or is it external to the jurisdiction of agency? My position is that no narrative is possible without some tacit axiology, simply because narrative is neither a value-free nor a purely descriptive act. The "value" that legitimates the narrative project is in a sense anterior to the project itself, and in another sense it can only be realized as a function of the narrative process.[55] The success or failure of the narrative is to be measured in terms of its closeness to the intended trajectory; the produced value has to be read in terms of the intended value. Of course, the two will never totally coincide with each other, for that would amount to the preemption of history by pure Presence. "Value" thus presides over the narrative project (also, the identity project), both as an epistemological and as an ethico-political imperative. The imperative is epistemological insofar as the "subjects" involved in the process need to be able to think of their intended identity as a worthy object of knowledge, and ethico-political since the value is also related to questions of representation, hegemony, authenticity, correctness, and fairness. In short, it is utterly meaningless to disconnect identity politics from questions concerning the truth claims as well as the legitimacy of identity. One cannot by definition entertain an identity that is truthless or illegitimate, for "identity" is both an epistemic and a politico-juridical regime.

Furthermore, the thematic securing of any identity within its own truth marks the powerful moment when the for-itself of that identity is in addition transformed to an in-itself that can be acknowledged and respected by other identities.[56] Without this passage from its *being-for-itself* to its *being-in-itself*, any identity is doomed to a history of ghettoization (i.e., it will have a reality for itself within its own niche and no more). If identities are denied the legitimacy of their own truths (both in their own eyes and through the eyes of the "others"),[57] they are bound to languish within their histories of inferiority, deprived of their relational objective status *vis-à-vis* the objective conditions of other identities. To put it concretely, the self-image of an African-American has to be acknowledged as objective knowledge by non-African-Americans. The historical intelligibility of a subaltern/minority worldview is neither a matter of special-interests epistemology nor a function of some mysterious and esoteric insiderism. For any identity to participate equally and meaningfully in a comity of identities, it has to ensure that its knowledge is accorded objective validity by all other parties at the very outset of the meeting. Without such a recognition, some identities are bound to be equal and more than equal, whereas others will be perceived as less than equal, for lack of an evenly realized universality. It might be objected (and more of this later) that the self-identity of any identity is "for the other," but my contention is that historical differentiations need to be made between intra- and inter-identitarian notions of alterity. Such distinctions may not be necessary in the context of a perfectly realized universality, but clearly no one will claim that such a state has been attained.

If my reading of the essentialism–narrative nexus is correct, then it would seem that there is something disingenuous about the polarized choice offered by postmodern theory: essentialism or a pure subjectless process. This binary choice seems like the only option possible because postmodern theory considers the identity question purely from a philosophic perspective. In so doing, it represses the programmatic and intentional connections between *interests* and identity. What is left out of the discussion, of course, is the politics of representation.[58] Epistemology, theory, and philosophy are reified as absolute sites of revolution, cleansed of political and representational partisanship. Such a celebration of epistemological revolutions at the expense of organicity and the solidarities of representational politics ill-befits the needs of postcoloniality, and yet why is it that theorists of postcoloniality (myself included) take postmodern/poststructuralist lessons to heart in their attempts to delineate postcolonial subjectivity?[59] My focus here will be on some of the significant contributions made by Homi Bhabha in the area of postcolonial narratology. These interventions have been as much postcolonial in their intent as they have been postmodern/poststructuralist in their conviction. The cardinal question that comes up in Bhabha's case (and by extension, any theoretical work that uses poststructuralist epistemology to clarify issues in postcoloniality) is which is the tenor and which the vehicle? Which is the figure and which the ground? Which is the historical body and which the animating spirit: poststructuralism or postcoloniality? What does it mean to articulate the two "posts" together?[60]

Whose Knowledge and Whose Politics?

The deconstructive dissemination[61] that Bhabha proposes as a resolution to contemporary identity crisis works on two levels. On a political level, "dissemination" stands for the dissipation of the legitimacy of nationalist regimes and their "imagined communities."[62] On a philosophical level, dissemination works as the radical postponement of *Identity as such*; in the place of identity we have the notion of displaced hybridities.[63] If radical theory deconstructs and defers Identity, history rebukes and calls into question the sovereignty of nationalism. Interestingly enough the figure that connects the two levels is narrative. In Bhabha's reading, the narration of the nation is a historical failure; but more consequentially, it is an allegorical failure of the "always already" variety. But why is it a failure? Is it a failure for specific historical reasons, or is it the failure intrinsic to the very form of the project such that historical circumstances do not really play a part in the determination of the outcome? Is the narrative failure of nationalism just another name for an omni-historical cognitive failure? The question that Bhabha does not raise (and this is consistent with his own stated intention of dealing not so much with the histories of nationalism, as with the temporality of Identity in a general sense), and one that Partha Chatterjee would raise with tremendous rigor and specificity, is the following: which particular agent of nationalism failed, through its performative, to achieve pedagogical authority on behalf of the people? The failures of different agencies such as neocolonialist, comprador, the indigenous elite, the subaltern, the nationalist male, the nationalist female, are all conflated into one monolithic failure. What then follows is an idealist refutation of all pedagogical authority, and consequently no account is provided of how certain "intentions" went awry in their performance, or how certain intentions were not truly representative of the people. There is no way to read diagnostically and meaningfully into the gap between the performative and the pedagogical. Quite in keeping with the Lacanian thesis that the very possibility of meaning is grounded in the radical possibility of miscommunication and misrecognition, Bhabha's thesis capitalizes failure absolutely, overlooking in the process the ongoing historical tension between any specific act of knowing and the omni-historical horizon of failure and negativity. Bhabha's theoretical model (more psychoanalytical than historical) thus loses the ability to learn something from failure.[64] Learning from failure is possible only when failures are understood as relational phenomena that help in evaluating the distance between intentions and achievements. But the essentialization of failure by Bhabha trivializes the significance of specific failures as they occur during specific times for specific reasons.

It could be argued that there is some justification for launching an all-out global critique of nationalism, for isn't nationalism in disrepute the world over, including the West? And besides, isn't it unfair to talk about the West as though it were one undifferentiated bloc? First of all, nationalisms the world over are defunct only in theory, but not in historical practice. And as my opening to this chapter argues, nationalism is hale and kicking in the first world, including the USA. Yes, indeed, the West is not one homogeneous formation (there are all kinds of "differences within"), but my point is that during colonialism the West was orchestrated as a unified effect, with telling consequences for the non-West. But more importantly, yes, there is an East–West divide, but this divide was not the doing of the third world. On the contrary, discourses of modernity and nationalism found it convenient to play the East–West game as a way of dealing with other cultures.[65] It is galling for the third world to be told that the West suddenly no longer exists, just because the West has willed it so: yet another example of the West's ability to unilaterally change the very name of the game whenever it freely chooses. The "West" is not just its localized name, but also the history of its travels and pernicious effects on other histories, and unless this aspect of the historical effects of the West on the rest is acknowledged as part of its identity,[66] East–West cooperation, by way of the "post," is bound to be entirely superficial.

The problem not addressed by Bhabha is that decolonized people, after their overthrow of colonialism, are faced with the crisis of agency. Bhabha's theory of postcoloniality does not acknowledge the basic non-coincidence of postcolonial *interest* with poststructuralist epistemology. Although through his elaboration of concepts like "sly civility" and "mimicry"[67] Bhabha has helped us to understand how the native is always in an antagonistic–deconstructive relationship with colonialist discourse, he never goes beyond the strategy of playing the master's game against him/her;[68] nor is he interested in ascertaining if there are other knowledges besides the master discourse of the West. Bhabha does assert that he is interested in producing through theory a "third space," but here again, the third space, as a movement of deconstructive displacement and "difference," falls well within the epistemological jurisdiction of Western discourse. The third space that I am interested in is an emergent macropolitical space (complicit neither with the West nor with fundamentalisms that are after all reactive to the West) with its own independent knowledge claims. To Bhabha, however, it is enough to theorize postcoloniality as a lack that frustrates the plenitude of metropolitan theory. Take postmodernism/postconstructivism away from Bhabha's theory, and instantly postcoloniality disappears also. In other words, there is no sense of *constituency in the theory* apart from the *constituency of theory*.

One way to account for this excessive dependence on poststructuralist theory is to invoke Bhabha's diasporan location as explanation. Living in the West and being an integral part of theoretical, cultural, and academic developments in the West, how can one's theory not be constituted by one's location as well as subject position? This explanation is not only quite insufficient, but it also trivializes and vulgarizes the profound significance of the very term "politics of location."[69] Clearly, by "location" we cannot mean something as impoverished and debilitating as one's actual and physical location. Locations are as factual as they are imaginary and imagined, and as physical as they are prepsychic, and as open to direct experience as they are to empathic participation. Location and identity, and location and knowledge are not mutually implosive, but mutually ek-static. And besides, locations are never simple, but rather multi-layered realities overdetermined by diverse cultural and political flows. In a postmodern world that is almost a virtual product of protean and multi-directional transfers and relays of information bytes and knowledge chunks, it is just a little bit shabby to claim location as an alibi for one's nonpresence in other realities. The "politics of location" is productive not because location immures people within their specific four walls, but because it makes one location vulnerable to the claims of another, and enables multiple contested readings of the "same reality" from a variety of locations and positions. As Lata Mani develops this notion so thoughtfully, location is a heavily mediated concept, and unless the many mediations that interpellate location are studied in all their interconnectedness, locational analyses will be no more than exercises in defensive self-absorption.[70]

Like any location, diasporan locations are characterized both by an "expressive totality" and the reality of uneven and relatively autonomous mediations that constitute and account for the totality.[71] The provocative question is always this: how is the totality spoken for or represented? How does the straddling-many-worlds experience result in a "home" and how is the ethnoscape of such a home produced into knowledge?[72] To take a hypothetical example: my taste in music could be primarily Carnatic music and jazz, secondarily Hindi and Tamil film music, and, at a tertiary level, contemporary rock and Western classical music. My affinities in literature could be primarily contemporary multiethnic literature of the USA; secondarily, canonical British and American literary works; tertiarily, contemporary Tamil bestsellers. My lifestyle may privilege the two-career nuclear family ethic, but my values may well endorse the extended family system. I could be a fierce champion of individual rights and the right to privacy, but on another level I am an uncompromising opponent of capitalism and the privatization of morality. I could be a secular atheist who participates in Indian religious events for cultural and ethnic reasons. I might scoff at nationalist ways of denominating realities, and at the same time I could be a passionate Indian, but under the third world umbrella. In other words, I could be hyphenated more than once and in more than one direction. In each of these configurations, the relationship between experience and identity is differently achieved: in some through physical intimacy and proximity, and in others through psychic and emotional solidarity. Some realities are real in a physical sense, and others imaginary. Different spaces get collocated through the logics of nearness and distance: there are multiple accents and patterns, and often, clashing priority agendas. As I have argued elsewhere, this profile of multi-historical hybridity operates hierarchically, whereby some of the elements that constitute hybridity have a greater say than others in giving it a name.[73] Thus, if my culinary preferences were exclusively South Indian, my cultural identity generally Indian, but all my cognitive–rational–intellectual value systems secular Western, it is inevitable that in an overall sense I would be more Western than Indian or South Indian. This is simply because the domain where I have chosen to be Western, the domain of cognition and rationality, is more determining in this last instance of my totality than any of the other domains. My very awareness of my Indianness in those other areas will be the result of a cognitive production, itself not Indian in its mode of operation. Within such a conjunctural "cross-hatching," to use Gayatri Spivak's ringing phrase, epistemology plays the honored role of speaking for the hybridity. In Bhabha's version of hybridity, the expressive historical totality in the final analysis is articulated by poststructuralist epistemology.

Bhabha's reading of a poem by Jussawalla is an interesting example of how metropolitan theory rereads a postcolonial dilemma as a poststructuralist aporia. In his analysis of the semantics of the letter/spiritual symbol "OM" (a religious Hindu symbol which raises the further question: what is the significance of a Hindu symbol to different secular Indians, the Hindu Indian, the Christian, the Parsi, the Sikh Indian, etc.?), Bhabha felicitously subsumes "OM" within poststructuralist–deconstructive procedures without ever acknowledging, let alone analyzing, the indigenous genealogy of that profound symbol.[74] My concern is not with the "correctness" or the "insiderness" of one genealogy and the "incorrect alienness" of the other, but rather with the nonchalant manner in which Bhabha's reading denies the poem its intense "double-coding."[75] The rich symbolics of a different culture automatically become the pretext for metropolitan theoretical virtuosity. Could poststructuralism by any chance be a problem here? Is it conceivable that Derrida, Lacan, and Foucault may at best be distracting when applied to postcoloniality? Could there be other epistemic starting points for the elaboration of postcolonial complexity?

I do not want to be misunderstood as an ideologue who would resist at any cost the "interruptions" and "readings against the grain" of the kind advocated and practiced by Gayatri Spivak.[76] There is a great and urgent need for transnational and transcultural readings, but these readings have to concede the reality of other knowledges. Transcultural readings are the very turf where the legitimacies of different knowledges should be contested, and not an arena where readings take on a purely epiphenomenal significance long after the question of knowledge has been settled in favor of metropolitan knowledge.[77] Unless and until "other worlds" are recognized not merely as *other histories* but as *other knowledges* that question the legitimacy of metropolitan theory,[78] no substantive common ground can be coordinated between postmodernism and postcoloniality. The postmodern concern and solicitude for the "other" has to step beyond the pieties of deconstructive–psychoanalytic thought.[79]

The vexing issue facing postmodern epistemology is how to reconcile a radical incommensurability among multiple knowledges and knowledge games with the dire need for a politics of mutual recognition – analogously, how to honor multiplicity and heterogeneity without an understanding of the very terrain of connectedness that makes heterogeneity visible in the first place. The category "recognition of the other" is posited at the level of cognition and epistemology; ironically, the very level at which "incommensurability" is also posited as a motif intrinsic to the postmodern condition. If there is radical incommensurability, then there can be no recognition. If recognition is to go beyond the mere phenomenal and/or empiricist acknowledgment of the mere facticity of the "other," then a way has to be found to transcend this incommensurability. Without such a transcendence in the name of a potentially multilateral universalism, we cannot even begin to pose the problem of how to read one history in terms of another. Neither the relativist postmodernist impasse nor the liberalist invocation of multiculturalism in the name of the dominant One serves the postcolonial need for equitable transactions among different histories and different knowledges.

To repeat myself, it is at the level of knowledge that the postcolonial subject has sustained crucial damage. Caught between two knowledges (one not one's own, and the other one's own but lacking in historical–political clout), the postcolonial subject remains a purely reactive subject: its *for-itself* rendered exclusively a function of its existence *for-the-other*, its *for-itself* hampered from producing its self-version as a form of a universal *in-itself*. Lacanian proponents may well claim universal purchase for their theories of alterity, but in the case of the postcolonial subject we cannot afford to forget that the Self–Other conjuncture has been mediated by the structure-in-dominance of colonialism that is historical and not a mere matter for allegory. As Partha Chatterjee has convincingly argued, decolonization by way of secularism has been a poisoned remedy for postcolonial peoples.[80] For them, secularism represents political victory at the expense of epistemological self-esteem. The difficult and unenviable task facing third world intellectuals is that of upholding secularism as a political ideology while at the same time critiquing secularism as a form of epistemological dominance. As Madhu Kishwar develops her thesis in essay after essay,[81] it is not a question of denying Western influences, some of which are beneficial, but rather a question of affirming one's own knowledge base in a global context that views "experiences" as "underdeveloped" and "Eastern," whereas the epistemic categories that make sense of "experiences" are deemed to be of the West. Furthermore, an unquestioning acceptance of secular modernity often comes in the way of third world projects that return in a revisionist mode to their own past – a past in fact invented by modernity in Manichaean opposition to its own spirit. These projects of return to one's own traditions have become epistemologically unfashionable, thanks to the postmodern insistence on identity deconstruction. It must be stated that the revisionist return projects are not necessarily characterized by nostalgia or by a fundamentalist impulse, but the need to separate the truth of one's own traditions from the significances attributed to them by the colonizer. Are the truths of Islam and Hinduism no different from the form they have been given by Indologists and Orientalists? What are the realities of one's tradition, good and bad, when viewed from within the tradition? Are there traditions other than the ones set up by colonialism in its attempts to essentialize and inferiorize indigenous cultures? The fact of the matter is that modernity effectively delegitimated the Hindu critique of Hinduism and the Islamic critique of Islam. It is as though such critiques did not exist at all, and the only critiques available were through the deracinating modernist theories of knowledge. As we have already seen, capitulation to modernist ideology preempts possibilities of one's own history and one's own knowledge: the center of one's reality is always made to lie elsewhere.

As we look at hybrid realities the world over during a period of increasing demographic and cultural overlaps, it seems sensible to question modernity's claim that it is the *Interpellation of all interpellations*. Can the claims of modernity be relativized and contextualized with reference to the criteria of relevance as experienced in the third world? Can the travel of modernity to the third world (to borrow from Said's notion of "traveling theory") be anything other than an "epistemic violence" of local theories and knowledges? This negotiation between "the local" and "the global" is an all-important issue that unfortunately receives no attention in postmodern theory that lives and dies by the logic of binary opposition: local *or* global. Controversial issues the world over raise this question repeatedly: when is global/universal policy or law relevant and when is it a violation of local traditions and laws?[82] On what grounds can "intervention" be justified morally and epistemologically? If global law is involved, on whose terms will the law be drawn up and promulgated? Should some areas be made available for global jurisdiction, while others are left to the authority of local norms and values? Given such a diversity of epistemic–juridical–moral spaces, how are events, situations, and experiences to be understood both *within* and *across* the legitimacies of discrete spaces? This problematic of space and spatiality has received (and rightly so) extraordinary theoretical attention in postmodernist theory.[83] And as I attempt to conclude this chapter, I would like to turn to the politics of space as empowered by postmodernist theory.

Unlike existential phenomenologists like Martin Heidegger and Jean-Paul Sartre, who invoked time and temporality as radical agents of change, postmodernist theory suggests that temporality is a spatial–discursive matter, and that when we say "time" or "temporality" we do not signify some raw, feral, and preconstituted force, but a very specific structuration of time (nationalist time, women's time, industrial or pastoral time, etc.) produced discursively into a binding episteme. Foucault's brilliant notion of *dans le vrai* sums up this idea of truth in history as a matter of spatial subjection. Ideological time is nothing but discursive epistemic space. Such a notion of spatialized time interrogates the unilinear teleology that underlies so much historicism. The sense of space, both physical geopolitical space and in an epistemic sense, cuts across and fragments the idea of identity evolving through history into a plenitude. Heterotopic and disjunctured realities are as much history as the history of rooted locatedness.[84] As Foucault's early work attempted so bravely, it is the advocacy of *discontinuity as history* that pits postmodernism against traditional historiographies that privilege the inherence of identity in non-moving origins. Postmodernism thus offers a dire threat to discourses of identity. If identity is nothing but a narrative effect and if, furthermore, narratives themselves are instances of unavoidable cognitive failure, then surely "identity" is neither viable ontologically nor defensible epistemologically. Hence the need in Foucault to "think a different history" and to write the history of the present, which requires different tools, strategies, and a different sense of space. This spatial revolution could be valorized as an entirely formal project (and I would not endorse that option), or better still, empowered as a historical project of imagining different spaces for different histories and knowledges that have been subjugated for too long – constrained to exist in darkness as gaps, holes, and "ineffables" within the body of a dominant historiography.

The Politics of Spatiality

It all depends how and in what interests postmodern spaces are to be imagined and activated. In the name of what principles should postmodern spaces be coordinated? Postmodernism at its best champions the phenomenology of lived experiences and verities against the authority of top-down identity regimes and their deceitful historiographies. These realities need to imagine their own discursive homes; homes that are not as yet real in history. These spaces need to be "imagined" in excess of and in advance of (avant-garde in this sense) actual history in the name of experiences that are real but lacking in legitimacy. Each of these lived realities, such as the ethnic, the diasporic, the gay, the migrant, the subaltern, etc., needs to imagine its own discursive–epistemic space as a form of openness to one another's persuasion: neither totalized oppression (where, for example, "nationalist time/history" presumes to speak for all other times/histories), nor relativist isolation whereby each history remains an island unto itself.

Given the aegis of the "post," what kind of new spatiality is to be conceptualized so that different histories can, in and of their very being, be responsive to the realities of other histories? How can the decentered spatial politics of the "post" help us understand the representational identity politics of specific groups and their interconnectedness? By way of responding to these questions, I go to a novel by Amitav Ghosh, *The Shadow Lines*, a work that goes a long way in developing such a dialogic cartographic imaginary.[85] It is well beyond the scope of this chapter to do justice to the complex perspectives on nationalism and the diaspora that are historicized in the novel. I would merely like to sketch a few of the important formulations on the space–location–identity problematic that Ghosh develops in his novel through a strategy of polyvocality and heteroglossia that is a lot more multi-historical than the kind of metropolitan ventriloquism one finds in the works of Salman Rushdie. Here, in schematic fashion, are some of the insights in the novel:

1 Spaces are real precisely because they are imagined.
2 The imagination of spaces acknowledges both the need for and the limitations of fixed spaces.
3 The transcendence of fixed spaces is motivated globally but executed locally.
4 One does not have to be an insider to understand the reality of any specific space; all spaces are reciprocally ek-static/exotopic.
5 The meaning of history is a function of narrative.

  6   All realities are "versions" in their epistemological grounding, but all too "real" in their political effects; hence the need to have "one's own" version.

  7   One can, through global empathy and the practice of a "precise imagination," understand and experience realities other than one's own.

  8   Understanding history is a deeply interpretive procedure and not a matter for a fact-based empiricism.

  9   Histories are never discrete; in fact, when any collectivity looks into a mirror to obtain a reflection of itself, the mirror operates both as a mirror into one's self and as a window into other selves.

10   Distinctions are to be made between a longing for the other's reality based on violence or exoticism, and a genuine dialogic longing based on possibilities of reciprocal and equal transcendence.[86]

11   The deconstruction of the "shadow lines" of nationalist divides is to be achieved by a transnational populist force that calls into question the adequacy of nationalist regimes by way of the authority of lived experiences and reciprocal realities.

My brief focus here will be on the manner in which Ghosh's postnationalist, traveling text calls for a thoroughgoing critique of existing discourses and regimes of Identity. But unlike a Rushdie text, this very call for deterritorialization is located in multiple histories: colonialism, nationalism, and only then transnationalism or the diaspora. There is no joyous counter-memory at work here; all three histories, each with its different but related center, are made to commingle in a variety of relationships. This substantive critique, to use Lacanian parlance, is interested in the overthrow of the mighty Symbolic by the Imaginary.[87] Ghosh's text demonstrates the utter poverty of the regime of the Symbolic, and argues for the need for a different political Imaginary. In a historical sense, the Symbolic stands for the authority of nationalism as interpellated by the nation-state that insists that all other and prior imaginary relationships and identifications (be they gender- and sexuality-based, or class-, religion-, ethnicity-, and community-specific) be mediated and alienated into knowledge by the symbolic authority of nationalism that, like the duplicitous Lacanian phallus, exercises total command precisely because it cannot be *had* by any one group, and yet can perform its representative–pedagogic function with seeming neutrality. Consequently, the symbolic of nationalism is thus turned into a perennial and incorrigible "lack" that can be critiqued perennially, but never transcended in the name of a different alternative.[88]

Like a number of feminists who have refused the notion of such a total interpellation by the Symbolic (in the name of the father), Ghosh, too, rejects the attractions of the negative critique, which in the ultimate analysis prolongs the same and "enjoys the symptom." Ghosh's fiction suggests that there is a pressing need for "imaginary" self-identifications of peoples across the world, and that such a need is by no means naive or pre-theoretical. The "imaginary" compels us to rethink our existing affiliations that have been founded entirely on an epistemology of alienation: the alienation of the Imaginary by the Symbolic.

Perhaps I must hasten here to point out a few things about "imaginary self-identification" so as to anticipate a number of canonical Lacanian objections. First of all, the act of self-identification through the mirror is "imaginary," and not real, and adulthood is all about the realization that identifications are indeed as imaginary as they are necessary. Secondly, the imaginary realm is necessary so that human beings may measure and evaluate the extent to which they have or have not attained their imaginary self-identity. Without the Imaginary there is no way of appraising the distance between who we are and who we want to be: all that we would be left with is the fetishized authority of the Symbolic accountable to none other than itself. Finally, the Imaginary, unlike the Symbolic, is a historically vulnerable mode of operation and not the "name of the Law." The mirror, as Ghosh develops it in a fictional world where voices resonate off each other and different worlds "image" one another despite distances in time and space, avoids the error of a dominant universalism based on one's self-image, as well as the perils of a chic relativism that uses the mirror as a form of self-enclosure. The mirror turned into window becomes a mirror–window dyad that does not allow the relational–historical structure of the Self–Other conjuncture as it operates both within and athwart cultures, to ossify into One Self–Other configuration as warranted by the dominant world order. As a result, the Self–Other problematic is posed as a multi- and inter-historical issue and not as a philosophic issue rooted in the rectitude of the dominant world order. There are "selves" and "others" operating within and across cultures, there are innumerable "comings" and "goings," "arrivals" and "departures" that refuse to make sense within a single historiography.

The spatial vision offered in *The Shadow Lines* is as imaginary as it is experiential. Between events and their meaning, between peoples and their destinies, a gap has opened up, and it should be the ethic of new historiographies to imagine new spaces that will connect legitimately the world of experience with the language of meaning. These spaces are the spaces of the "post" that are transformative of the status quo. This transformative imagining of relational spaces is equally an attempt to enfranchise different knowledges with historical reference to one another.

This way of imagining the "post" seems to me to be more worthwhile than the fashionable global regionalism/localism that is being promoted currently in the name of the universal commodity form. It is in the interests of a capital-driven postmodernism to cultivate and support localism in far-off places, only to reclaim these localisms as part of a universally vendible global localism. We cannot also afford to forget, given the asymmetry of power relations, that the West retains the power to decide when the "other" is like "us," and when not, so that the very cultivation of the "politics of difference and heterogeneity" is subservient to the dominant demand for difference and heterogeneity. It is "access" that postmodernism is after, and consumption is its basic premise. Localism and specificity should be available to the metropolitan gaze so that the remotest spot from the most underdeveloped sector of the third world may begin to satisfy the "epistemological thirst" of the metropolitan center.

This entire chapter has been a tentative effort to separate out the emancipatory possibilities of postmodernism from its colonizing potentialities, and to articulate coalitions between East and West, between First and Third. I have also tried to argue that the valence of postmodernism cannot be decided upon without reference to the accountability of postmodernism to the rest of the world. For postmodernism to have any kind of meaningful travel across the world, it has to present itself to the world as a finite ideology based on specific interests and not as a value-neutral and ideologically free form of knowledge or human condition, and be prepared to face challenges from other knowledges from other parts of the world and consent to have its self-story narrativized by the "others." This turning of tables (or what Gayatri Spivak has termed suggestively "the anthropologization of the West") is historically necessary before the time-spaces of the "post" can begin to reinvent and reimagine a truly equal and multilateral universality. Without a change of direction, the "post" will only serve to exacerbate existing asymmetries. Perhaps postmodernism is also post-Western in ways not available to the metropolitan consciousness.[89]

In the words of Samir Amin, as he "imagines" a more egalitarian universal society, such a "society will be superior to ours on all levels only if it is worldwide, and only if it establishes a genuine universalism, based on contributions of everyone, Westerners as well as those whose historical course has been different."[90] A universalism liberated from dominance, and captive no more to the ventriloquism of the West.[91]

2
The Use and Abuse of Multiculturalism

The Multicultural Who?

Given the number of pages that have been devoted to it, it seems that multiculturalism as discourse has come to stay. By that I mean it has achieved a certain discursive duration that should not be confused with historical or experiential duration. Why make this distinction between multiculturalism as a historical reality and multiculturalism as a discursive event? As Michel Foucault has taught us with insistent rigor, the movement into discourse of any reality, and its eventual epistemologization within that discourse, are matters of high ideological significance. After all, what would it mean to say that we have suddenly discovered the multicultural nature of the world we live in? Wouldn't that be an abominable cliché, much like Columbus' discovery of the New World? Of course, the world has always been multicultural, but that is not the issue. The real question is why the insistence now in the first world, for the last decade or two, on multicultural*ism*? How has this new *ism* taken on such prominence, and what are the ethico-political and cognitive underpinnings of the mainstream advocacy of multiculturalism? How identifiable are the interests that drive the multicultural train on its way towards inclusiveness?

The significant difference, in the aftermath of massive decolonization all over the world and the migrations of peoples across national and cultural boundaries, is that multiculturalism is increasingly perceived as a crisis. Different realities "have leaked into one another," to use Salman Rushdie's phrase, and the first world is replete with the presence of the third world, its identity now interrupted by subaltern and minority "difference." It is no longer a mere academic or statistical awareness of the reality of multiple cultures all over the world but "thank God each culture is in its own place"; rather, it is a more troubling and lived awareness that the spaces where "we" live are no longer cordoned off from "their" spaces. If colonialism in its heyday instituted a hegemonic awareness of an Us–Them divide, in the postcolonial situation "they" are "here" with "us" in the very heart of metropolitan contemporaneity: Algerians in France, Islamic neighborhoods in London, Indo-Pakistani-Bangladeshi presence in England, and a variety of "ethnic" and immigrant life-worlds within the heartland of Euro-America. In the context of the USA, whose internal history of racism and xenophobia is different from that of colonialism, the problem of immigration has to do with people of color: not just "black" or "native" Americans, but a whole continuum of alterities – yellow, brown, and so on.[1]

Not only is alterity, in all its ontological generality, right at our doorstep, but we also have a variety of determinate alterities sharing "our" budget, "our" economy, occupying "our" marketplaces and cultural thresholds. Since all of this is happening here and not elsewhere, mainstream culture is being forced (a) to experience multiculturalism as a crisis that will not allow business to go on as usual, and therefore (b) to do something about it by taking the initiative. Mainstream discussions of multiculturalism have been part of an opportune and instrumentalist strategy to contain the crisis in the name of and from the point of view of the dominant regime. Now that "they" are "here" as fellow sharers of our civic and political space and as fellow sovereign citizens, what should "we" as dominant subjects do? Should we change, rename and re-narrativize ourselves from their point of view, initiate a perilous dialogics that will not allow us to shore-up our privilege, or assume a certain avant-gardism of representation whereby "we" can speak for the other and in doing so, include the other on our terms? Mainstream discourse on multiculturalism, with its assimilationist ideology, has clearly opted for the avant-gardist course of action, and as a result we have seen a rapid proliferation of diversity workshops, heterogeneity seminars, and sensitivity training sessions in academic and corporate sectors. The purpose here is to render differences intelligible to the mainstream and in the process maintain "our" anthropological relationship with the other. In other words, differences are not meaningful in themselves except as raw material to be made sense of in our laboratories of significance (they need our coding); and furthermore, we don't need to explain to them who we are or why we are who we are. The onus of intelligibility is on them as immigrants, diasporans, and ethnics, and thank God we are here to effect that translation into mainstream sovereignty.[2]

It is quite obvious that the discourse of multiculturalism is floundering at a very basic, even ostensive level. For lack of a radical decentering and for lack of a critical transcendence of the binary politics of Us–Them and Self–Other, the mainstream discourse on multiculturalism remains captive to the regime of the dominant One. The highly overdetermined opposition between the One and the "many" remains unproblematized, undeconstructed. Let us take, for example, a town hall meeting where the majority are Euro-Americans, and the minority is available in the bodies of a few African-Americans, a few Hispanics, a few Latino/a/s, and a few Asian-Americans. In such a context, it is the minority position that gets named and essentialized as the multi-culturalist position, whereas the "unnamed" majority is designated as the pro-tector and guarantor of diversity even though ontologically and politically the majority is not a member of "diversity" or "difference." In a move of strong ide-ological disavowal, the majority masquerading as the fully actualized One covers up its own internal history of difference, heterogeneity, and "becoming," and initiates what Jacques Derrida called "a centered play" or stratagem.[3] The majority position remains outside the politics of heterogeneity even as it directs the politics of multiculturalism. The "multi-" is that which has come after, and this latecomer is cast as the object of solicitude, patronage, and representation by the One. To state this in specifically American terms, and here I am echoing the profound contributions made by historians such as Howard Zinn and Ronald Takaki, it is assumed that the normative national measure of American identity is the Euro-American mold, whereas non-Western ethnici-ties are factored in as American only to the extent that they give in to and accept assimilation on terms already axiomatized by Euro-American presence.

I have opted to frame the issue of multiculturalism in the context of the politics of representation, since the contestation is indeed about the perspec-tival legitimacy of representation. The historical reality of the "multi-" has never been in question, but what is in question is the point of view from which the multivalent realities are spoken for and actualized. The multiculturalist ini-tiative as sponsored by the dominant culture sidesteps the question of what it would mean for the dominant regime to be narrativized and rendered visible from the points of view of the many and the unassimilated. Rather than pose the issue in dialogic and relational terms, the unilateral dominant mandate on behalf of multiculturalism fixes the many as the object of a paternalistic benev-olent representation. The "multi-" continues to carry the mark of alterity within a dominant model that refuses possibilities of reciprocity and mutual narrativization. In other words, nothing has changed in the house of Euro-America.

Where and how does multiculturalism inhere in any given society? Who is the "exemplary" multicultural subject and can this subject be identified in the way in which we identify, say, the American subject or the Euro- or Afro-centric subject? Is multiculturalism a property or an essence that is carried effectively by some subjects, such as the subalterns, the ethnics, and the minorities? Would

I be persuasively multiculturalist if in addition to *being* an Asian-American I performed in *other* ways and sported *other* tastes and styles in the way I dress, behave, make friends, eat food, or enjoy music? My point is that so long as multiculturalism is perceived as a subset of the Identity theme (and its inevitable entanglement with the binarism of Self and Other), it is doomed to failure. Within the aegis of identity politics, multiculturalism can at best tantalize the Self with the exotic distance of Alterity, all the while making sure that this distance will never be negotiated in the name of a coeval relationality.[4] The only options are to "eat the other", to use bell hooks' ringing phrase, become the other through an act of histrionic virtuosity, or just ignore the other as non-negotiably different. All these options are hopelessly locked within the Manichaeanism of the Identity–Difference game. I would like to suggest that any honest attempt at embodying multiculturalism as social value and praxis has to step beyond the reified rhetoric of Self and Other, of Identity and Difference, in a spirit of decentered multilateralism. For starters, multiculturalism has to be thought of as an eccentric and exotopic field that is not to be mastered by the will to dominance of any one subject. The only way to honor and enter the multicultural field is in a spirit of self-reflexivity, self-consciencization, and submission to that radical alterity that founds all social process in opposition to egocentric ideals of self and other.[5]

Let me try to elaborate the problem in terms borrowed from Lacan, by way of Žižek.[6] My fundamental purpose in this excursion is to argue for the reinstatement of the category of "universality," certainly not universality in its old fashioned dominant attire, but a relational and perspectival universality that is always in process. In other words, it is crucial to reformulate the category or the space of the universal as the objective semantic horizon that enables the multilateral activation of multiculturalism. If multiculturalism is a field whose radical alterity is not reducible to identity politics or to the narcissistic fixity of subject positions, then the only way to attempt a worthwhile multicultural politics is through a rigorously cultivated accountability to the Other: not the frozen and reified "other" glorified and reviled by Manichaean thought, but the alterity of the *socius* itself, and consequently the always unacknowledged "other within." The first challenge proffered by a rigorous practice of multiculturalism is to the category called "recognition." If recognition is a kind of mirroring and confirming process by which any given identity, collective or individual, affirms itself by looking at itself in its own "imaginary mirror," avoiding or disallowing in the process the legitimacy of "other mirrorings" of itself, the exotopic logic of multiculturalism as field insists that the egoistic *naïveté* of a self-entrenching mirroring be demystified, not just in the name of the Lacanian Symbolic, but also interrupted and problematized by "other mirrorings" of itself and self-recognition. The symbolic alterity that I invoke here has an ethical authority that is binding on all the members of the "multi-" continuum, but this authority functions in the form of a constructed *a priori* (i.e., an *a priori* constituted by the "multi-" that is willing to disclose the historicity of its own construction and authority). In other words, this form of ethical apriorism can only be the ongoing and interminable result of a critical practice undertaken as a perennial accountability to the other.

Let us say, for example, that a Hindu experience (based on the ideology of Hindutva) wants to recognize itself as authentic or legitimate. The standard procedure would be to use the transparency of an ideologically or canonically sanctioned Hindu imaginary or mirror that would confirm or question the "Hinduness" of the experience. But what if Hindus insisted that their act of self-recognition be routed necessarily through a Christian, Islamic, or Zoroastrian imaginary as well? This conscious and defamiliarizing attempt at connecting "one's" ontological integrity to the ethico-political legitimacy of the other's gaze opens up the blocked connection between inter- and intra-identitarian modes of thinking and in the final analysis deconstructs the practice of identity as a form of enclosure. Critiques undertaken of "one's" identity can now move beyond a narrow range of provincial filiations and naturalizations. Of course, as can be anticipated, there can be no end to the process of mirroring once it is set in motion, but the choice of mirrors can always be made on the basis of historical contingency and polemical urgency.[7] Thus, in the contemporary Indian context of the ascendancy of an aggressive communalist Hindutva, it becomes imperative to mediate Hindu self-cognition by way of the Islamic imaginary. Similarly, the Palestinian gaze has to be built into the visual field where Israel presents itself to itself. The ethical obligation can always be embodied in response to determinate historical hostilities and antagonisms, but the point to be made is that this obligation of vulnerability to the other's gaze is as much ethical as it is political. Here, we have to be very careful about how we coordinate the ethical with the political.[8]

If my (i.e., any "one's") self-cognition (all cognition is re-cognition, since cognition inevitably raises the issue of doubleness and alienation, reality and the mirror image, naturalness and consciousness through knowledge) is validated merely and exclusively in the eye or gaze of a determinate other, what results is a dyadic oversimplification of the alterity of the field. The moment the category "in the name of" is filled with the authority of a particular gaze or perspective, the "real" spirit of "in the name of" is betrayed for reasons that are exclusively political, strategic, or opportunistic.[9] In other words, the open and nameless categorial space of "in the name of" gets usurped by the dominance of a specific name. What we then have is a false or pseudo-formulation whereby the Hindu is made to feel that her adequate "self-same" reality is being invaded and alienated by the Islamic gaze. Out of this sense of hurt and indignation comes the fanatical desire to repossess one's self-cognition and wrest it from the other's perspective. What started out as a dialogic move gets enacted as a conflictual or antagonistic operation where it becomes increasingly necessary to shore-up and embattle one's self-image against visualization by the other. The highly valuable self-knowledge or insight that the Hindu could have arrived at through a radical exteriorization (other-originated knowledge) by the Islamic gaze is now rendered hostile or impossible. What is left is the boring and sanctimonious drama of one version against another in the absence of a deeper "Other" grounding.

As any elementary psycho-sociological study will tell us, social reality is made up of the following dimensions:

1 Self as experienced and legitimated from the point of view of the Self.
2 Self as experienced and legitimated from the point of view of the other.
3 The other experienced and legitimated from the point of view of the Self.
4 The other experienced and legitimated from the other's point of view.
5 Most significantly, an "objective" theory of reality that grounds and gives meaning to the dialectical–differential play of meaning between Self and other by way of a multilateral accountability to the big O.

Any theory of multiculturalism, if it is not to drown in the quicksand of solipsism or fall prey to extreme and irreducible particularism, has to deal with the twin issues of objectivity and universality. Objectivity diagnosed (and rightly so) as the privilege of a dominant perspective that anoints itself as the perspective of all perspectives has been retired in favor of a swarming multiplicity of solipsistic and reciprocally unintelligible subjectivities. Correspondingly, universality has given way to radically heterogeneous locations and subject positions that refuse implication in relational macro-narratives. But what about a hermeneutically sensitive objectivity realizable as "common ground" and a relational, decentered, and multilateral universalism based on the assumption that persuasion among perspectives is possible as well as desirable? To put this in the context of the multiculturalist debate, on what objective–universal ground can the identity and value of any one group experience be rendered valuable and intelligible to another group, i.e., without recourse to the politics of exotic difference or the strategies of a monothetic mainstreaming?

Calling the Shots: Who and From Where?

Let me try to explore this by means of a concrete example. Here is a situation that transpires *ad nauseam* in the lives of passionate tennis spectators such as myself. The US Open is on and the television coverage is as exquisite as it is long and inclusive. I am watching a sizzling down-the-line Agassi forehand ("Oh my God! Did it just catch the outer edge of the line or not?"), and it has been called "out." I want to make a decisive judgment call, from where I am, and here it does not matter whether I am watching it live or on television. So I say, "From where I am watching, the ball *was* [and I pause in confusion, and in the name of an all-consuming phenomenological honesty], hmm, the ball *seemed* in." The very syntax in which I phrase my call dramatizes the tension between the "objective" fall of the ball and the perspectival perception of that very fall, from where I was watching. I feel compelled to hesitate (both as a rhetorical strategy and as an admission of perspectival probity as finitude, for after all I cannot pretend that I saw the fall as I might or could have if I had been occupying a different perspective), between the objective rigor of "the ball was in" and the subjective ambiguity or skepsis of "the ball seemed in." Why do I even feel compelled to make an objective judgment call and at the same time detract from the potential verity of my statement, all in the name of per-spectival distortion or misrepresentation? After all, in this situation, to follow Nietzsche and the phenomenologists, am I not my perspective? Would not the act of doubting my perspective and its attendant truth claim amount to dis-crediting my claim to have a say in the matter? The epistemological ambiva-lence in my response suggests that it is possible to assert in a categorial or formal mode my right to my "seeming truth" as it is visible to me, and at the same time entertain skepticism regarding the truth content of what I see and the appropriateness or otherwise of the very perspective of which I am the ver-itable occupant. The thesis of phenomenological perspectivism enjoins me to experience my point of view and its interiority as "truth" or as a version of truth, while at the same time something in my mode of phenomenological wit-nessing whispers to me that by the law of perspectives there will indeed be other perspectives on the same event and that each of these perspectives will have its contingent say on the matter. Therefore, in deference to that law, I am constrained to speak in a double register (for without acceptance of that law of perspectivism my own perspective will have no cognitive or epistem-ological legitimacy) and announce and thematize my perspective as limitation, as embodied finitude.

Is it possible then that I can see erroneously and falsify the event as a func-tion of my situatedness? Is it possible to evacuate my perspective of its truth content without formally renouncing that perspective, in order to honor, accommodate, and understand other perspectives and to sustain the possibil-ity of an objective call? But then what do I do, or how do I negotiate with other perspectives or with an Objectivity that is not experientially available to me? This profound tussle has always been at the heart of phenomenology: how to reconcile the reality of situated and embodied truths with the possibility of an objectivity that cannot by definition be situated (i.e., if by situated we mean caught up within the subjective finitudes of perspectivism). After all, Objectivity, too, has to be a spectacle seen from a certain perspective, and if that is the case, how is this perspective different from all other perspectives?

Perhaps a quick rehearsal of the phenomenological intention is in order, and here I would be privileging the model proposed by Maurice Merleau-Ponty in his *Phenomenology of Perception*. The purpose of phenomenology was, in the act of going back to "things themselves," to effect a reciprocal relationship between the reality of perspective and the reality of objectivity. Rather than celebrate objectivity as a form of apriorism, the phenomenological intention was to find objectivity in the perspectival. Objectivity is given, not as an *a priori* given, but given to perspectivity. The next step is this: since perspectives are heterogeneous, myriad, and non-totalizable, to question a canonical and closed-off notion of objectivity in the name of heterogeneous perspectivism. Next comes the tension between objectivity as totality and perspectivism as subjective finitude. Rather than pose the two as implacable antagonists, phenomenology enlarges and reinvigorates objectivity by making it inexhaustible and forever new (hence the appeal of phenomenology to artists who wanted to speak perennially from "the now," and who wanted to avoid sclerotic closure passing itself off as normative objectivity). The "back to things themselves" manifesto undertaken both in the name of a "primordial" reality and as a critique of maps that usurp the place of reality (a critique of the inherent narcissism in all epistemology and thereby the indirect celebration of "objectivity," for here we cannot afford to forget that phenomenologists, and Merleau-Ponty in particular, were Marxists as well and the phenomenological defense of objectivity is compatible with Marxian materialism) recasts objectivity as an inexhaustible horizon that is constantly made and remade by the play of perspectives. Objectivity does not transcend subjectivity, nor does it situate itself apodictically beyond the play of perspectives; instead, it gets reformulated as a given that is to be achieved in and through the exercise and play of perspectives. The ontological status of objectivity is reconceptualized as an epistemological property of perspectives, which in turn are mandated to look for objectivity as a function of their never-ending negotiations among themselves. In this way, Merleau-Ponty attempted to protect and sustain the given nature of objectivity by phenomenologically calling into question the hubris of methodology, while at the same time he rendered objectivity itself compatible and harmonious with the nature of perspectival investigation.

The point to remember is that at no time does phenomenology inflate the claims of subjectivity to question the status of objectivity. The problem, rather, is how to reconcile the two through phenomenology as process. It is in this context that Merleau-Ponty resorts to the use of "the pre-personal One" that is neither reducible to egocentric finitude nor "absolutizable" into the One of Omniscience that transgresses all perspectives. It is in the name of the pre-personal One that is available to each "person," that "objectivity" is co-thinkable as a horizon by all the perspectives (i.e., subjectivities that constitute the phenomenological continuum). Phenomenology thus makes it possible for any embodied personal gaze to operate simultaneously on a double visual register: the personal and the pre-personal. The latter is neither owned nor automatically instantiated by the former. The latter grounds the former as the very precondition of its acuity. To state this in the context of perspectivism, my perspective can honor itself only if it honors a perspective different from mine, but this can happen legitimately only if both perspectives acknowledge grounding in a third term which is nothing other than "objectivity as horizon." Objectivity is therefore neither pre-perspectival, if by that we mean the categorical non-availability of objectivity to perspectival investigations, nor post-perspectival, if by that we mean the final balancing of all perspectives in an act of transcendence that renders objectivity a home where all perspectives lose themselves. Rather, objectivity is a horizon in process that makes perspectivism intelligible to itself.

Lest I be misunderstood as positing objectivity in violation of the intricacies of hermeneutics, let me clarify. The position from which the "objective call" is made is not a post-hermeneutic position. To go back to the fall of the ball: replays from a variety of angles can indeed tell us which angle is most objectively suited for which call. Hence, different lines persons for different calls. Among the many possible angles, there is indeed an angle that sees the fall "objectively," or should I say, as the ball sees itself. The objective position *vis-à-vis* that particular event does not coincide with reality itself; rather, it is the best analytic–interpretive position available on the event. And here "objectivity" is also intended in a Marxian vein to suggest that an objective description would be able to reveal the inner or the systemic truth of a situation diagnostically, rather than remain arrested at the merely subjective or experiential level.

To illustrate this more concretely: let us think of real life situations, such as someone being denied entrance to an elite company, a woman experiencing the glass ceiling, someone being systematically subjected to ethnic slurs. In each of these cases, class, gender, and ethnicity might be the appropriate objective points of entry to help us understand the incident in all its complexity; that is, understand it in a way that is deeper and "more correct" than the surface characteristics of the incident might allow us to do. For example, we might be persuaded prima facie to believe that the racial–ethnic situation can be resolved on the basis of interpersonal generosity and give and take, but a more objective analysis reveals "the ethnic" or "the racialized" nature of the situation, and such an analysis is indeed "more correct" than a superficial fix.

What is Correctness?

With the term "correctness" we have reached the sore heart of the multiculturalist debate. Whatever one's position on multiculturalism, both the resistance to and the advocacy of multiculturalism are encoded as responses to the problem of "political correctness." Very often, within the binary divide that I have already tried to describe, the unassimilated (Them) are perceived as beneficiaries of political correctness, and the already assimilated (Us) are cast as helpless victims whose conscience is being twisted and wrung in excess of any possible conscious wrong doing, so that the benefits that accrue from "political correctness" may be extorted from their reluctant acquiescence. Here again, it is as though the Us had no part in the fate of the Them except when forced to have a part on the basis of "political correctness." In all this exaggerated and misdirected focus on PC what is forgotten altogether is the possibility of persuasion among groups, identities, and constituencies. Also forgotten is the relational, cooperative, and systemic nature of social accountability. After all, correctness without an underlying persuasion is at best cosmetic, administrative, and procedural.

As we have already seen, the meaning of multiculturalism is far from transparent. It is indeed a contradictorily coded term that, depending upon how and from what point of view it is articulated, stands in for a range of contradictory social phenomena and values. Multiculturalism could be developed along lines of social justice, egalitarian democratic participation, and the ideological yet multilateral production of social consensus and dissent.[10] On the other hand, multiculturalism could be commodified and aestheticized and packaged as an exciting consumable collage: brown hands holding yellow hands holding white hands holding male hands holding female hands holding black hands in a spirit of post-historical contemporaneity. It is the latter super-capitalist manifestation of multiculturalist *zeitgeist* that ought to be resisted vigorously and without compromise. This consumerist version "spectacularizes" multiculturalism, and in doing so promotes the insidious belief that all the different groups occupy an even playing field, encourages historical amnesia, and by creating an immanent spectacle (seeing after all is believing in this day and age of technological virtuality) conceals the actual center of power that remains external to the constitution of the collage and thereby controls and directs the representational politics that undergirds the frame of the collage. The tacit (and, one might add, seductive) ideology of the collage as aesthetic lies in its seeming transcendence of the regime of representation. The seduction of the aesthetic form lies in its ability to create an intense and intimate sense of "speaking" and expression from within the collage, while at the same time cutting the connection between "speaking" and "speaking for," reducing expression to a response of unmediated participation and pleasure. The ideology of the collage form effectively silences, in the name of immediate authenticity and visual pleasure, any kind of second order reflexivity.

If the frame of multiculturalist collage were to speak, how would it speak: as one voice, as many voices, symphonically or cacophonously, as voices speaking simultaneously on one or multiple registers, or as voices taking turns according to a prior and invisible measure of prioritization and gerrymandering, or as voices interrupting one another? What would be the cognitive/epistemological preconditions for the collage to make sense as heterogeneous babble or as unified performance? Would the different components be intelligible to one another, and if so, on what or whose terms? What is the synecdochal logic at work here that negotiates between the autonomy of the parts and the integrity of the whole? A prematurely postmodern celebration of the collage form will only tend to valorize the semiosis at work in the form as a kind of desirable post-representational triumph. And one should be wary of this tendency. It is precisely because the collage seems so aleatory and value neutral in its organization and self-presentation that it achieves its own kind of didacticism. As an under-theorized form, the collage does not produce a second order knowledge-as-critique of the structural and systemic relationships that are at work within the frame, despite the deracination that realizes the collage as collage. Lacking a multilateral syncretic awareness of the interconnectedness among its ingredients, the collage merely reproduces the ideology of the status quo. It goes even beyond: by virtue of its seductive tactic of spectacularizing differences within the same frame, the multicultural collage disarms diagnostic readings of "how it is framed."[11]

It is only by rigorously insisting on the politics of representation that we can steer the multiculturalist debate towards such dire social issues as equality, distributive justice, and reparation and compensation for crimes and injustices of the past, and the ongoing influence of the past on the present. For it will not be enough to say that a collage-style deterritorialization has already enabled the "multi-" to speak and to believe that such speaking has rendered obsolete the relationship that each different culture has to itself representatively and representationally. The big O or the symbolic alterity that is doing all the interpellation of the collage is accessible differently and differentially to the brown hand, and the black hand, and the yellow hand, and the white hand. On whose bidding did the different bodies "choose" to come together in the context of the frame, and what about possibilities other than the one provided by this frame? Unlike a coalitional model that would have for its prerequisite the condition that each member within the coalition be substantively dialogized and re-semanticized with reference to all other members of the coalition, the collage model does not promote intra- and inter-historical dialogues within and between constituencies. As a result of its inability to reconceptualize the relationship between the one and the many, between sameness and difference, the multiculturalist frame as collage misreads both the egalitarian ideal that underlies distributive justice and the recognition politics undertaken in the name of difference.

If the collage model of multiculturalism is erroneous, what indeed is the right model? I would like to advance the thesis that multiculturalism cannot be in complicity with business as usual, and that there are some things to be taught and learned here, and some things to be corrected and rectified. Rather than run away in fear from the very term "correctness," radical theorists of multiculturalism need to align "correction" with "persuasion," ethical as well as epistemological, historically and contingently, with the idea of realizing "common ground" among identities, groups, and constituencies by re-formulating the very nature of "interest" and its inherence in the politics of perspectivism. So why is the term "politically correct" so abhorrent? Is rectitude such a bad quality after all? What about political fairness or justice? Aren't we as human beings interested in "correct" evaluations of situations, i.e., so long as the correctness is not a matter of ideological servitude that abuses the "means" in the name of the "ends," or a form of doctrinaire rigor mortis, so long as it is not a top-down concept that refuses to historicize its own meaning and value? Why is the freedom "not to want to be correct" more basic and fundamental than the necessity "not to be wrong"? Say you are in a group and some one says something about a "gal/chick/babe," or an "Indian gift," or a "fag/dyke," or an "Oriental friend," or about somebody "welshing" somebody else, and you find yourself intervening firmly but non-magisterially (do you really have the choice not to intervene?), and let us say your critical comments are resented in the name of personal freedom and you end up being accused of "political correctness." What do you do now and what are your options – you who seemed so pedagogically sure of yourself and have now been found guilty of a solecism, perhaps even a violation? Do you, for fear of impinging on the freedom of the others to remain who they are (for after all, no one is obliged to be non-racist, non-ethnocentric, or non-sexist), disavow and recant the "correctness" of your intervention? My point is that non-interference on one's part would have been absolutely "wrong" and "incorrect," precisely and proportionately to the extent that their utterances were "wrong" and "incorrect." The much-vaunted procedural sense of freedom that guarantees everyone's right to persist in his/her biases and isms is the result of a profound misreading of the relationship between "freedom as content" and "freedom as procedural or formal possibility." The autonomization of freedom as a formal guarantee is a relative and not an absolute autonomization.[12]

To go back to my example, what are the possible explanations for the incorrect speech?

1 They were not aware of the history of any of the offensive terms, and therefore they are innocent and unaccountable as individuals. Furthermore, they had not put the offense in the words themselves: the epithets were already there, sanctioned by historical usage. Response: ignorance is not innocence, and this is an example of a hurtful sanctioned ignorance. Learn self-reflexivity and auto-critique as a necessary component of human speech and articulation. Unlearn your innocence and change your behavior accordingly. As for accountability, by definition the term implicates the individual in processes and concepts larger than the mere present and the notion of an isolated individual consciousness.

2 They were aware that the terms were suspect and yet used them because, after all, everything is not political, and besides it is not always easy coming up with the right terms. Response: there indeed are other words, go learn them. As for everything not being political, go tell it to the people you denigrated by your slurs; or think of yourselves as the potential objects of similar slurs. The mark of the political is contestation, and believe me, your verbal behavior is eminently contestable.

3 Sure, they knew it was wrong, but it was OK in present company since no such "other" was present. Response: this is sheer hypocrisy. How can you know that something is wrong and still commit the act? And surely, the authority of right or wrong has nothing to do with who is there unless you conceptualize right and wrong in terms of mere opportunistic behavior.

4 We can and will say what we want and bracket the nature and the content of what we are saying. This is a free country. Response: such a defense of freedom is fatuous and is totally devoid of any complex historical understanding of what it means to defend freedom as a formal right.

The point that I want to thump home, even at the risk of being branded an ideologue, is that any discussion of freedom that evacuates the concept of its fraught history and its painful genealogy of determinate causes and values is itself a grave injustice to the "cause of freedom."

The correction that is being made is not made in the name of any one individual, group, or constituency that has arrogated to itself the privilege (based on suffering: Jewish, Palestinian, feminine, subaltern, or whatever) of omniscience and eternal correctness. All corrections are historically contingent and the perspective that initiates the correction is itself not invulnerable to error and oppression. No perspective has a monopolistic hold over the ethico-political capital of humanity. Rather, the correction is made in the name of a transcendent human principle or value that is more worthwhile and precious than the egotism or the moral righteousness of any one group. And besides, the correction is made not in the name of a finished or immaculate ethics, but in the name of a process of becoming:[13] a process that is directed towards the idea of respect of all, for and by all. The correction is made in a spirit of critical solidarity and the point of view from which the "correction" emanates is neither permanent nor free of historical taint and sedimentation. Corrections can be made on the basis of partial and contingent knowledges, and there is no everlasting ontology to the perspective that provides the correction at a determinate historical conjuncture. The content of the correction is not claimed in the name of some transhistorical truth or principle, but rather, the very moment of "affirmative correction"(affirmation since the correction does say a loud "yes" to a certain idea or principle of justice) opens up its own precarious history.[14] Thus, what could be deemed near formulaic or programmatic pronouncements by NOW, Manavi, the ACLU, or the NAACP on matters pertaining to gender, race, sexuality, or the politics of women of color, in fact, could be made to historicize themselves with reference to "where they came from." The truth as well as the ethico-political acuity of the position taken is inseparable from the historical actuality of the conditions of production of that very truth. In other words, the voice that speaks through the correction can only be contingent in its authority. There need be no contradiction between the universally realizable nature of the ethico-political attitude and the historical limitations of its perspectival production.

Let me now address the relationship between correction and persuasion. When we are talking persuasion, there are no winners and no losers: it is not a wretched zero-sum game. When Gandhi insisted on making a distinction between the personhood of a Britisher and the colonial politics of the British Raj, and when he affirmed time and again that it was his mission to persuade the British that it was immoral and deeply harmful to their own interests and psychic well-being not to grant India its independence, he was indeed trying to set in motion an ethics of transcendent alterity that went beyond the immediacy of the colonizer–colonized divide and the political investments and interests of such a structuration. It was in the name of the Other that persuasion flowed from the weak to the strong, from the colonized to the colonizer. What is crucial to observe here is of course the directionality of the flow of persuasion. Surely, British colonialism had fabricated its own rhetoric of persuasion to convince the native of her inferiority and hence her unavoidable depend-

ence on colonialist epistemology and pedagogy. But the purpose here of persuasion was coercive–dominating and was premised on the obliteration of one
set of principles altogether: no dialogue or reciprocity here. Part of the challenge indeed is to differentiate among the motives that underlie persuasions
and productions of consent. It is indeed tempting at this stage to digress into
an elaborate discussion of the master's desire and freedom and the slave's, by
way of Hegel and Judith Butler, but that would indeed be a digression. For my
purposes here, I would just like to emphasize that ethico-political thinking
should avoid the circular and question-begging logic that declares that ethical
imperatives are to be determined by "interest." It is certainly ethical of me to
entertain strong self-interests, but this does not mean that all my self-interests
are always already ethical. There can be no "ethical thinking" unless it is on the
basis of a critical and other-oriented transcendence of the self. What needs to
be worked out is the nature of the relationship between "ethical self" and
"political interest."

Ethical Persuasion and Political Interest

Is there a "self" beyond interest, a self that has a reality before it has been constituted as such by "interest?" Conversely, what are the conditions under which
interests get embodied and instantiated as so many selves? Is this a mutually
constituting–constituted nexus,[15] and does this reciprocal constitution take
place without excess and slippage? In other words, is the "self" entirely
reducible to "interest" and is "interest" the only analytic that makes the "self"
intelligible to itself? But what about "ethical" situations where self-interest has
to be directed against itself, either in the name of a greater and transcendent
good or in the name of a "species-interest" whose authority is more binding
and legitimate than an atomized self-interest? What about the ethical constitution of the self and its hyphenated connection with the self as politically constructed? If the political paradigm attempts to clinch and gain closure for the
self in terms of discrete and isolable interests, the ethical imperative points
sternly in the direction of the Other, understood both as determinate others,
and more significantly, as a radical–categorial alterity that underlies the bina-
rized self–other political configuration. It is this dilemmatic and aporetic
tension between the ethical and the political poles of persuasion that I wish to
explore in the pages that follow. It is my objective to activate the hyphen that
connects the ethical and the political within the figurality of a relationship in
difference, and to try to open up the "occlusion of the Other" that takes place
so habitually and unself-reflexively in the realm of political representation.

At this point, let me restate the non-identical relationship between persuasion and correctness. Whereas "correctness" focuses on questions of authority and prefers end-state orientations (as in "we want to get closure in the debate by announcing who got it right and who was wrong; case closed"), "persuasion" is criteria and process oriented and opens up the possibility of the "correct answer" to multiple "ownership," all in the name of a transcendent ethical alterity. The task of persuasion, to borrow from Gramsci, is permanent and perennial, whereas the objective of correctness is egocentric correction without the benefit of self-reflexivity and auto-critique. Whereas the rhetoric of correctness would have its practitioners believe, in a kind of positivistic hubris, that once they have reached "correctness," all alterity has been dissolved, and hence they can speak from within the plenitude of the correct rhetoric, the language of persuasion acknowledges the need for an ongoing and contingent correctness, but fosters in the ethical subject a critical and long-term (utopian if you will) attitude towards correctness and the historical construction of correctness. Lest I be misunderstood as posing the ethical and the political as adversarial categories, or as suggesting that the ethical subject is "disinterested" in projects of correction, let me repeat and say that ethical persuasion includes "correctness," but its mode of legitimation follows a different path from that of political triumph and conquest. .

To begin then with the political mode. What indeed marks "the political?" For starters, we might say that the political begins with the activation of "perspective," and along with perspective comes "interest." In opposition to metaphysical and humanist notions of universal representation that believe in the "disinterestedness" of knowledge, the discourse of the political-as-ideological drives home the reality that all representations of truth and knowledge are unavoidably interested and perspectival. Nietzsche and Marx, each in his own way, conceived of the political as agon, as an arena of contestation.[16] Marx went much farther than Nietzsche in asking the following question: given the brute reality of "classed" interests, how should dialectical materialism go about producing a class as perspective that will in the end universalize itself as the true and necessary spokesperson of the "species-being" of all humanity?[17] Gramsci's demystification of the so-called "traditional intellectual" and his theory of the "organic intellectual" legitimated in the name of subalternity go a long way in this direction. The political is born in conflict and in opposition to the dominant–repressive regime; furthermore, "the political" and "interestedness" are mutually coextensive, and the only way "the political" will disappear, as in the withering away of the state, is when a genuine uiniversalism has been realized in the name of all humanity; that will also be the moment when representation will have been rendered superfluous. Meanwhile, take away the notion of conflict and of antagonism and their corollary, the notion of "winning and losing," and the category of "the political" is instantly eviscerated and devitalized. More than persuading, more than elaborating common ground, the political purpose is to defeat the enemy. Labor and Capital collide; feminism and patriarchy are at loggerheads; colonizer and colonized are in implacable opposition, and so on. Change, progressive dialectical change through an ongoing production of theses and antitheses, is produced through the playing out of antagonisms and conflicts, and there are well defined winners and losers. The purpose of dialectical materialism is to motor the "right agency" (the proletariat) towards its actualization of *its* perspective as *the* universal perspective. Are the other classes to be persuaded or defeated?

Though "winning" or "having to win" has to be at the very heart of any political project, three fundamental questions loom on the horizon:

1 How to turn winning into an act of persuasion so that the effects of winning may be realized permanently in the heart of all humanity?
2 How to build into the political project of winning a component of ethical vigilance that will not flinch from blowing the whistle when the right revolution goes wrong?
3 How ultimately to valorize the revolution, not just in terms of winning and losing, but in terms of a value or direction that "wins" even when actual history is marred by the defeat of the just or when "winning" turns into a dystopic nightmare?

Walter Benjamin was well aware of these dangers, hence his poignant declaration that "Every document of civilization is equally a document of barbarism." Hence, too, his insistence on "rubbing history against the grain," and his perennial distrust of the winner's mode and the winner's historiography. It was as though in his attempt to ethicize dialectical Marxism, Benjamin was suggesting that genuine universal human triumph would consist in putting the very category of "winning" and "losing" under erasure. Real ethical winning would consist of a systemic interrogation of the very category of "winning," i.e., if historical materialism were to effectively differentiate itself from the hubris and barbarism of other developmental narratives. In other words, Benjamin chooses a "weak form" of winning, a winning in the name of an undying and abiding marginality. The "angel of progress" has to confront the debris that is mounting sky high, in the name of progress; and the angel has to face the past to make the future whole. Lest winning degenerate into a pyrrhic phenomenon, the revolutionary agent of history has to problematize the very modality known as "winning" so as to prevent the repetition of the Same. The Same is fated to be repeated unless the practice of politics as end-oriented is subjected to a rigorous ethical scrutiny anchored in the "purity" of the means, to use Gandhi's term.

As for the ethical model of persuasion, as I have already been saying, the ethical imperative honors the legitimacy of political interest, but its real purpose is to keep the latter honest and to keep providing it with a conscience, endlessly. The ethical imperative insists that the "means" be as legitimate and unexceptionable as the "ends," that the means be capable of justifying themselves autonomously. Whereas the political model takes persuasion for granted or believes that it is automatically effected as a by-product of the main event of "winning," the ethical model invests in persuasion absolutely and unconditionally. This pedagogy of persuasion has for its disciple both the colonizer and the colonized, the master and the slave. The political arrangement short-circuits the flow of persuasion by arresting it within the winner–loser structuration, whereas ethical subjectivity is open and vulnerable to the call of the big O: a call that is irreducible to the egocentric needs of political correctness. To persuade any self against its ostensible self-interest is indeed the essence of the ethical mandate.

One way of demonstrating the ethical principle at work, in conjunction with "political correctness," is in the context of the phenomenon of so-called reverse discrimination. Let me quickly analyze the semantics of the phrase "reverse discrimination." There are two parties: the discriminator and the discriminated; and of course there is the reality of discrimination.[18] In the past there was the practice of discrimination and such a practice was legitimated, at the expense of the discriminated, in the self-interest of the discriminator. What I want to stress here is that there was a time when discrimination was a "valued" practice: its error and enormity were neither obvious nor axiomatic. In other words, the moral and political overthrow of the apartheid regime was not "always already" inscribed, negatively as it were, in the body or the history of discrimination. When discrimination was on, the agents who were practicing it were doing so cognitively, intentionally, and conatively (i.e., they believed in the rectitude of what they were doing). The "discriminated" suffered miserably; their humanity abrogated, they protested, went to jail, kept the movement going in the face of brutal repression, and after years of struggle that often seemed hopeless, eventually succeeded in dismantling the system of apartheid. The ethico-political "value" of "anti-discrimination" was therefore produced historically and agentially. It was not some *a priori* truth whose time had come quite immaculately. There is no inclusive universal and undivided "we" that authored the truth of anti-discrimination. The truth was produced antagonistically by the victims of discrimination in total and absolute opposition to the regime being executed by the discriminator.

The irony of so-called reverse discrimination is that of repetition, a repetition without learning. Tables are turned, positions reversed, but the phenomenon of discrimination persists. It is as though it is quite impossible, once and for all, generally and universally, to outlaw discrimination. Instead, we need to go through the same historical process on behalf of each and every oppressed and discriminated group, invent the wheel *ab ovo*, *ab initio*. How then can a cognitive transition be made from a discriminatory world into a post-discriminatory world? How is such a critical transcendence to be achieved with a sense of history and historical accountability? Clearly, it would be quite disingenuous to claim that a critical transformation to a post-apartheid or a post-racist or a post-patriarchal temporality can take the form of a clean break with the past. The injustices and inequalities of past histories ought to be redressed and remedied, uneven and biased arenas need to be divested of bias, profound political and psychic traumas need to be named and healed, lost histories need to be recovered and dignified. Indeed, the past has to be corrected in certain ways and remembered "counter-mnemonically" before an egalitarian future for all can be envisioned. It must be obvious by now that I have been using the phrase "so-called reverse discrimination" to indicate my profound disagreement with the proponents of that thesis. For these are the same people who hastily misread the "ethic" of affirmative action, and in doing so revert to a naive and non-ideological notion of the "political," and grossly oversimplify the asynchronous relationship of the ethical to the political.

The debates over so-called reverse discrimination and affirmative action raise fundamental questions about universal humanism as a transperspectival ideal, about how to get there via the practice of a perspectival politics, and about the nature of bias and the bias to end bias altogether. My position is neither that reverse discrimination cannot take place and that the oppressed in their turn cannot become oppressors, nor that affirmative action can do no wrong and therefore needs to be perpetuated. Rather, my argument, in light of the articulation I have been attempting between the ethical and the political, is that terms like "affirmation," "discrimination," and "bias" need to be subjected to a rigorous historical and theoretical analysis. In what follows I will be using the word "bias" on multiple registers: (1) to mark "bias" as something wrong and injurious that requires correction (i.e., the unself-reflexive practice of bias and the consequent worldviews); (2) "bias" as progressive partisanship whereby *bias as bias* is thematized and understood as such, resulting in the partisan need to "end bias"; and (3) bias as understood in the hermeneutic tradition that scandalized positivism by asserting that "prejudice" is intrinsic to the activity of human comprehension and interpretation. I would then be claiming that bias is both corrigible and incorrigible, and that the correction of bias cannot be divorced from the rhetoric of advocacy and that of perspectivism. Here are a few questions. Is it logical to equate the bias to end all bias with a particular instance of discriminatory bias? Isn't a bias undertaken on behalf of the oppressed in fact not a bias at all? How is the long-term or utopian goal of ending all bias to be coordinated with the immediate historical goals of correction and remediation?

Affirmative action can be perceived either as a mechanical procedure or as a mechanism backed by the authority of persuasion. Let us take a look at the term: affirmative action. Some value is being affirmed, said "yes" to on behalf of somebody or some group, but in the name of all humanity. An analytic as well as historical distinction needs to be made between the axiology of "in the name of" and the polemical valence of "on behalf of." When redress and historical reparation are made "on behalf" of say, a woman of color, it must be remembered that this correct and just act is being undertaken "in the name of" all humanity. The blank that follows "in the name of" is not to be filled by a determinate name such as the African-American, the lesbian, the Chicana. The ethical imprimatur of "in the name of" is in fact a radical namelessness and is spoken for by a radical alterity that in speaking for all guards against the usurpation of that open space by the sovereignty of any one determinate name. But the "nameless" dignity of all humanity, or of the "species-being," whose value is enshrined in all human beings as the Other, has to be spoken for and produced as a contingent principle in different historical conjunctures by determinate, named human groups. Thus, when Gandhi or King or Susan B. Anthony or Mandela speak, they speak for all humanity; and when advocacy is practiced on behalf of the Haitian man brutalized by the police, it can only be in the name of all humanity. No winners or losers here. A white male understands why "his" job went to an equally qualified "person of color" because his ethical subjectivity tells him that it should be so. Whereas a narrowly interested political spin on affirmative action creates the belief that the person of color got the job at the expense of the white male, an ethical understanding brings the "self" out of its cocoon of "interest" and makes it vulnerable to the call of the Other. In such vulnerability rests human weal spoken for on behalf of the weakest link, but in the name of all. It is only on the basis of specific, situated acts of partisanship and advocacy and perspectival commitment that the Other in each self can be honored and affirmed.

As we consider the ethico-political authority of any human "value" that we consider universal, it is important (1) to consider the relationship between the cause that carries the value and the immediate historical agent of that cause, and (2) to acknowledge the "produced" nature of the value in question. Though the "value" may well be universal, we cannot afford to forget that the burden of producing that value, as the *telos of their cause*, was borne in history by a particular group of people and it was through their embodied experiences of pain and struggle that the cause attained its universality. Furthermore, the ideal in whose cause a particular people suffered and struggled was not already available in some essential form, only to be made manifest by historical struggle. On the contrary, it was the struggle that produced the ideal. To put it in Foucauldian–genealogical terms, the universally binding authority of values such as "freedom" and "equality" should not be separated from the traces that produced them in the first place. In other words, careful distinction needs to be made between a glib, unsituated, utilitarian universalism and a historically fraught perspectival universalism. Without this distinction there is the real danger that perspectival truths will get prematurely universalized, and as a result, historical prices will remain unpaid and obligations and acknowledgments will be obliterated.

Let us take for an example the ironic logic by which both Mandela and de Klerk become recipients of the Nobel Prize for Peace. Within the systemic logic of binarity, the semantics of the slave and that of the master are ruthlessly conflated and we arrive at the following preposterous premise: the enunciation of the slave's truth requires, is even dependent on, the truth of the master.[19] That the two truths and the will to power behind each of these truths are differently and adversarially charged is overlooked within the coercive synchronicity of the master–slave binary. That the ANC and the State were "enemies" is conveniently forgotten. What comes to pass is a bland and polemic-purged celebration of the overthrow of apartheid in which Mandela and de Klerk become benign co-producers of a post-apartheid South Africa. Did de Klerk ever say sorry and did his party confess to a horrendous *mea culpa* and ask for forgiveness? No. Instead, a value born in suffering and conflict, a value so tenuous and contingent that it might well not have seen the light of day, is now suddenly a universal value, shorn of its perspectival prehistory. As Mandela and de Klerk share the same podium (and I am not saying that they should not; indeed they should, but with a difference), the history of where each of them came from is erased and forgotten in the name of a natural and dominant humanism. It is far from my intention to argue that the ANC is beyond reproach or that by mere extension of its ethico-political authority accrued during the period of apartheid, its exercise of sovereignty on behalf of the people of South Africa will be free from blemish. If anything, the onus is now on the ANC as protagonist in history to guarantee that there will be no "reverse discrimination" and that there will be no abuse of power in the name of the people and no garnering of privilege in the name of its own illustrious path. Here again I am reminded of Mohandas Gandhi's farsighted ethical prescription that the Indian National Congress Party should disband itself immediately after India's attainment of independence. As far as Gandhi was concerned, the rationale of the Congress Party to exist had vanished the moment India attained independence, and it was not Gandhi's desire that the party should shore itself up politically in the name of political power. Gandhi's mode of action was consistent in its emphasis that the ethical demand was of a higher order than political expediency. Whether it is the context of affirmative action, or multicultural democracy in post-apartheid South Africa, or the integrity of postcolonial politics in the new nation-states of the third world, more important than the calculus of power sharing and strategies of aggrandizement and appeasement is the deep-down reality of ethical persuasion. No! the whites and the Afrikaners did not lose while the blacks won. The triumph was universal. My contention is that the dominance of the political model militates against the realization of a deeper ethical persuasion and, as a result, the wheel has to be invented over and over again. Each group within the *socius* continues to identify wins and losses purely in terms of its own narrow and provincial self-interests. That a political loss for a certain self and its interest can be an enormous moral triumph and lesson is overlooked in the heat of the present political moment. Self-interest based on restrictive identitarian ideologies comes in the way of a relational–universal commitment to the big O.

So why is persuasion so difficult, and why is it much easier to be interpellated by political interest than be hailed by ethical demand? How does one persuade the other, or the other persuade the one, without arrogating to itself the authority of rectitude? Why should one listen to the other in the absence of a self-interest to begin with? Why, in short, should I listen to you if there is nothing in it for me? And this is even more difficult: why should I cultivate vulnerability to the other when I know beforehand that it will result in my loss of privilege? I have been attempting to show all along that there is a yawning disconnection between the self-centered schemata of the political game and the Other-oriented flows of ethical idealism and ethical subjectivity. Is there some "disinterested" way in which epistemology can make it untenable for thought to coerce, colonize, dominate? Can epistemological persuasion take roots in the delicate hyphen that connects the ethical to the political and thereby inaugurate new and non-objectifying modes of knowing? Is it possible for such an epistemology to realize mirrors as windows and vice versa? Under what conditions does a mirror that reflects me back to myself act also like a window, thus enabling a movement out of the self, beyond? Correspondingly, under what conditions does a window that lets me into the world of the other also act as a mirror where I can see myself? What is the epistemological imperative that realizes the window as mirror and vice versa, and furthermore, what forms of recognition are enabled in a setting where windows and mirrors interiorize and exteriorize each other? These indeed are the questions that need to be asked if multiculturalism is to be realized as a multilateral initiative, if it is not to regress into the ugly rigidities of binary identity politics.

What happens when a group or constituency attempts to identify itself through an act of representation (i.e., self-representation)? We might make the case, in a Cartesian vein, that there is no self without a mediating process of representation. What matters more than the factual pre-theoretical reality of the group is the representation that the group makes of itself as an act of cognitive necessity. As any self, individual or collective, seeks to "subjectivate" itself as an object of knowledge, it both reasserts and transgresses its originary intimacy with itself.[20] Central to the act of epistemological self-production are the need for recognition of the self and a critical alienation from the self. The recognition would not be possible without the alienation. There is both a comforting mirroring effect and a symbolic alienation. A group has to be able to recognize itself in its own imaginary even as it avoids the *naïveté* of identification with the mirror image. The recognition has to work for and on behalf of the group. A self-knowledge that is all alienation would be irrelevant and non-utile, whereas a knowledge that is all imaginary self-identification would be filiative in the worst restrictive sense of the term and hostile to possibilities of critical growth, movement, and self-transcendence. Knowledge then should be neither "home," where the home is merely a natural given, nor a cavalier deracination that leaves no room for contingent belongings and solidarities. To borrow usefully from Edward Said, knowledge should be another name for the perennial cultivation of criticism in solidarity and of the opening up of an in-between space.[21]

Between Recognition and Representation

But what about the status of this self-recognition in the context of other gazes? If, as Charles Taylor rightly points out in his highly influential essay "The Politics of Recognition," social realities are negotiated and achieved dialogically, how then do I factor in these other perspectives that emanate, not from me, and yet are integral to my self-definition and recognition? Moreover, how do I differentiate between those gazes that harm and objectify me and those that are generous and respectful of me, given that both kinds of gazes are formally legitimate? Clearly, I cannot insist, and it would not be healthy for me to do so, that the other's cognition of me should coincide with my cognition of myself. Also, I cannot compel the other's gaze to take as its axiomatic starting point my recognition of myself. What I can do, however, is to ask that even as the other exercises her freedom to narrativize me from her point of view without any juridical–normative interference from me, that she take into account in her recognition of me my recognition of myself – that she be aware that I am not a blank slate and that my cognition of myself is germane to her visualization of my reality. What I am trying to say in a poststructuralist vein is that there is no putative or originary self outside the field of cognitions, visualizations, and representations. In this sense, then, selves actualize themselves as perspectives acting on other selves and all perspectives enjoy equal formal validity. My point of view on myself does not enjoy any kind of primacy, privilege, or intrinsic infallibility. But what my perspective can demand of other perspectives is that they allow me similar latitude when I gaze at them, and that they honor the reality that I do exist unto myself within my perspective as an object and subject of knowledge. This acknowledgment is procedural and does not entail that the other has to concur with me in the contents of my self-recognition. In other words, the other cannot, without being guilty of hypocrisy, tell me that she honors me and at the same time display lack of awareness of my self-knowledge. Honoring me substantively and not just tokenistically would be to honor me within my narrative. Failure to do so can only result in what Spivak, with characteristic eloquence, has called "epistemic violence." The violence or violation here is not that an essential self has been "dissed" by another, but rather that a particular perspective and its knowledge have been preempted and silenced by the dominance of another perspective. At this point I would like to recall my earlier claim that multiculturalist realities have to resist representations as offered by a world structured in dominance.

The politics of recognition has to be articulated with and informed by the politics of subalternity. To put this in the context of the argumentative tenor of this entire chapter, the politics of recognition needs to be played out between the utopian and trans-ideological invocation of a relational universalism and an active and critical awareness of the representational failures and injustices of the status quo: on the one hand, submission by all selves, in a spirit of reciprocal coalition, to the alterity of the big O; on the other hand, the responsibility of subaltern "selves" to offer resistance and battle to the reality of structures in dominance. A politics of recognition voided of advocacy and partisanship would be nothing more than a mainstream gesture and nod towards difference. The fact of the matter is that some cultures have been recognized more than other cultures; some cultures have had recognition as a *fait accompli* while others have had to struggle against heavy odds. To restate this in the context of my earlier discussion of an absolute and unearned universalism and a perspectival universalism, the politics of recognition would have been unthinkable except from the point of view of subaltern and subjugated knowledges. It is only against the backdrop of an unevenly realized cognitive human landscape that the politics of recognition takes on any kind of meaning or significance. The critical task is to detach the morality of recognition from its anchorage in the visuality of dominance, to detach it from the *gaze as dominance*. To answer the question "Recognition by whom?" I would say, recognition in the name of a radical alterity and on behalf of the ones who have not been allowed to speak. The insistence on multilateral recognition is not in the name of the authenticity of any one group's self-image, but in the name of a categorical and systemic fairness and openness that rigorously guards against the possibility of "recognition" becoming the exclusive function of any one particular gaze. It is rather like an anti-trust provision against cognitive and epistemic monopoly and control. The politics of recognition is at work as a Derridean "double session":[22] on the one hand, the call for rectification and remediation of existing inequities and imbalances, and on the other, a utopian affirmation of openness as such.

In an otherwise engaging and deeply thoughtful essay, " The Politics of Recognition," Charles Taylor makes the critical mistake of equating the need for recognition with the clamor for authenticity.[23] What Taylor forgets to include in his calculus is the dire fact that the subalterns are those who have been obliged to undervalue "their being for themselves" so that they can be "somebody" in the gaze of and for the "other." Whether the example is that of an immigrant Chinese woman who renames herself as "Jane" to promote easy intelligibility to the "other," or that of an intransigent "ethnic" value that has to be mainstreamed before being admitted to sovereign national status, the issue is this: subaltern self-image has been constrained to realize itself adversarially against itself, indoctrinated to accept as chronic the disjunction between its reality and the intelligibility of that reality, and compelled to internalize the other's gaze as its gaze upon itself, whereas its point of view on the "other" has been thoroughly shorn of any kind of political valence or legitimacy. What we have here is the politics of unilateral non-reciprocal recognition: the politics of objectification. What kind of a self am I to myself if all I can be interested in is pleasing someone else's demands of me? What kind of self am I if in my encounter with the other I am always the one who is named, framed, looked at? What kind of a self am I if my very ontological reality is the absolute function of the other's gaze? What kind of a self am I that I am not able to influence the other through my self-image or persuade the other to see himself as a function of my gaze? These questions are symptomatic of a situation where recognition has gone awry, where the heterogeneous mirrors and windows of recognition have been replaced by mirrors of dominance. In such a context, the antagonism is not between the spurious and the authentic, between the extrinsic and the intrinsic, but rather between perspectives that have had and continue to have their say and those that have not as yet represented themselves. Subaltern constituencies do not know themselves, nor are they in touch with the meaning of their realities more directly or more authentically than any other group. As a matter of fact, it is this hasty and sloppy coupling of subalternity with authenticity that has depoliticized the subaltern cause and rendered it ever more vulnerable to the histrionics and theatricalizations of the dominant culture. The issue rather is that there is a "relative inside space" that pertains to every group including the subaltern, and in the case of the subaltern, the integrity of this space has been violated over and over again, and it is this right to speak for that interiority that is in question. It is not the celebration of that "inside as such" as the mystic *arche* and *telos* of some inscrutable authentic truth, or a validation of that interiority as a form of identity politics that runs counter to the vagaries and contingencies of the processes of representation. Quite to the contrary, it is the struggle for positional/locational/perspectival articulation. The subaltern cannot speak because she is always speaking from "elsewhere," lip-synching to some other tune. Dominant groups on the other hand, not any more or less authentic, have succeeded in exteriorizing their interiority as universal objectivity and in ideologizing their form of indigeny as universal cosmopolitanism.[24]

The subaltern demand is for permission to narrate a certain story from a certain place and a certain position, so that the story and "where it came from" can be made sense of together: in other words, not the exoticization or the alteriorization of "where it came from" in isolation from "what it is saying"(this would result in the fetishization of the subaltern body), nor a liberal or mainstream assimilation of "what is being said," deracinated from its subaltern "origins"(this would be a way of exorcizing the subaltern body altogether). The radical nature of subaltern speech is such that in its very drive towards amelioration and eventual hegemonization it would wish not to obliterate or transcend subalternity as perennial perspective. To work again with an example: let us say a controversial situation arises within an "ethnic" community regarding a certain cultural practice. We can either instantly dismantle the "inner" ideological space within which the controversy has taken shape, instantly force the issue out and open into universal–secular jurisdiction, resolve the issue, and in the process chalk up a triumph over the inadequacy, provincialism, or backwardness of the ethnic code or worldview; or, we can exercise patience and develop a sense of hearing and attentiveness so that we may come to understand how that issue is being mapped and parsed within the "ethnic" world. The intention here is not to laud the correctness of the insider code and assign it unquestionable relevance on the basis of its interiority, and indict any secular intervention as invasion and aggression. The objective is to acknowledge that there indeed is a productive "inside" space and to insist that whatever value or principle is produced as an act of self-understanding within that space (the ethnic way of knowing as against the cosmopolitan way of signifying) be admitted as substantive evidence along with other forms of evidence. For after all, how can the cosmopolitan secularist be so self-assured that the "ethnic" is incapable of self-critique and of quarreling antagonistically with his own tradition in search of better and more humane answers? Why does the project of amelioration and progressive critical self-consciousness have to bear the cosmopolitan/modernist imprimatur? When the self-image of a dominant culture meets up with the self-image of a subaltern culture on a world historical stage, the former all too easily destroys all subaltern defense on behalf of itself and prescribes its own mode of cognition as the answer to the subaltern question.

The issue that I am trying to delineate here is the delicate issue of insides and outsides, of insiders and outsiders. I am not an advocate of insiderism in general, but having said that I find it of paramount importance to add (1) that the whistle be blown loud and clear whenever a dominant culture or economy practices insiderism on behalf of its own interests; (2) that the subalterns reserve the right to practice insiderism in the scrupulosity of political interest whenever the dominant partners renege on their promise not to be "insiders"; and (3) that great care be taken not to misidentify the dialogue between the subaltern and the dominant cultures as the dialogue undertaken in the name of radical alterity. In other words, within the ethico-political continuum, the subaltern cannot afford to depoliticize its cause on a false guarantee that the world that is structured in dominance will somehow honor its ethical commitment to alterity, the big O. Here, too, I wish to stress the importance of the hyphen that differentially connects the ethical to the political. If the absolute ethical demand made of human subjectivity is that it be vulnerable to the gaze of the other, how does one deal with a situation where the "other's gaze," as in patriarchy, racism, colonialism, is "unethical" to start with: unethical because the intention of the gaze is to deny reciprocity and break trust with the big O. Just as it was unethical to obey the "legality" of Jim Crow laws, here too the ethical choice is not to honor the gaze of the unethical other. I bring this up only to point out that the subaltern subject has to keep making sharp situational decisions about where to cultivate ethical vulnerability and where to practice a politics of uncompromising resistance. The subaltern project cannot afford to surrender "its perspectival political value" to the gaze of the dominant as other unless and until the dominance of the other has been thoroughly politicized and ethicized by subaltern value.

As I have already indicated, while discussing these issues it is important that we do not conflate the two terms "identity politics" and the "politics of representation." Whereas authenticity would want to inhere in identity as its implicit cognitive precondition (identity and authenticity are thus mutually transfixed), the politics of representation forces identity out of its naive imaginary rendezvous with itself into the open space of representation: a space that is external to identity and is yet responsive to its historical needs and demands. My utopian long-term tendency is certainly post-identitarian, but not anti-identitarian. I make this distinction in the context of an uneven world where identity politics can have a strategic role. At the same time, there is an urgent need to step beyond the binary world of Identity–Difference, Self–Other, into a horizon where recognition and representation interact in that charged critical space where the Self–Other problematic can be rethought quite radically.

I have been commenting obliquely so far on Charles Taylor's profound contribution to the multiculturalist debate. It is time now to initiate a more focused dialogue with his work. Taylor's essay begins by yoking together the impetus behind multiculturalism with subaltern demands and with the subaltern insistence on nationalist recognition.

> A number of strands in contemporary politics turn on the need, sometimes the demand, for *recognition*. The need, it can be argued, is one of the driving forces behind nationalist movements in politics. And the demand comes to the fore in a number of ways in today's politics, on behalf of minority or "subaltern" groups, in some forms of feminism, and in what is today called the politics of "multiculturalism."[25]

Taylor goes on to acknowledge how misrecognition can indeed be a profound way of disrespecting a people and their culture. This is indeed a rousing way to begin an analytic essay on the merits and pitfalls of multiculturalism. It attempts to historicize multiculturalism and give it a local habitation and a name. And yet this beginning is full of slippages and hasty conflations that remain to haunt the entire essay: an essay that despite its erudition and tough-minded thinking is unable to bridge the gap between its philosophical base and its putative political trajectory. For starters, it is not clear why Taylor lumps together nationalism and a variety of subaltern and/or minority movements including feminist and ethnic movements. I am assuming, for lack of evidence to the contrary, that by nationalism Taylor denotes nationalisms of the third world (or for that matter the vanishing second world) that seem to be engaged in the virulent politics of self-affirmation and hegemonic identity politics. Taylor seems unaware of Partha Chatterjee's ground-breaking work on nationalism that brings to view the Us–Them mentality that underwrites most contemporary discussions of Eastern and Western nationalisms.[26] Not having availed himself of Chatterjee's thesis (a thesis that cannot be overlooked in any discussions of the ethico-political status of nationalist sovereignty), Charles Taylor would seem to be theorizing from within one of two possible worlds:

(1) a world that contains a postnationalist first world (a world that has been so successful in achieving national status on its own behalf that its nationalism is not marked any more by the ideology of national*ism*) and a third world where nationalism is rampant, rightly or wrongly, or for whatever reason; or (2) a world where there is nationalism that has no need for recognition (i.e., the good kind, as in Western nationalism), and there are those other recognition-driven subaltern nationalisms. At any rate, having articulated the term "nationalism" in an ostensive mode, Taylor has to acknowledge the reality that he has situated himself and his logic in a world where there *is* nationalism: good or bad, resistant or dominant, normative or idiosyncratic.[27] The fact that he identifies nationalism and its passions with subaltern and minority movements is a clear indication that he is thinking of third world or developing nationalisms and not Euro-American nationalisms. So where does this leave his rhetoric? Either he must hold the view consciously or unwittingly that nationalism has been transcended and "post-historicized" in and by the first world, or that there is indeed a Euro-American kind of nationalism, but this variety is not driven by the need for recognition, unlike subaltern nationalisms that are intrinsically and essentially recognition centered. His rhetoric also does not own up to the historical reality of a binary world structured in dominance with asymmetry and unevenness as its hallmarks, and by not acknowledging the implication of his own discourse in the deep-structure logic of an asymmetrical binarity, Taylor ends up, despite his best intentions, positing multiculturalism as a minority or subaltern issue with no ethico-political bearing on the goings on of the dominant/majority culture.

Taylor cannot mean that there is no nationalism "here," whereas it is alive and kicking in the subaltern zone – that would be just too blatantly counterfactual. Here is the point. As Partha Chatterjee has so ably argued, in the case of non-Western nationalisms the vital relationship between the *thematic* and the *problematic* is disjoined and therefore differently realized as a chronic form of "derivativeness." In the first world or Euro-American context, however, it is assumed that nationalism has been achieved organically and therefore it is a thing of the past: a stage that has been achieved and transcended within the teleology of a developmental logic. As for recognition, Western nationalism has been so thoroughly confirmed and recognized, and exported as exemplum to the rest of the world through colonialism and imperialist domination, that it has been naturalized to the point of invisibility. Not only has the dominant historiography of Western nationalism recognized itself in its own imaginary–symbolic mechanism, it has also "universalized" its mode of self-recognition. Having been successfully recognized as the "dominant–universal" paradigm, it has no need for recognition. In aligning subaltern needs and demands exclusively with the politics of recognition, Taylor ends up perpetuating the divide between dominant and subaltern, and what is even more injurious, protecting the dominant historiography from subaltern critique and disavowing the profound relationality between the two formations. It is almost as though the conditions of intelligibility of the two are just not sharable: there is *us* and there is *them*, and "we" as humans experience motivations that are different in principle from the ones that "they" experience.

It is interesting that, despite all this, Taylor understands that misrecognition can and does function as a form of put-down among societies. Now, what can "misrecognition" mean unless it is measured against a normative backdrop of what is *not misrecognition*? In what is to follow, it is important to remember that whatever is being said on behalf of "the subaltern perspective" is true for perspectives in general, and so "the subaltern question" is after all not a special interest attempting to muddy up and complicate some general law, but rather a diagnostic instance that brings to light what is seriously wrong with the mainstream/dominant discourse on multiculturalism. There are several possibilities here:

1   We can talk about recognition along the lines of content or substance and on that basis say something like this. A subaltern sees "this" when she looks at herself and it is this image she has of herself that is to be recognized from every other point of view on subaltern reality; for, in some inviolable and proximal sense, this is the correct answer. This option would attempt to shore-up "recognition" from the exteriorizing possibilities of representation.

2   We could maintain that recognition does not have to do with the rectitude of any pre-established, pre-perspectival, or pre-representational content that is secure in its autochthonous integrity, but rather with the freedom with which any group is able to inaugurate, maintain, and legitimate a point of view or perspective on itself. Such a perspective may not pre-know on the basis of a completely worked out political ideology what it may "contain" as its "proper content," but suffice it to say that the orientation of the perspective speaks for a certain "interest" even though the forms of historical embodiment of this "interest" have not been determined aprioristically.

3   Since recognition, whether it is subaltern or dominant, is always already dialogized, and furthermore, since the importance of "recognition" to any group or self can never afford to bypass the exteriorizing modality of "representation"(i.e., without representation there can be no recognition), the best option is to in-mix the urgencies of recognition with the politics of representation. The reason for this option would of course be to ensure that the intra- and the inter-aspects of self-reflexivity and self-recognition

of each and every perspective are worked out relationally and coevally with the intra- and inter- dimensions of every other perspective.

My recommendation is that options 2 and 3 be combined judiciously and strategically in the name of an egalitarian, multilateral practice of multiculturalism.

In the foregoing analysis my purpose has been twofold: on the one hand, to resolutely affirm subaltern perspective *as* perspective, rather than canonize it as a fulfilled vision or "content"; on the other hand, and with equal resolve, to reject the ghettoization of subaltern interest in the name of authenticity, separatism, or identity politics. Recognition and representation: how do these modalities intersect and how do they address each other? To recap, it is in the nature of "recognition" to want to naturalize "representation" in the name of a "natural" identity and thereby own or fix that "representation" in a self-entrenching, even self-securing manner. In other words, the Hindu would like to secure his self-image in the name of a sacred axiology, which over a period of time and through repeated ideological ritualization procedures becomes a "natural" Hindu blueprint that refuses to historicize itself as representation and in the process invalidates/delegitimates "other" representations of "its selfsame" identity. "Representation," on the other hand, insists that identities are necessary "subject effects" and, furthermore, that the alienating process of representation cannot be owned in allegiance by any identity. One can and should of course make value judgments about the nature of different representational truth claims based on their "interest" and the nature of "their will to knowledge," but the play of representations both within and among identities cannot be terminated or "shorted" in the name of essence, primordiality, or the dictates of a "natural" identity. Once we situate the practice of multiculturalism within this barely coordinated space between "recognition" and "representation," a space that honors the need for recognition without at the same time circumventing or censoring the play of representation, we are in a position to approach the problem of "correctness" contingently and processually, rather than in the name of a fixed and transcendental truth. The politics of representation and not identity politics becomes the focus of social transformation. To put it in the context of my critical discussion of "perspectivism," the focus is not on the pre-orchestrated and pre-ideologized "content" of a perspective (i.e., "what is inside" the perspective), but on the right of each and every perspective to enter into an egalitarian multilateral relationship with other perspectives. To put it even more specifically in the instance of "the subaltern as perspective," the claim is not that subalternity, by virtue of its being subjugated, knows its own truth ahead of its own representational practices. Nor is it an easy case of empathy, whereby "you will know my truth if only you stepped into my shoes." Perspectives do not give birth to their "knowledges" immaculately, and neither are these "knowledges" guaranteed as an extension of their "being." And even more significantly, the trap of liberal or neoliberal empathy has to be avoided at all cost, and here is why. Liberal empathy encourages the naive view that positions in life can be exchanged easily on the basis of a humanistic imagination, and all that is required of any class is a fertile enough mode of visualization that will enable it "to be in the place of the other," and then everything will be all right. This empathic view depoliticizes the real political distance between classes and instead endorses a politics of political lip-synching or theatrical ventriloquism. So long as I can effectively "imagine" myself in your position and effect such an epiphany of being across real political divides, I can "become you" and then real differences can be obliterated in the name of a trans-ideological humanism. As we can tell right away, such a perverse theory of empathy can only emanate from dominant positions as part of their benign attempt to speak more effectively for the "other" by virtually becoming "the other." But in fact real political change occurs only when possibilities of transformation are not tied to the specious premise of "identity interchangeability." In other words, "I" do not have to "become you" to be able to understand and respect "where you come from" and the ethico-political urgencies of that starting point. If anything, liberal notions of empathy, by promoting a facile belief in possibilities of "becoming the other" in an aesthetic–histrionic vein, demolish the necessary "distance of difference" and thereby exonerate each perspective of its accountability to the "other." "I" do not have to change in response to "you," since I have already solved that problem of accountability by demonstrating my histrionic desire and passion for "wanting to be you." I hope I am not laboring the point, but what needs to be remembered at all cost is that positions are not to be rendered mutually transparent through empathy. Even if "you" got into "my" shoes, you will not automatically see it "my way," simply because I too do not see it "my way" just because "I am me." The fact of the matter is that for "me to be me" cognitively and theoretically, I need to produce "my way" through an act of representative labor: I just do not have or own my way as an extension of my being.[28]

Despite his best intentions, Taylor's discourse ghettoizes subaltern world-views within their own "authenticities." It also effectively removes recognition and representation from the reality of mutually imbricated histories. Consequently, the all-important question of "what to do with misrecognition between and among cultures" remains unasked and unaskable within Taylor's analytic. In Taylor's multicultural universe, the dominant and the subaltern can never meet, leave alone address each other. The subaltern demand for recognition by the dominant other comes across instead as a fractious, truculent piece of adolescent behavior: the subaltern is after all throwing a tantrum –

"Please see me, notice me . . . or else." The tantrum, of course, cannot have any critical effect on the "adult" dominant discourse. What we get instead is a Manichaean world in which "recognition" is phenomenologized in the name of subaltern authenticity, and "representation" is carried out in the name of the dominant regime. The dominant historiography is exempted from recognition, whereas the subaltern is exiled from representation. In strongly identifying the subaltern demand with the need for recognition, Taylor in a sense pathologizes subalternity as a chronic practice of identity politics. The subaltern, from Taylor's perspective, is an outsider to the politics of representation. The unfortunate but inevitable upshot of it all is that "misrecognition" never gets diagnosed as a phenomenon that is both necessary and "corrigible" within a multilateral and relational field of representation where recognitions and representations are bouncing off one another without final recourse.

When Taylor does attempt to instrumentalize his reading of recognition and misrecognition to help him reach an evaluative stance regarding affirmative action, he comes up with statements like the following that to me are totally inexplicable:

> To proponents of the original politics of dignity, this can seem like a reversal, a betrayal, a simple negation of their cherished principle. Attempts are therefore made to mediate, to show how some of these measures meant to accommodate minorities can after all be justified on the original basis of dignity. These arguments can be successful up to a point. For instance, some of the (apparently) most flagrant departures from "difference-blindness" are reverse discrimination measures, affording people from previously unfavored groups a competitive advantage for jobs or places in universities. This practice has been justified on the grounds that historical discrimination has created a pattern within which the unfavored struggle at a disadvantage. Reverse discrimination is defended as a temporary measure that will eventually level the playing field and allow the old "blind" rules to come back into force in a way that doesn't disadvantage any one.[29]

First of all, there is the unproblematized and axiomatic use of the term "reverse discrimination," as though the reverse directionality of discrimination has been substantiated historically and institutionally. As I have been arguing all along, the nature of the uneven playing field is much more complicated than Taylor would allow it to be. Secondly, here too, Taylor attaches "discrimination" as an issue, not to the politics of representation, but to his pet peeve, subalternity as a fierce and unappeasable form of identity politics. Thirdly, Taylor conflates the language of distributive justice with that of cultural and/or ethnic difference (more of this later). And finally, and this blows me away, Taylor talks about "the old blind rules" prior to all the fuss about affirmative action. What on earth can he mean by "the old blind rules?" When, pray, in the heyday of humanism, were the rules blind? Was there indeed a past, American or otherwise, some golden age of which we are the pathetic and politically tainted postlapsarian inheritors-as-traitors, when justice was blind? My understanding all along has been that all revolutions and subaltern movements have been articulated on the premise of "a blindness to come," and not as a recuperation of "a blindness that has never been," except as the mighty ruse of dominant regimes. It is difficult to believe that a thinker as astute and progressive as Taylor would make the mistake of equating the philosophical claims of liberal humanism with the realities of historical practice, or that of reading history in the name of a regressive Utopia.[30] How could "blindness" be prior to the history of biases and discriminations? Here indeed we see the limitations of Taylor's discourse. Taylor is first and foremost a philosophical humanist, and as a humanist he would rather privilege the notion of "value" as something inherent and aprioristic, rather than as something that is produced *a posteriori* through perspectival historical conflict and antagonism. Rather than implicate his axiology in its own constitutive and genealogical contradictions, Taylor opts to speak in the name of a past and already realized blindness or bias-lessness. Unlike, say, a Foucault, who would never practice an ethics of justice in the name of an ideal truth or censor a genealogical analysis of the very history of truth (and Gramsci for one would go along with Foucault here, whatever their other differences), Taylor spirits away the ideological nature of value production in his humanistic account of the pursuit of truth and justice.

Sameness, Difference, and Justice

Time now to address a specific theme that has been hovering around this entire chapter: sameness and difference. My point of entry for this discussion will be Nancy Fraser's book *Justice Interreptus*, which combines, often brilliantly, the concerns of a political activist with the methodological rigor of an academic intellectual.[31] Unlike Charles Taylor, whose subject position is unmarked (he is a trans-ideological humanist philosopher), Nancy Taylor is identifiable as a post-socialist feminist profoundly influenced by aspects of poststructuralism and postmodernism. Unlike Charles Taylor, Nancy Fraser makes effective analytic distinctions between the cultural politics of difference and heterogeneity and the discourse of distributive justice whose aim it is to achieve the eradication of differences in the name of equality. Fraser is worried, and rightly so, that "our" society is experiencing an agonizing schism between the politics of difference that deploys race, nationalism, ethnicity, etc., and perpetuates these "particularistic" categories through their usage, and the teleological drive of distributive justice that – in employing categories such as gender and class – would in fact look forward, deconstructively as it were, to a future of "sameness" where these categories will have withered away, having lost their particularistic or special meaning and significance. Fraser's useful insistence throughout her book is that in practice these two forces or directions are often contradicting each other, addressing each other; and therefore we should not succumb to the temptation of practicing one or the other. Fraser is passionate in her call that social critical thinking should read the two movements, despite their analytic separability, dialectically and with relation to each other, so that some viable common ground may be coordinated in response to both pressures.

Let us see what such a common ground might look like, and from what perspective such common ground might be coordinated. First off, it is useful to make the observation that there is nothing inherently wrong with difference or being different. Peoples and cultures are different; and the all-important issue is how to receive and practice difference relationally and non-hierarchically; in other words, how to create a society that will not evaluate some differences more positively than others. Furthermore, practicing or embodying difference (a great example is the project of dwelling rigorously and passionately in "the hyphen" without succumbing to total integration on either side of ethnic hyphenation, i.e., sustaining difference along multiple axes without totalization) does not have to take the form of an ideologically reductive and a non-porous identity politics whereby "I am Afrocentric" whereas "you are Eurocentric." Differences and heterogeneities can be practiced openly, relationally, and as invitations to a rich and ongoing heteroglossia, rather than be primed as raw material for some grand unification or cultivated as hotbeds of separatist thought. The problem, as Jacques Derrida's work has been teaching us over the years, is when "difference" is construed and parsed in the name of identity, rather than allowed to realize itself differentially. And indeed it has been Derrida's project, in coining the term "differe(a)nce," to go beyond the binary structuration of the self–other problematic towards another kind of opening into human ontology. Foucault's work, too, has tried to wean difference away from its canonical status of "secondarity" or "supplementarity" towards a real and inalienable difference. If every identity within the self–other grid is inescapably marked by "difference," then it becomes utterly meaningless to mark only certain identities as "being different," such as the Jewish difference, or the gay difference, or the Arab difference. It becomes meaningless to ask "What does Jesse want?" or "What is the nature of ethnic difference?" Difference loses its stigma: we all are different from each other and from ourselves, both intra- and inter-historically, both in inter- and intra-identitarian ways. The mainstream, too, is ethnic and different, and therefore there is no need to militarize "identity" bureaucratically or otherwise against the onslaught of "difference." There is no "one" who is not "other" in the most fundamental sense of the term. Such a relationally heterogeneous understanding of "difference" deconstructs the self–other paradigm and enables representation to work along multiple axes rather than along the time-honored identitarian axis that always ends up on behalf of dominance and in violation of subalternity. Now, is such a practice of heterogeneity commensurable with the norm of distributive justice?

Consider for a moment the possibility that after generations of persuasive consciousness-raising and progressive legislation, "blindness" has been achieved and a level playing field brought into existence, and categories such as gender, sexuality, race, class, ethnicity, etc. have been successfully superannuated. Thus, in the workplace, one is just a human person, plain and simple, in the eyes of the law. In such a context where distributive justice has been achieved for and on behalf of all, what would it mean for "one" to desire to be perceived as African-American, Chicana, or lesbian? Would these categories as cultural markers of difference feel quite irrelevant now that distributive justice has "equalized" or "samed" every one, or would these markers exercise their significance in the "relatively autonomous" realm of culture and cultural semiosis? Would these categories enjoy representational legitimacy within their own contingent borders of experience and intensity? Would names have any valence at all? Would some names evoke a general–universal response, while other names still connote a narrow and a more provincial range? There being no determinate other, would a name which after all has the socializing function of making the self "callable" and "iterable" by the other have any functionality at all? In other words, how completely and without residue will the politico-economic sphere have spoken for the symbolic–cultural realm as well?

My own inclination is to maintain the tension in the name and in the naming process rather than assume that the distributive process will have worked out the differences within the symbolic/culture sphere. The problem here, as Nancy Fraser aptly points out, is that the domains of distributive justice and cultural difference are deeply intertwined. Though for purposes of analysis and selective social action it is possible to focus on one or the other, or assume that economic and political redistribution will automatically affect the cultural realm, in the context of lived reality such assumptions tend to oversimplify the nature of the relationship between the two realms. Let us face it: is it even possible to claim that distributive justice can be realized in analytic isolation from the affirmation of cultural value? Is it not quite likely that a person of color may have been empowered into equality on one level, and at the same time be made to feel "culturally inferior" to the culture of Euro-

America? How does the culture card get played out in the context of distributive justice? Did the Chicano have to "officially" renounce his bilingual heritage in favor of an all-American branding before he received "equal respect?" Did the Bangladeshi worker with a thick accent have to straighten out her spoken English before she became equal? What is the cultural price that has to be paid to pave the way for the implementation of distributive justice? Unless one follows an unregenerate base–superstructure model that believes in economic determinism of "the last instance," one has to accept that cultural difference does come in the way of the actualization of distributive justice. To put it simply, the fact that the African-American and the Asian-American and the Latino and the Chicana are all "equal Americans" in the eyes of the law, wonderful as that is, does not imply that the cultures of American citizenship and sovereignty have changed.

Let us say that as an Asian-American I feel "equal" with every other American. But as debates in feminist theory have pointed out, "equal" is not the same thing as "same." I retain the right to be "different" on certain levels and registers, and on these levels and registers I do wish to be seen, perceived, and experienced as "Asian-American" and not just as "all-American." I want my difference to be prized and respected and even thought of as a "different" role model for all-America. I am not American the same way in which my neighbor the Italian-American is American, or for that matter my colleague and her way of being Arab-American. Each one of us would want "where she has come from" to be respected during the all-American moment of national contemporaneity. So what does it mean to say that labels will have no significance once distributive justice has been achieved on behalf of all? Only that I do not have to parade or demonstrate my particularism or hide it in certain public contexts, such as the workplace. Just being "me" in a nondenominational way is all that is required of me: no bias, no discrimination of any kind. This is because "I" am not a special interest category any more in need of special advocacy or a polemically charged representation. This is indeed the utopian moment where representation fades away, having achieved its goal of universal equality. But as I have already tried to explain, this way of delinking economics and politics from issues of culture and symbolic identity perpetuates a schizophrenic tension within the social psyche. Just think of minorities who cannot afford to be "who they are" in public for fear of exposure, ridicule, and incomprehension. The minority citizen goes back to her private sphere where she can cultivate her "inner self" in grand isolation from the world "out there." Though "represented out there" she is still not being recognized there: recognition still remains an "inner need."

What has been missing so far in this discussion is "the imagined community of nationalism," the "community of all communities" that claims to align representation with recognition. In other words, the ideology of national sovereignty claims that the citizen, in consenting to be "interpellated" by nationalism, is also receiving full "recognition" of her entire being. Other and earlier affiliations will be sublated within the national form, dangerous particularisms such as ethnicity will be eradicated or reterritorialized so that everybody will feel equally empowered as national sovereign citizens. But this is the lie of nationalism, and this lie takes the ideological form of "assimilationism." When I say, after I have become a US citizen, that I am now the same as or equal with, I also need to add "same *as my fellow American*" or "equal *with my fellow American*."

What is my point here? It is quite simple: that even universal human rights such as equality and justice are mediated and made available through a nationalist ideology/morphology. Much as Charles Taylor and others may wish to transcend or discredit the claims of nationalism as ideology and in the process "find" the third world as the dumping ground of nationalist frenzy, the truth of the matter is that even "here," equality, justice, and other "human" rights are constantly parsed and made sense of within a nationalist syntax. America and the developed nations are no exception to this rule. Thus, when we see the Russian leader and the Chinese leader give each other a bear hug and aver that human rights are not by definition more basic than national rights, I suggest that our critical response be ambivalent: no doubt a shudder of fear on behalf of human rights that could easily get trounced in the name of national sovereignty, but also a rigorous attitude of skepticism towards an ideology of human rights that disavows its implicated prehistory in national rights. Just as minorities need to be wary of assimilation, since assimilation is always spoken for in the name of the status quo and the dominance that it conceals, so, too, subaltern and developing nations need to be wary of first world disclaimers in the name of non-ideological, postnational human rights. Given the ideological duplicity of the verdict that nationalism has been a success in the first world but a bloodbath in the third, subaltern nationalisms have to dedicate themselves to the twin task of (1) striving towards a multilateral and relational universalism and human rights as they pertain to such a universal worldview, and (2) calling into question the ideological motivation and the will to power behind first world initiatives on behalf of universalism. In other words, subaltern nationalisms cannot let their guard down and be willing to be led down the path of "dominant universalism." The intricate challenge to be undertaken multilaterally, of course, is to see through a variety of "masquerading universalisms" and attempt to bring into existence a fair and decentered universalism, a universalism of the future, and not a regressive universalism. To put this in the context of my present framework, much as the first world might deny it, the developmental evolution of human rights in the West has everything to do with the success of nationalism in the first world: nationalism is well and alive in the first world. It has indeed become the privilege and prerogative of the first world to take the initiative on issues of universal human rights: a privilege based not so much on its own record, but rather on its successful post-national status.

The problem with terms such as "justice" and "equality"(and here I am following a Foucauldian mode of genealogical investigation) is that they are as historically sedimented and contaminated as their opposites: "injustice" and "inequality." Thus the term "equal as an American" marks a tension between a nameless drive towards equality and the ideological horizon of what it means to be American at a given historical conjuncture. Mere procedural calls in the direction of equality do not eliminate the inequalities that constitute the present moment. Thus, in the phrase "equal as an American," equality has already been standardized in a certain American way, and the problem is that this American way in itself is symptomatic of multiple equalities. Unless the "American" in "equal as an American" is itself submitted to rigorous deconstruction, the phrase becomes an endorsement of the status quo. In the context of ethnic hyphenation and American citizenship, what this means is that normative American identity has already been prescribed in certain ways as "equal," and therefore the newest "ethnic" entrant into the national equation has to bear the brunt of that normativity without the power to alter that normativity in any way. The Asian-American is now naturalized as an American, but America has not in any way been Asianized. Whereas "Euro-America" is well preserved within the national equation or the "imagined community" called "America," African-America and Asian-America are not at all sure of such preservation: hence the necessity of the hyphen and of the markers of difference. Subaltern and minority movements have to pay special attention to the politics of recognition precisely at that moment when it seems like they have "made it" (i.e., achieved success within the representational paradigm made available by the dominant discourse). To have been represented but not to be recognized is not a particularly palatable recipe for self-esteem.

Multiculturalism as ongoing multilateral negotiation cannot be merely procedural. It is also profoundly ideological. The facile and historically insensitive division of cultural significance into procedures that are value neutral and contents as ideologically fraught begs the very question of multiculturalism. The difficult task is to discern to what extent these so-called value-neutral procedures themselves are carriers of historical burdens and vehicles of ideological change. I am not saying for a moment that there is no need for neutral procedures or that procedures are doomed to unself-reflexive partisanship; rather, procedural and axiological questions need to be raised simultaneously and interconnectedly. Procedures and their vaunted neutrality were after all not created in a vacuum, but were incubated and hatched within very specific ideological horizons. Even though the purpose of the procedure may well have been to transcend an ideological bias, the procedure is a critical embodiment of a certain historical tension. The neutrality of procedures cannot be universal or for all time; they can at best be contingent and relational *vis-à-vis* the circumstances that gave birth to them. Procedures like, say, the Miranda right, were instituted to protect certain rights or to prevent certain abuses of power, and were therefore directly implicated in "the contents" as well as the political power dynamic of the situation. Procedures, the best we know, need to be used critically and self-transformatively rather than be practiced in the name of an unproven universal neutrality. Often, in an unequal world, as Bakhtin would have it in the context of the linguistic sign, the contest is over "what is a procedure" and not merely about what the procedure safeguards. As Charles Taylor almost reluctantly admits in the context of *The Satanic Verses*, it is not enough to advance the separation of religion and state as a universal thesis when there are other contradictory worldviews that sternly disallow such a separation. Most worthwhile debates are not about the meaning of the book or the text, but rather about "what it means to read a book." Given the fact that the meaning of the book is inseparable from the procedures of reading that made the book significant in the first place, it is impossible to legislate universal meaning, unless a false methodological universalism is claimed on behalf of one methodology at the expense of other methodologies.

With some of this in mind, let us take a look at the all-important connection between liberalism and multiculturalism. Should multiculturalism be articulated and accommodated within the ideological horizon of liberal humanism, or should it take up the task of demystifying liberalism and reveal it for what it is: yet another ideological structure, and not the "human" and therefore trans-ideological axiology it pretends to be? Should multiculturalism depend upon the patronage and protection of liberalism for its own successful implementation, or should it make visible the constitutive axiological contradictions within liberalism and thereby impel liberalism towards its own ideological auto-critique? Charles Taylor, in his discussion of liberalism, makes the very useful point that liberalism should be thought of as a range – a range whose inclusiveness has very definite limits. The questions then are: what sort of platforms, positions, and coalitions are permissible within the range, and why? What are the reasons for excluding certain other positions, platforms, and coalitions from the range? What is the ideological relationship between the reasons for inclusion and those for exclusion? Do the latter reasons constitute a form of alterity that cannot find a place within the jurisdiction of liberal reason? How does liberalism, from within the plenitude of its ideological horizon, adjudicate and preside over the dividing line between reasonable and unreasonable? I am quite intentionally casting this problem in the language of "reason," since the politics of recognition requires the backing of Reason. After all, some recognitions are considered rational and reasonable, and others deemed irrational and unreasonable. It is not coincidental that we talk about nationalisms in terms of their "reason" and rationality, and "rogue" nationalisms are precisely those movements that have abandoned the path of universal reason and progress, or worse still, are virulent instantiations of unreason.

It is on the basis of the assumption that liberalism is the authentic inheritor of universal reason that liberal humanists take pride in their ability to articulate their ultimate manifesto of tolerance and inclusiveness: I may disagree with you, but I will defend your right to disagree with me. But of course it will not occur to the liberal that perhaps in response to this manifesto, the subaltern murmur could well be "Who are you to defend my right to hold an opinion different from yours?" Only a dominant ideology will have the hubris to "officially allow" difference to exist. For lack of an ideological–critical understanding of itself and its relationship to the other, liberalism, after all is said and done, remains a glorified version of a laissez-faire mode of thinking. Caught up obsessively, even monomaniacally, in the "neutral beauties" of its own procedural reason, liberalism is unable to provide a satisfactory genealogical understanding of its own procedurality. Nor is it interested in following through, ideologically and semantically, the reasons why the other's point of view is different. Any substantive and dialogic engagement with the other's perspective might well result in the loss of liberalism's self-esteem and authority; therefore, it is much safer to invest in purely procedural defenses of the other's legitimacy. That the other's desire or demand may well beg the question of the authority of liberalism is a thought unthinkable within the complacency of liberal humanism. "What if I am wrong and the other right?" is also a form of auto-critical curiosity forbidden to the conscience of liberal humanism. A liberal will have no difficulty in upholding the right of the terrorist to believe in terrorism, but it is impossible for the liberal even to think for a moment that under certain circumstances the terrorist may well be a freedom fighter waging guerrilla warfare against the tyranny of reasonable state sovereignty. Having comfortably evacuated procedure of all traces of value, partisanship, advocacy, and political–ideological commitment, and furthermore, having successfully suppressed the inherence of "procedurality" in already preexisting ideological formations such as the state and contractual obligations built on unevenness and inequality, liberalism is occluded from a radical understanding of the meaning of "freedom" and the history of its "becoming." To put it in the context of the recent controversy over the meaning of *The Satanic Verses*, liberalism, despite its vehement claims of universal procedurality, is incapable

of coordinating a critical–dialogic space where a secular–cosmopolitan inter-
preter of the Rushdie text can substantively understand where all the rage and
indignation is coming from. And here it is not a mere matter of agreeing
and disagreeing and of honoring disagreement like a real sport, but rather of
"understanding one's own understanding" of the matter in active relationality
with other understandings of the same crisis. It is also a matter, despite one's
own putative procedural superiority, of wanting to understand in a general way
how meanings, interpretations, and procedures (including one's own) are historically bounded, both internally and with reference to one another.

The Politics of Comparison

How then is "value" recognized and legitimated in a multicultural context, and
how is it to be affirmed simultaneously as a production that is both intra- and
inter-historical? How does any self or one go beyond the easy pieties of procedural affirmation of the other's value towards that vulnerable clearing where
the other's value becomes really audible to the self? The very concept "value"
instantly yokes together a certain universalizing urge with the realities of a
regional finitude. In other words, "value" will not be valuable unless it is universally intended (i.e., not hoarded as one's own), and at the same time "value"
carries with it its own historical–contingent markings, as in phrases such as
"Christian values," "Islamic values," or "secular values." Moreover, since the
worldly propagation of values has had everything to do with questions of
dominance and submission and with inequalities of power and prestige,
some values have become strong and others weak. To put it differently,
the ideal–philosophical intentions of "values" are inseparable from the
actual–material histories of their propagation and dissemination. For example,
it may well be or not be that "Western" or Judaeo-Christian "values" are better
than or more profound than Islamic or Hindu "values," but how will we ever
know intrinsically, now that the relationship between these values has been
clinched in the name of colonialism and modernity? In a world structured in
dominance, clearly modern values seem more worthwhile than say communal
or ethnic values. But this is the story of value as rendered by the victor. What
about a multi-valent and multi-temporal valorization of the multiplicity of
values and their historical development in different cultures, philosophies, and
worldviews? These questions immediately land us in the problematic area
called "the politics of comparison." What kinds of comparisons are possible in
a multicultural world that intends to honor difference without objectifying it
or without resorting to a hierarchical calculus?

Taylor has some of these comparatist challenges in mind when he comments episodically on Saul Bellow's evaluation of the significance of Zulu literature. Is it conceivable that a culture may have the potential, but may not as yet have produced anything of universal value, Taylor asks. Is it OK and politically correct to opine that Zulu, though potentially capable, has not as yet delivered a Tolstoy to the world? So what does this say about Zulu culture and the Zulu language and their impact on the world stage? Taylor sounds clearly unhappy and repressed that because of reasons that have to do with political correctness, we are forced to discern the tinge of Eurocentrism behind Bellow's remarks. I agree with Taylor that multicultural hermeneutic generosity should not degenerate into an illiterate and stupid celebration of "everything that is" in every culture, for that would amount to a dismal abnegation of evaluative accountability in the name of multicultural amity and solidarity. Clearly, Bellow, or for that matter any ordinary citizen of any one culture, should have the inalienable right to evaluate, often negatively and drastically, the artifact of another culture. It is also understandable how such an evaluation will have to be necessarily mediated through comparatist lenses. So far, so good; and no problem. But where Taylor falls short is when he assumes that a normative comparative framework is already in place. But what is a comparison, and how does a comparison establish a normative framework on behalf of both or more parties involved? Who is initiating the comparison and why? Is comparison a neutral ground purged of prior affiliations and partisanships, or is comparison itself the tacit instrument of these preexisting tendencies? Where is "the one" when one is in a comparison? Who is being represented within a comparatist paradigm? How should comparatist credentials, both along lines of belonging and of scholarship and expertise, be cultivated and held accountable, and accountable to whom or what: to Tolstoy or to Zulu culture, or both, or neither? These are questions that do not seem to bother Taylor. Why, for example, should Zulu culture produce a Tolstoy? Why the centrality of the novel form? Here again, what is conveniently not acknowledged, or what is disavowed, is a certain dominant universalizing tendency: a tendency passed off in the name of a comparison. My point is that comparisons are undertaken in the name of values, values already anointed with universal aroma well before the historical dynamics of the comparison itself. Lest I be misunderstood, I am a huge and passionate admirer of Tolstoy, but that is not the point. The issue is how and by what logic a certain kind of comparatist balance or imbalance is empowered to negotiate "universal value" among the different players that comprise the comparative field. How and why and on what basis should a Zulu artifact be compared with a cultural object produced, say, in Paris? Should Zulu culture produce a Tolstoy before it can successfully stake its claim for honorable comparison? And here is the problem with the logic of comparatism. Zulu culture is not equipped, or shall we say directed towards, the production of a Tolstoy. But we have already mobilized, in a stringently normative mode, Tolstoyan fiction as a mediating value between "our" culture and "theirs." Either the Tolstoy norm is irrelevant, in which case the comparison falls apart (they are not comparable to us, or we are not comparable to them), or the Tolstoy norm is used coercively and unethically to inferiorize Zulu culture and penalize them for their "incomparable difference" from us. If they are not like us in a certain way, or if "what they are all about" cannot in some way be construed within our patterns of excellence, they are either inferior or unintelligible in and for their very difference.

As I think about these issues I am suddenly reminded of a comparative evaluation I was used to hearing as a boy growing up in India. Telugu, a rich and euphonious language spoken in the South Indian state of Andhra Pradesh, was often referred to, in an honorific vein, as "the Italian of the East." Both Italian and Telugu were obviously considered "sweet and musical" languages, and it is on the basis of that linguistic sweetness (which is the tenor of the comparison) that the languages were being identified in terms of each other. And yet this comparison is not without its own hierarchical assumptions. Why not call Italian "the Telugu of the West?" In whose image is the comparison being initiated and who indeed is being honored by the comparison? Why is Telugu being named and regionalized as Eastern/Oriental while Italian remains unlocated and universal as the standard bearer of linguistic euphony or sweetness? Telugu is to feel honored by the comparison, whereas Italian is not constrained to feel any glory in having been associated with Telugu. The comparison assumes that linguistic musicality has already been idealized or exemplified by Italian well before the claims of Telugu were even considered in that light. Telugu is in the position of the younger African brother who can at best emulate his already well-accomplished and standard-bearing European brother.[32] I am not arguing that the comparison should be set right by instantly making Telugu the standard bearer and Italian the follower. The point is that in a world structured in dominance, comparisons are initiated in the name of those values, standards, and criteria that are dominant. Once the comparison is articulated and validated, the values that underwrote the comparison receive instant axiomatization as universal values. In another related example (and here I have in mind Salman Rushdie's blithe and ill-informed verdict on the value and quality of fiction produced in South Asia in the last fifty years), what we find at work is a comparatist unilateralism partly based on arrogance and partly on ignorance. Rushdie assumes that quality fiction being written during the second half of the twentieth century ought to be a citizen of the modernity–postmodernity continuum, or else it is naive as literature. Here, too, the comparative standards are applied unilaterally, non-reciprocally, with a panache that is all too typical of dominant norms, i.e., norms that refuse to historicize themselves with respect to other histories and literary–cultural traditions. Let me just reiterate that behind the will to comparison lies the will to judge and evaluate; unfortunately, the judgments and evaluations, so long as they fall prey to dominant norms and expectations, do not enjoy multilateral legitimacy.

However, Taylor's use of the Saul Bellow example points us in the right direction, for there can be no serious multicultural experience or multicultural perception of value without a responsible theory of comparison. As I have already tried to indicate, a comparison is an attempt to make a useful and strategic "identification" (without such an initial identification, it would just be a case of the proverbial "apples and oranges") within an overall context of difference and heterogeneity. There is some valuable commonality between A and B, and hence the comparison. But the comparison by no means exhausts or speaks for the entire being of either A or B. We may perhaps best think of a comparison in terms of a Venn diagram that sharply brings into relief the comparable overlap between two identities even as it makes visible the non-overlapping areas of each. A comparison then may be seen as a selective vivification of a certain relationship or resemblance between two identities. Let us say hypothetically that a novel in Urdu is being compared to Salman Rushdie's *Satanic Verses* on the basis of a shared narrative characteristic – say magic realism. A number of questions arise. Why even make the comparison? Who is initiating it? Why not focus on the dissimilarities, or better still, why is "magic realism" the kind of generic phenomenon that is considered important enough to be stressed when it is found in two otherwise very dissimilar works? I am using the example to point up the reality that the term "magic realism" has already found strong and resolute metropolitan favor and hence its way into the universal lexicon of literary terms and genres.[33] The comparative value of "magical realism" is indeed being derived from its metropolitan preeminence and prestige. What makes the Urdu novel suddenly interesting and exciting in the metropolitan gaze is the fact that it participates in a kind of "realism" that has become valuable to metropolitan perception. The metropolitan gaze is certainly not interested in those other aspects of the Urdu novel that have to do with characterization, political content, and a myriad other details that conform to the more traditional way of telling a story. What the comparison does is to hoist the Urdu novel into the realm of metropolitan visibility. And the question has to do with those parts that have nothing to do with metropolitan recognition or visibility to the metropolitan gaze. Once the comparison is initiated, it also causes a certain kind of representational instability. In other words, though a comparison may be intended as specific and delimited, it begins to speak for the entire work. In being compared to a prestigious metropolitan work, A, does B, the novel from the third world, lose touch with itself? What is the nature of B's relationship to itself after it has been partly but significantly reterritorialized by the comparison with aspects of A? What happens to the internal relationship, within the organicity of B, between the "compared part" and "the uncompared part"? Does the work continue to be of a piece with itself despite the comparison? Does the comparison instill in B a divided sense of self: one part avant-garde and deserving of metropolitan attention, and the other part mired in the backwardness of third world realities? And this is precisely what I meant by representational instability: of the two parts that now constitute the work, which part speaks for which, and is the act of representation legitimate? This problem of vulnerable organicity does not confront A, the metropolitan work or text, since the reality of "complete development" in the first world has ensured the synchronicity of part and whole on behalf of its artifact. The comparison, so to speak, does not draw the metropolitan work out into a region where it does not *naturally belong*. The politics of comparison, insofar as it pertains to the metropolitan work, only further augments and solidifies its oneness with itself. As a result of the comparison, it is not made to feel ill at ease or experience any kind of disruption from its original or primary sense of belonging. The effect of the comparison on B, the work from the third world, is quite different. We must remember that the third world represents the kind of uneven development unthinkable in the first world, and in such a context of underdevelopment, comparisons with the first world only tend to exacerbate the already existing realities of unevenness. Having now been mediated by the comparison with the first world mode of production, B finds it increasingly difficult to connect meaningfully with those "other" aspects of its being that lie outside the framework of comparison with the metropolitan mode of production. The comparison sets up a paradigm of false or irrelevant avant-gardism that really does not speak for the entire work. Resisting affiliation with the metropolis is all the more difficult since such affiliation begets immediate prestige and global visibility. To put it in the context of developmental rhetoric, the urban realities of the third world are made to choose between their transnational allegiances with other urban centers the world over, and their accountability to their own rural and semi-urban hinterlands. Needless to say, the glamor lies with deracination and transnational allegiances rather than with conscientious accountability to "backwardness." As Kumkum Sangari puts it thoughtfully in her essay "The Politics of the Possible," the double-coding that presides over the significance of the postcolonial work is all too easily yanked into a kind of metropolitan monocoding, and as Anthony Appiah has observed, it becomes difficult to sort out the "post" in "postcoloniality" from the "post" in postmodernism.[34] The problem for the subaltern work is how to maintain representational and representative integrity in the context of an underlying double consciousness. The response cannot be: eliminate double consciousness or forswear representative integrity. It is not an either-or situation. On the contrary, the subaltern work has to make double consciousness work on a double register of significance: on the one hand, implicate the dominant paradigm but from the perspective of subalternity; on the other hand, empower subalternity without at the same time falling into the *naïveté* of radical separatism or the identity politics of authenticity.

I hope that my critique of the politics of comparison will not be construed as a whining protectionist ploy on behalf of the sovereignty of third world or postcolonial valences and meanings. My point has been to insist that comparisons, however well and generously intended, take place only within the existing regime of multinational dependencies and inequalities. The comparative framework by itself is incapable of addressing, leave alone redressing, the imbalances of the so-called "universal value" it is based on. If anything, comparisons are symptomatic of the uneven flows that characterize the realities of current global exchange. So rather than tacitly place trust in the semantics of comparison, it behooves comparatist cultural critics and theorists to problematize the structures and apparatus of comparatism, even as they continue to compare and contrast cultures with one another. For the comparative framework to function dialogically and multilaterally, it has to be weaned away from the rigid exigencies of identity politics and the binarity of the self–other divide. For it is indeed important and worthwhile for a member of any one cultural group to be able to rate, evaluate, and prize (on the basis of a rigorous comparison) the contributions of one culture more than that of another culture. After all, as Taylor points out, it may be the case that a particular culture might well have achieved more than another culture in a particular domain at a particular moment in history, despite the fact that all cultures have equal potential and intrinsic worth. But to say this is to merely scratch the surface of the problem. A number of questions are just not raised by Taylor. What does "potential" mean in general? How is potential to be evaluated proleptically with reference to its intended teleology? How are teleologies developed within and between cultures? How does the teleology of one culture become intelligible to another culture? How discrete are different histories, given the dominant and globalizing sweep of colonialism, imperialism, and modernity? Is it possible even notionally to imagine what Asian or African teleologies might have been realized if colonialism had not made its aggressive and invasive impact on these cultures? I am not attempting to invoke here a pristine vision of indigenous culture in dire opposition to the history of colonialism; nor am I unaware of the heterogeneous and hybrid appropriations of Eurocentrism in the colonies that have resulted in unique modes of resistance and struggle. I am merely emphasizing that when a European work is compared in cavalier fashion with an African artifact, we need to keep in mind the horizon of a differently shared past. In other words, we cannot afford to believe in the reality of a legitimate value system that makes the comparison possible; instead, we must initiate the comparison tentatively and experimentally with the intention of rewriting the existing system and its inevitable skewedness. We can either look at comparatism as a practice that is founded on the assumption that the issue of universal value that operates among and within cultures has already been normativized consensually or otherwise, or we can conceptualize comparison as but the beginning of a complex, uneven, and multilateral investigation about "the value of value" and the meaning of value. It is the latter option that I would strongly advocate. For comparatism to be honest and accountable in multiple directions, it cannot pre-know the truth of its own value; nor can it be mired in the self-serving practices of "centrist" orthodoxies and pieties. To invest responsibly in the double task of believing in and acting on "universal value," while at the same time opening up axiology to critiques from within and without – that would be the most exciting and transformative way to think of comparison in a multicultural world. In other words, the project of comparison has to be subsumed within the larger and more inclusive endeavor of producing a relational universality as a process without end.

With something like this in mind, Charles Taylor makes significant references to Gadamerian hermeneutics and advocates the desirability of the fusion of horizons: a fusion that, it is to be hoped, will neither assimilate difference, nor exoticize it, but invite it radically into the very heart of identity, so that identity will be no more, in the traditional sense of the term.

> To approach, say, a raga, with the presumptions of value implicit in the well-tempered clavier would be forever to miss the point. What has to happen is what Gadamer has called a "fusion of horizons." We learn to move in a broader horizon, within which what we have formerly taken for granted as the background to valuation can be situated as one possibility alongside the different background of the formerly unfamiliar culture. The "fusion of horizons" operates through our developing new vocabularies of comparison, by means of which we can articulate those contrasts. So that if and when we ultimately find substantive support for our initial presumption, it is on the basis of an understanding of what constitutes worth that we couldn't possibly have had at the beginning. We have reached the judgment partly through transforming our standards.[35]

Before I attempt to evaluate Taylor's application of Gadamer to the multicultural situation, it might be useful to rehearse some of the main features of Gadamerian hermeneutics. Emerging from the Heideggerian problematic of the historicity of the Dasein and the historicity of understanding, Gadamerian hermeneutics raises two related issues: one between Truth and Method, and the other between Self and Other. If truth is not trans-hermeneutic, then (a) how do we secure the objective legitimacy of truth, (b) how do we adjudicate among the partial truths of multiple interpretations, and (c) how do we argue for the validity of the hermeneutic method if the method itself is disjunct from the temporality of the truth? Correspondingly, how should the hermeneutic method make possible the alignment of "the language of being" with the "being of language," i.e., make possible through a non-invasive epistemology of *Gelassenheit* the uncovering of Being? In other words, how can epistemology be realized non-anthropocentrically as an "opening" or a "clearing," so that Being may be housed in that clearing? Gadamer was in fact unpacking in a programmatic and pedagogical manner the disconcerting problem with which Heidegger had scandalized the world of philosophy: the circularity of human understanding. How can the Dasein, in the act of understanding itself in relation to the world, go through the circularity of historical understanding, rather than avoid the circularity *à la* the positivists who chose not to "situate the questioner within the question" and thus avoided a troublesome self-reflexivity, which to Heidegger was the very hallmark of rigorous thinking? The Dasein has to thematize its own historicity before it proceeds to understand Being and Time, and to be able to do this, it has to realize circularity as a form of transformative hermeneutic understanding. Interesting connections are being made between the forestructures of historical understanding and understanding as such. Both Heidegger and Gadamer thematize the prejudicial nature of all understanding and in doing so operate against the grain of Eurocentric reason. Reason cannot cleanse philosophical investigation of its prejudicial base. Reason and prejudice need to be thought through together in the context of the hermeneutic circle and the Dasein analytic. A radically autonomous and self-reflexive awareness of "prejudice as prejudice" now becomes an integral part of the hermeneutic production of truth. The all-important question facing the hermeneutic philosopher is how far can self-reflexivity go and does self-reflexivity guarantee the truth of the Other without violation and anthropological invasion? In Taylor's terms, how is the fusion of horizons effected through the historicity of understanding? Is the self transcended and the other affirmed? How is the "other" celebrated in all its radical alterity even as it becomes available horizonally for the understanding of the Dasein? Has the other now been known in radical transgression of the certitude of the self? Does the horizonal nature of the hermeneutic transaction between Self and Other bring into being a new continuum of meaning, reducible neither to self nor other? Is there a point where auto-critical self-knowledge merges seamlessly with a non-invasive access to the other? If the other can be experienced or known only on the basis of the categories of the self, what exactly happens at that conjuncture where there is a fusion of horizons? Is that the conjuncture of the perfect dialogue characterized by pure reciprocity without recourse? Does the self–other dichotomy lose its valence in the face of an emerging synthesis? Does the fusion of horizons produce a third and grounding meta-horizon or tradition that effects an overarching synchronicity that now represents both self and other?

As we can notice, for Heidegger, all these questions are ontological and not historical. The ontology of the Dasein, it is assumed, speaks for all histories – European as well as non-European. Heidegger shows no awareness that the historical period from within which he articulates the "universal" project of the Dasein is in fact the heyday of a world structured in dominance where the only thinkable universalism is that of dominance. Heidegger fails to notice that the distinctions he chooses to make between the Dasein and the Dasman and his deservedly famous articulation of the "ontico-ontological difference" are still trapped within the episteme of Eurocentrism. Consequently, his philosophical discourse fails to make the critical distinction between the self–other problematic as intra-historical and the self–other problematic as inter-historical. The intra-historical dialogue that Eurocentrism has with itself gets hypostatized as the universal mode of negotiating with the alterity of Being. Heidegger's thinking, though replete with political consequences, disavows the embeddedness of the philosophical in the political.

The Gadamerian project, however, is much more pronouncedly Eurocentric in its assumptions and objectives. Gadamer demonstrates unequivocally that the teleology of Heideggerian destructive hermeneutics is indeed the creation of a new and "authentic" temporality freed of the sclerosis of a stale and inauthentic tradition. In other words, Gadamer's hermeneutic intention is to reclaim the European tradition in the name of a perennial Heideggerian authenticity. The search is for a radical and yet self-sustaining Tradition that will, through the process of *aletheia*, take the spirit of Germany/Europe back to the proximal authenticity of Being; an authenticity that has been objectified and covered over by positivistic thought.[36] Both Heidegger and Gadamer are deeply invested in the project of a Eurocentric renewal whose purpose it is to articulator and align an authentic contemporaneity with the demands of a primordial phenomenology. It is in this context that Heidegger deploys his particular brand of Hellenism: a Hellenism prior to its official ideologization by the tradition of Western ontotheology and metaphysics.

Gadamer's own trajectory as a philosopher became more and more conservative as his search became more and more canonical: the search for the eminent text and the eminent tradition that will authentically restore the European philosophical and literary tradition back to itself. I am not saying that this act of cultural conservation is a bad thing in itself; after all, every culture does attempt, in the very act of renewing itself, to guarantee for itself a continuous and unbroken *longue durée*. However, the universal philosophy that speaks in the name of the universal Dasein is in fact instrumentalized and realized as a Eurocentric political and cultural project; and unless one concedes without a struggle that Europe is the center of all humanity, the European hermeneutic project needs to be problematized rigorously at that very moment when it presumes to speak for the universal Dasein.[37] The fusion of horizons that Gadamer is talking about is an intra-historical fusion that takes place within the episteme of Eurocentrism. The real problem is that we do not know as yet what it means even to begin to think about a tradition between cultures; all articulations of tradition function within the assumption of an "essence": European, Hindu, Western, etc. There is nothing in Heidegger or Gadamer that even remotely resembles an attempt at historicizing Western philosophy with reference to the rest of the world. Also, the Self that was seeking to fuse itself with the Other was nothing but the contemporaneity of European thought trying to synchronize itself with its own authentic origins. The histories of colonialism and imperialism are effectively smothered in such a fusion, simply because this hermeneutic philosophy disavows the connection of the West with the Rest. Unfortunately, the very humanism that was being taken to task by Heidegger for its objectification of "the being of Being" remains unproblema- tized in its political manifestation as Eurocentrism. In other words, the philo- sophical task of reimagining an authentic universalism remains complicit with the political safeguarding of universalism in the name of Eurocentrism. Just as in Conrad's *Heart of Darkness*, here, too, the alterity of one's own past as horizon gets conflated with and therefore begins to speak for the alterity of the "other" of a different history and culture. The prehistories of London and the Thames are effortlessly synchronized with the contemporaneity of the Congo and the Nile, and the African is recognized with cavalier ease as the younger and much less developed brother of European man. Eurocentric universalism is thus posited on the thesis of a false and dominant avant-gardism: no coeval narrativization here, and no acknowledgment of the mutual imbrication of European development with non-Western underdevelopment.

What about Fusion?

Yet there is much to be learned from the hermeneutic project for, after all is said and done, the fusion of horizons is a desirable end, so long as the fusion is submitted simultaneously to intra- and inter-historical criteria and rigor.

When Taylor, for example, makes the distinction between our appreciation of a raga and our musical understanding of a well-tempered clavier, he is certainly nodding in the right direction. Not only do we need to acknowledge the categorical and structural differences between the two values, but having done so, we should be interested in the possibilities of transformation of "our" values in the face of "other" and equally legitimate and persuasive values. It is only on the basis of such a thorough and reciprocal transformation that genuine or substantive or qualitative fusion can be differentiated from cosmetic and depthless versions of easily consumable hybridity. Such transformation is imperative as a prerequisite for the production of a multilateral and relational universality that has nothing to do with Us–Them divides and the sclerosis of binary cultural politics. So it is understood that not only should "our standards" be transformed, but also standards as such need to be transformed on the basis of contributions and criteria from multiple cultures. The qualitative jump from "our standards" to "standards as such" can be made only if the ideological and aesthetic conditions under which "standards" become appropriable as identity characteristics are themselves submitted to thorough critique and deconstruction. To take the case of raga appreciation, the raga is no more the property of an "Oriental" than the well-tempered clavier is the birthright of the "Occidental." It is only by positing the raga and the clavier as semantically rich domains of complexity and expertise open to all potential practitioners and performers and *rasikas*, that we can even raise the issue of "whose understanding does justice" to the raga and the clavier. The raga and the clavier "belong," not along lines of filiation and nativity, but along lines of affiliation, disciplined acquisition and cultivation of taste and value. Ultimately, the raga and the clavier rightly "belong" to those that understand them, and not just those who happen "to be born" with them. I will come back to this theme of necessary reciprocal defamiliarization as I conclude this chapter.

The reason for an ongoing interest in the transformation of standards, as Taylor correctly points out, is that distinctions need to be made between civilization and barbarism. I would strongly identify with Taylor's concern, so long as two qualifications are made: (1) that we acknowledge that civilizations and barbarisms are ubiquitous; (2) that we refuse to think of the two as mutually exclusive categories and instead (along with Walter Benjamin) think and understand that every document of civilization is equally a document of barbarism. Whether a culture is monocultural or multicultural, there can be no argument about the necessity of critique and critical standards and criteria by which a culture adjudicates what is valuable and what is not, what projects are well directed and which ones not, and which artistic and cultural contributions are profound, progressive, and real, and which ones superficial, retrogressive, and apocryphal. So from what platform or forum of objectivity can such questions of "value" be raised? At this point I would like to reemphasize some of the concerns that have been the basis of this entire chapter: the question of "value" in a multicultural milieu; the tension between centrist/identity politics and the politics of a relational and sharable universality; and the tension between subjective and objective orientations to historical meanings and realities.

The right thing to do here is to raise equality itself as an issue, rather than celebrate it uncritically as a universal end. Something like a disequalization of the "equal," along Foucauldian lines, has to be attempted so that the "unequal" history of equality may be fully thematized, and the error of associating "equality" with the normativity of dominant standards may be avoided in the future. As Foucault has demonstrated tirelessly, the so-called conversation among "equals" is already the result of the regime of a normativizing discourse that has found a separate place for "unequals," so that the "equals" may enjoy their conversation without interruption. Any egalitarian principle of action cannot afford to forget the reality that the politics of equality is not exempt from either the practice of exclusion or that of hierarchical worth. For example, if and when a third world country is invited as an "equal" to a conference of the G7 countries, such an invitation is already posited on the "inequality" of the third world country and the coercive assumption on the part of the developed countries that, for the third world country, achieving equality would have to be synonymous with resembling or looking like or catching up with the first world countries (i.e., along an inevitable learning and growth curve called "developmentalism").[38] And if we keep in mind to what extent "developmentalism" itself has been the root cause of unevenness the world over, it becomes difficult not to be suspicious of programs of emancipation that continue to serve as vehicles for a dominant universalism. In a real sense, the third world country does not have to demonstrate its potential for equality by successfully internalizing the developmental teleology prescribed by the first world; there are indeed other teleologies, and if we shift perspectives radically, it is quite conceivable that along other and different axes it might well be the first world that is deficient and the third world quite adequate. The strategy then should be to open both issues of value and objectivity to multiple sets of criteria and multiple axiologies. Rather than be complacent with evaluating works exclusively within their areas of provenance or nativity, the multicultural critic has to open up the valence of the work to multiple points of view and multiple gazes. Since no work or artifact, in an increasingly globalized world, is ever quarantined within its own narrow and provincial history, it would be worthwhile and instructive to analyze the story of a pair of Nike sneakers from the point of view of its poor Asian maker, or for that matter open up, say, the effectiveness of the American platform as it develops during an election year to criticisms and appreciations from a non-American populace. It would indeed be interesting to factor into the notion of the domestic popularity of a presidential candidate the story of how he or she was received by foreign presses and audiences. The "global" intention here is of course to prevent the trumping of any one narrative by another and the foreclosure of "value" from any one point of view. By according credence to a non-American perspective within an American frame, not only are we complicating what it means to be American, but we are also finding a way to honor "the other within." In keeping the question of the value of "our" narrative open to other evaluations and appraisals, there lies the possibility of raising the question of "value" at a meta-level. Rather than debate if American values are superior to African values, we can now analyze and understand symptomatically what it means to raise the question of "value" as an African or an American, as a single unwed mother or as a corporate suburban parent. Adjudications of value can be productively turned into auto-critical analyses of the perspectival–ideological underpinnings of value (i.e., a relational and multilateral investigation into the nature of value), rather than a dominant–universal imposition of value.

My position is that in a globalized world where realities are unavoidably cross-hatched, overdetermined, and located across multiple sites, the question of value has to be posed simultaneously as a question of methodology and perspective. Thus, if *The Satanic Verses* is lauded in the first world along a specific axiological axis (I am using this tautologous locution just to point up the question-begging irony in the situation), why is it that the same text is reviled in the world of orthodox Islam, i.e., along a different and seemingly incommensurable "axiological axis?" Asking such questions in a reciprocal and dialogic spirit could result in a broader and more inclusive understanding of how "the value of value" develops differently and differentially in various parts of the world. Perhaps it might also help "us" to understand – as in the case of the fundamentalist Christian boycott of Martin Scorsese's movie *The Last Temptation of Christ* (1988) – that even "here" blasphemies do exist and there are devout religious believers who find secularism quite problematic. Such an understanding of "the value of value" can only serve to prevent the hubris of any one value system from deciding unilaterally what is valuable and what is valueless. The complex and daunting task of producing objectivity through shared and reciprocal labor can now be attuned to the multiple and heterogeneous barometers of subjectivity that constitute universal human experience. Just as I have argued in the case of universality, here too in the case of objectivity, perspectives, shorn of their parochial centrisms, have to come together relationally with the intention of realizing a negotiable objectivity; an objectivity that does not by fiat replace subjectivity, but one that is perennially in relationship with the protean subjectivities that make up the human spectrum.

If it is true that no one culture has it all and that every culture needs all other cultures to universalize itself, not in the name of the One, but in the name of a radical relationality, then it follows logically that each culture should act both as a window and as a mirror to all other cultures. Just as universality should not be conceived of as the final and definitive resolution of perspectivism, so too, objectivity is not to be made sovereign at the expense of an orphaned or marginal subjectivity. Objectivity is no less a construct than universality, and the ratification of objectivity is possible only on the basis of a range of subjectivities to whom objectivity is given as a potential and project.

To put it in the context of a multicultural universe, let us ask ourselves this question. How does the world look, what does it say, and how does it speak? Does it look white, black, brown, yellow, multi-colored, dotted, spotted, continuous, intermittent? Does it speak in English, French, Urdu, Tagalog, Tamil, Arabic, or Yiddish? Does it speak a standard language, or does it speak with an accent? Does it speak a "pure" language, or are its tones hybrid, pidgin, patois, creole? Does it speak a dialect or an idiolect? My point is that the world speaks in all of the above at the same time, and the result is not a regrettable tower of Babel that balks at the possibility of one world, but a one world trying to understand itself through its one own cacophonous, contradictory, and unorchestrated modalities. Whoever mandated that Objectivity has to be one and an eternally finished product? If anything, the project of producing objectivity has the obligation not to hide its traces, its anchorage in the memories, experiences, and subjectivities of the many, the multiple, and the heterogeneous. The same is true, *mutatis mutandis*, of the production of a relational and multilateral universality always in touch with the clamor of multiple perspectives. Instead of conceptualizing Objectivity and Universality as achieved regimes or states of normative being, it would be much more creative to think of them as ongoing processes of multilateral accountability to Alterity. Thus, objectivity and universality would be in the name of that nameless Otherness of humanity that is not reducible to the divisive seduction of identity politics. The space or the field in which these processes work themselves would be an open space where meanings, references, and values are to be worked out. What would indeed keep the heterogeneity of multiculturalism within the common ground of solidarity would be the desire, the commitment, and the obligation to realize universality and objectivity as an interminable possibility of process, undertaken from multiple perspectives.

Let me conclude this chapter with an anecdote. Years ago, in graduate school, a friend of mine who was doing his Masters in Comparative Music asked me with some measure of exasperation: "Man, don't you have a sense of time in your classical music?" I was stunned beyond disbelief: anything but that, I thought. Of all the possible bizarre misperceptions, and that too from a formal student of music. If anything, I had always felt that Indian classical music, Hindustani as well as Carnatic, had gone quite to the other extreme of autonomizing "time" and "temporal spacing" and percussive rhythm almost as an act of self-indulgence. And from my point of view, say unlike jazz, Western classical music had always sounded relatively amorphous, unstressed, and non-rhythmic when it came to questions of beat and rhythm. And then I began wondering: what could he have meant by "a sense of time?" Could he have meant something quite other than what I intend when I say "a sense of time?" The funny thing, it seems to me, is that in this dialogue both my friend and I had acted and responded so "naturally," as though "a sense of time" were something primordial, pre-discursive and unconstructed, culturally and systemically unmediated, immediately available as a "human" dimension. I had forgotten that each of us had been aestheticized and conditioned in certain ways, by way of our respective musical traditions, to something as basic and phenomeno-logical as "duration" and a sense of time. I had forgotten that each system of music semanticizes sound into music under certain conditions of theoretical and categorical production; and all this against a backdrop of radical aurality. What my friend and I had internalized as musical value, each in our own way, is the finitude of a certain aesthetic/semantic model and its untheorizable relationship (i.e., untheorizable from one single position) to the radical alterity of "sound as such."

How does this relate to the creative practice of multiculturalism as an open field? Let us think of an album such as Miles Davis' *Bitches Brew*, or Ilaiyaraja's *How to Name It?*, or Philip Glass's *Passages*, or Yehudi Menuhin and Ravi Shankar's *East Meets West*. What is at work in these works is a drastic technique of defamiliarization or de-naming, whereby the musical valence of a particular tradition is persuaded to lose its determination and instead find itself in the context of a radical and nameless aurality. Thus, what would it mean to hear a "swara" non-musically, as though it were not a musical value in the Indian classical music system? What would it be to hear "counterpoint" non-musically, as though it were not a form of musical structuration in Western classical music? What the defamiliarization does is to take a certain musical meaning out of its system and thus expose it merely as one among myriad, contingent, aural possibilities. Thus, when you hear Ravi Shankar and Yehudi Menuhin in dialogue, what you hear is neither the plenitude of the sitar within its own melodic horizon, nor that of the Western violin within its own harmonic horizon, but the staging of a fundamental vulnerability to aurality as such. In "real" fusion, what you hear is each system both announcing and denominating itself in the same instant. What is audible is a tenuous contingency that tells the listener that the sound is not like the celebrated *mot juste* in literature, but could indeed have been something "other." The sitar and the violin sound and achieve something different than they would have under their respective musical aegis. In fusion, each participant is persuaded both "to be," to practice itself as itself, while at the same time to pose its relationship to aurality as such as a question: at best, as a contingent and inconclusive resolution. The special feature of the fusion situation is that this act of self-problematization of each participant takes place alongside and simultaneously with a similar practice of self-problematization of other participants. To put it in terms that I have been using all along in this chapter, the fusion experiment is an attempt to interarticulate the transformative practice of vulnerability and openness between any determinate self and other with the radical practice of accountability of all selves to the big O. Put another way, the sitar and the violin are audible to each other as they problematize themselves both in relationship to each other and in acknowledgment of the transcendent authority of aurality as such. The dialogue between the two musical horizons is not an egocentric palaver, but a mode of surrender to the radical unknowability of aurality as such. Neither horizon claims to house the truth, but instead confesses autocritically, in the presence of the other, the finitude of its own quest. It is this mutual gesture of incompleteness that bears witness to the partial nature of each horizon and thereby enables the utopian dream of a transformative completeness. Hence the feeling, when one listens to honest fusion, of a rooted rootlessness and of a lostness in familiar location; of a profound loss of recognition at the very heart of one's name or being, and the enrichment of one's being in another's cadence. So, in fusion, who calls, and who responds? Perhaps the really worthwhile multicultural response should be "who knows?" – in the form of a question, but in the name of an answer.[39]

3
Globalization, Desire, and the Politics of Representation

What is the attraction of globality and why is its rhetoric so seductively irresistible? What is the nature of its authority? Let me begin by suggesting that the triumphalism of globality has to do with the fact that it seems to emanate from reality itself even as it speaks persuasively for that reality. As a *fait accompli*, globality presents itself both as reality and as a representation of that reality, all within a unified temporality. It is as though the very essence of reality is global; therefore, any attempt at interrogating globality would be nothing short of discrediting reality itself. How did reality get globalized so absolutely and normatively, and by what process did the space between reality and representation get closed up and claimed in the name of globality? Part of my purpose in this chapter is to put some pressure, historical as well as theoretical, on the ideological structuration of globality, and to examine how a profoundly uneven and relational category (i.e., globality), gets spoken for as though it were a thing, an essence, an incontrovertible property of reality itself. Consequently, my focus in the following discussion will be on the tensions between globality as perspective and content, globality as unipolar and multipolar, and globality as process and realized vision and product.

Fredric Jameson begins his essay "Notes on Globalization as a Philosophical Issue" with a schematic account of the phenomenon of globalization:

Four positions on our topic seem logically available. The first affirms the opinion that there is no such thing as globalization (there are still the nation-states and the national situations; nothing is new under the sun). The second also affirms that globalization is nothing new; there has always been globalization and it suffices to leaf through a book like Eric Woolf's *Europe and the People without History* to see that as far back as the Neolithic, trade routes have been global in their scope, with Polynesian artifacts deposited in Africa and Asian potsherds as far afield as the New World.

Then I suppose one should add two more: one that affirms the relationship between globalization and that world market which is the ultimate horizon of capitalism, only to add that the current world networks are only different in degree and not in kind; while a fourth affirmation (which I have found more interesting than the other three) posits some new or third, multinational stage of capitalism, of which globalization is an intrinsic feature and which we now largely tend, whether we like it or not, to associate with that thing called postmodernity.[1]

I do not intend to examine all four scenarios or offer an opinion on the classification itself. My focus will be on the "first position" that, according to Jameson, reads an oppositional relationship between the transcendent dynamic of globality and the territoriality of nation-states: so long as nations and nation-states continue to exist and exert hegemonic influence on geopolitical circumstances, globality and globalization are at best an ideological illusion. I would like to suggest, on the contrary, that there is indeed no contradiction between the logic of globalization and the self-interest of dominant nationalisms and nation-states. Just as, analogously, notions of transnationalism and internationalism are posited, not on the basis of any critical negation of and/or divestment from the ideology of nationalism but, rather, on the basis of a supra-nationalism that holds on to and consolidates the privileges and prerogatives of dominant nationalism; so too, globalization extends the regime of uneven development as it exists between developed and developing nations.[2] In typical fashion, Chomsky drives this point home with great polemical verve:

> Putting the details aside, it seems fairly clear that one reason for the sharp divide between today's first and third worlds is that much of the latter was subjected to "experiments" that rammed free market down their throats, whereas today's developed countries were able to resist such measures.
>
> That brings us to another feature of modern history that is hard to miss, in this case at the ideological level. Free market doctrine comes in two varieties. The first is the official doctrine that is taught to and by the educated classes and imposed on the defenseless. The second is what we might call "really existing free market doctrine": For thee, but not for me, except for temporary advantage: I need the protection of the nanny state, but you must learn responsibility under the harsh regimen of "tough love."[3]

Globality and Nationalism

Rather than posit globality and nationalism as adversarial projects, I would maintain that globalization takes the form of the dismantling of subaltern nationalisms by developed nationalisms. Globality and globalization are the Darwinian manifesto of the survival of the fittest: the strong nations will survive "naturally," for it is in their destiny of dominance to survive as nameless and unmarked nations, whereas the weak nations will inevitably be weeded out for lack of strong performance as nation-states. In other words, the strong nations will have earned the ethico-political authority to deconstruct the sovereignty of third world national rights precisely because they, the developed ones, have succeeded in actualizing this form of sovereignty. The developing nations, on the other hand, will be blamed for their inability to secure this sovereignty on their own behalf; furthermore, they will be blamed and penalized if they raise the flag of subaltern national sovereignty in revolt against the standard of dominant national sovereignty. Globality is indeed the name of that ideological structuration that seeks once and for all to realize "the world" as a worthy trophy to be held aloft by some nation-states on behalf of all.

If postmodern globality implies radical divestment from the politics of nationalism, such a divestment has different implications for third world nationalisms. When I use the term "postmodern" here, I wish to refer to the "anti-representational" strand of thought within the vast and heterogeneous repertoire of postmodernism. From within the context of the developed world, the movement from modernity to postmodernity is macro-politically continuous and "conservative," whereas in the context of the underdeveloped world, whose very claim to citizenship in the modern world is the phenomenon of "underdevelopment,"[4] the movement towards a postmodern economy of meaning is disruptive. In the case of the developed nations, the capacity for going global enhances their capacity for self-representation as powerful nation-states, whereas in the case of the underdeveloped nations, globalization attenuates and eviscerates their sovereignty as nation-states. Within the global postmodern space of advanced capitalism, what is problematized is not the representative and representational space of nationalism as such, or the legitimacy of representation *qua* representation, but the ethico-political rights of postcolonial peoples to realize themselves as sovereign nation-states.

Successful and dominant nationalisms are rewarded further, while subaltern and emerging nationalisms are penalized for wanting the very things that dominant nationalisms have successfully monopolized by merely getting there first. Nowhere is this hideous double standard more visible than in the case of nuclear power, where the developing countries with potential or demonstrated nuclear capacity are criminalized as "rogue states" in happy oblivion of the fact that "roguery" was initiated in the first place by the superpowers.[5] It is a case of the first and mighty criminal arrogating to himself the authority of the cop on the basis of his prior and therefore norm-setting entry into the realm of criminality and transgression. Nuclear capability and the CTBT (Comprehen-

sive Test Ban Treaty) are not my present concern. My concern is with the status
of representation as it inheres in the nation and the nation-state. As I have been
maintaining all along, global capital as motored by postmodernist epistemology calls foul on representation, and in so doing authorizes the belief that the
flow of capital in and by itself identifies people's interests the world over and
speaks for them non-ideologically. Such an assumption is as theoretically inept
as it is counter-factual. For indeed, even under the premise of transnational
and border-busting globality, protectionism and industrial and economic
policy are well in place; only, protectionism by the high and mighty is not
named as such, whereas subaltern protectionism is immediately demonized as
rabid nationalism. If the nation form is dismantled in the postcolonial context,
who then will speak for the peoples of the third world: Capital, NAFTA, WTO,
or the president of the USA, leader of the world entire?

Let us take a quick look at the opposition to the WTO talks in Seattle and
the IMF. As has been commented on by many writers and analysts, the opposition has been along multiple axes: strange coalitions in the face of a common
foe.[6] To summarize the scenario somewhat schematically, there is the so-called
ideological opposition between multinational and transnational corporations
and the sovereignty of nation-states, and there is the opposition between a
border-busting capital and a nationally administered labor pool. Multination-
als and transnationals, it is said, make mincemeat of the sovereignty of nation-
states; they merely instrumentalize the existing structure of nation-states, but
the real beneficiaries are the corporations whose only allegiance is to themselves and not to the ideological politics of nationalism. Prima facie, this argument sounds lucid and persuasive, but just a little reflection makes us aware
that this argument fails to make the all-important distinction between actualized and dominant/super nationalisms and emergent nationalisms. These
transnational arrangements, far from dismantling the unequal international
division of labor, only serve to perpetuate that division. Just as – by its very
definition – nationalism empowers division and not relational or empathic
solidarity; just as nationalism is posited on the fundamental assumption that
there are good nationalisms (Us) and bad nationalisms (Them), these transnational configurations reassert the supranational power of dominant nationalisms, thus making their nationalist ideologies transparent and invisible, and
necessitate an ongoing inferiorization of emergent nationalisms.

Take the simple instance of the loss of jobs. The jobs are not categorized as
"human" jobs, but as American or Canadian or Mexican or Indian jobs. The
leaders of the free world evince no embarrassment as they protect and represent their labor, their people power, and their right for a fair share of global
employment opportunities. It is inevitable that they do so, but they might as
well do it with ideological candor, instead of parading their recidivism into

mercantilism as a vigorous advocacy of free trade. It is obvious that first world national governments become interventionist when the ideology of free trade suddenly turns inimical to their own economic interests. Though the enemy may well be the same, when it comes to orchestrating a defense strategy against the enemy, the strategy becomes irreducibly nationalist in character and ideological register.

When did President Clinton ever show concern or alter foreign trade policy in response to dire job losses in Mexico or the Philippines? But when the Mexican peso tumbled, Greenspan and Clinton went into a quick huddle to help the Mexican economy so that America and American workers would not pay the price. In the unequal relationship between Mexico and the USA, not only should Mexico deliver the impossible goal of living up to US expectations, but it must also prepare itself to be demonized and castigated for its ineptness, should it fail. In a similar fashion, World Bank and IMF interventions in the economies of the third world have been undertaken in the name of a world system that represents the interests of the dominant economies.

The motivation here is neither benevolence nor altruism, but an egocentric concern of the dominant economics that somehow the weaker economies should be maintained in a state of systemic viability that is compatible with the growth patterns and objectives of the G7; even if such a form of viability endangers sustainable development within those poor and underdeveloped economies. And that is why most IMF and World Bank prescriptions for third world ills take the form of fundamental structural changes and redefinitions of priorities.

The logic runs thus: be viable for us (the system) so that you can be viable for yourself. What if there are genuine priority clashes? What if the local and national economic well-being of Indonesia requires strategic protection from rapacious foreign investment? Such questions are incompatible with the avant-gardism of a developmental globality that unflinchingly invests in the under-developed world with the intention of maintaining it in eternal dependence and heteronomy. Within such a vision of dominant globality the weaker economies are condemned to fantasies they can never actualize and to tele-ologies over which they have no direct agential control.

Thus, the ideology of dominant globality plays out a duplicitous ideologi-cal game: on the one hand, it insists that the entire world should think unipo-lar (i.e., the rest of the world should look like, resemble, emulate, and follow the Western lead); on the other hand, "they" remain forever the other. They can and should never be allowed to become us or like us, but they should bond with us like an indigent and hapless relative in need, who pathetically solicits our help (i.e., the bonding should keep in place the chasm of an unbridgeable and unactualizable desire). When they behave like us, they become a threat; so they need to be contained within a sanctimonious rhetoric of pedagogy that ensures their perpetual discipleship or apprenticeship. We are virtuous and immaculate in what we do, but they are flawed and roguish in their repetition of our protagonistic deeds on behalf of ourselves. To sum it up, globality shores-up dominance and continues the anthropological fantasy of maintaining the other in intimate and yet exotic followership.

Within and Without: Modes of Address

This in a nutshell is the lie of globalization: though the official blurbs maintain that the reality of globality is on the other and far side of the sovereignty of nation-states, in fact and in effect, the world invoked by globality remains structured in dominance, whereby subaltern nations are engaged in the chronic project of theatricalizing themselves as eternal laggards and "catcher uppers." The users of the "derivative discourse"[7] are paralyzed as the objects of derivative discourse, and as a result of this paralysis, the political agency of third world nations is effortlessly subsumed by the ideology of a post-representational globality. Globality, as it confronts the underdeveloped countries, marks the space of incommensurability where the international and the intranational modes of organization and community historicize their mutual asynchrony. Within the figurality of the postcolonial nation-state, the question that comes up is this: for whom does the nation-state speak, and to whom is its rhetoric addressed? Does the addressee influence, perhaps even constitute, the legitimacy of the rhetoric, or is the rhetoric ideologized without reference to an addressee? Moreover, how is the internal addressee different from the one without? How does the temporality of the nation-state form create insides and outsides? When the head of a nation-state speaks (and therefore the nation speaks, too), is the nation addressing its own people, or is it addressing other sister and brother nations with whom it enjoys ideological and morphological contemporaneity? Within such a Janus-faced figurality, where is the point of balance, or homeostasis, between exteriority and interiority?

When Jawaharlal Nehru made his memorable speech that marked the birth of India as a nation, was he addressing the Indian people who henceforth would fill the interiority of India, or was he addressing the national peoples and national heads of state, to whom he was saying, "here we are in your ranks now: equal and contemporary"? Within such an unavoidable double consciousness (I say "unavoidable" since baptism by nationalism necessitates such an entry into the world of internations), what are the safeguards against the selling away of "interiority" to the superior and prestigious demands of exteriority?[8] Third world nationalism, much more than Western nationalism, is in constant danger of capitulating its "being for itself" in deference to the demands of "being for the other" (i.e., the demands of a global internationalism). The global insistence that nationalism be deconstructed has a different impact on subaltern nationalisms than it does on dominant nationalisms. Therefore, unless nationalisms are destabilized the world over and a genuine alternative is found to replace the imagined community of nation-states, the third world would do well to focus on issues of representation, rather than place implicit trust in the post-representational flows of globality.[9]

If the discourse of representation operates on the principle that sovereignty needs to be produced on behalf of a people and their determinate and historically specific interests, the global network model assumes rather glibly that political issues of representation will be automatically taken care of in the name of capital and uncontrolled economic opportunism. Whereas the politics of representation does not attempt to exorcize the mediatory distance between the experiential and the political, the techno-global model attempts to "get real" by presuming to take the place of the real in the name of its own seductive immanence. Whereas the model of representation insists that the "political" can only be produced through a process of ideological interpellation, the techno-global model sells itself as the home of the political imaginary, thus severing all connection with the alterity of the ideological call.[10] The enticing aspect about techno-globality, particularly during these times of a general disillusionment with matters political and ideological, is that it promotes the belief that the political inheres in the model in a thoroughly transparent and trans-ideological manner. Reality matters, not the political; if anything, politics mars, disfigures, and polemicizes reality: that is the manifesto of techno-globality. And this message sells well, since it makes the promise that the political does not have to be produced any more and that a certain way of "phenomenologizing" the real will indeed take the place of the real.

The narcissistic imaginary of techno-globality, in not allowing the awkwardness of a jagged and contested *horstexte*, intends to celebrate its own immanent interiority as a form of experiential plenitude. In consonance with such a celebration of immanence, the techno-global model inculcates in its members a sense of inclusion that is in fact a facile substitute for the concept of agential citizenship. If inclusiveness has been the agonizing issue that all political movements and revolutions have faced all through history, the techno-global revolution makes a pseudo-problem of inclusiveness by suggesting that the network is indeed God's formal answer to the problem of "unconnectedness." Get on the network and *ipso facto* you are included, valorized, and politicized. The power and the persuasiveness of the network model lie in its ability to create space without ideological location or situatedness. In a sense, this could be termed the ultimate aestheticization of the political. No other phrase captures this tendency better than "global village": a phrase that looks back to the history of the village only to dehistoricize it in the context of techno-globality.

In an interview in *The Nation*, Noam Chomsky, responding to the question, "Can the master's house be dismantled by the master's tools?" suggested chipping away at the system as a real and critical alternative.[11] The other way would be just despair and apathy. Chomsky's suggestion is not unlike Chatterjee's notion of the "derivative discourse" or Ranajit Guha's concept of the "small voice of history." Derivative discourses and the small voices of history are incapable of achieving systematicity on their own behalf. The best they can do to authorize their own sense of agency is to chip away, by "signifying" their intentions on a preexisting and often alien text. These political actors are incapable of writing their own scripts; they can at best "turn the pages" of the dominant script in a certain way, as suggested by Derrida. Is this enough? Is anything else possible other than "a war of position" *à la* Gramsci? As we try to evaluate the possibilities of "signifying" and "chipping away," it would be worthwhile to consider critically the nature and the phenomenology of tools in general. What are tools, and what is the nature of their inherence in specific ideologies, "isms," and worldviews? Are tools a kind of methodology definitively anchored in the theories and the epistemologies that gave rise to them, or are they detachable in a purely pragmatic and opportunistic interest? To what extent are tools faithful to their origins? Finally, does any body or group really "own" tools except in a purely functional and instrumental way? There are two related issues here. One, to use Ralph Ellison's suggestive phrasing,[12] is the thinker–tinker relationship, or to put the same thing in Marxist terminology, the theory–praxis relationship. The other is the issue of achievable agency.

As for the relationship between the nature of tools and who is using them, the postcolonial situation presents itself as a complex and interesting instance. If both modernity and nationalism are historicized as a derivative discourse in the third world, how can the derivative discourse be owned agentially (as against just being assimilated or instrumentalized) by the non-West? How bad and crippling a stigma is "derivativeness" and is there any way of redemption over and beyond derivativeness?

Can derivativeness be negated, or is there a way of working through and beyond derivativeness into a realm of originality and one's own-ness? To avail ourselves of Partha Chatterjee's compelling insight once again, can anything be done at all at the level of the political that can erase the mark of epistemological derivativeness? To use Nestor Canclini's terminology, is it enough that non-Western cultures choose to enter and exit modernity in their own way and in accordance with their own needs and priorities?[13]

Why privilege epistemology to such an extent that it begins to underestimate the power of the political? Is it really necessary for the third world to come up with its own organic and integral epistemology as a precondition for a successful resistance to Eurocentrism? Where and how should the third world signify its valence both as "something in itself" and as a form of difference from the paradigm of Euro-American modernity? The postcolonial predicament can be stated thus: how to achieve political unification on the basis of double consciousness? If we look to Edward Said, two possibilities emerge: hope in traveling theory and in possibilities of contrapuntal meaning.[14] The moment theory travels, its origins are immediately de-sacralized, relativized, and rendered contingent upon the realities and circumstances to which it moves. A theory "born" in the West can become a tool of resistance in the non-West. Hybridized, heterogenized, mimicked, and shot through with difference, metropolitan theory is submitted to a process(to conflate Spivak with Said) of catachresis, as a result of which every metropolitan articulation is simultaneously realized as a postcolonial articulation.[15] Yet all of these strategies remain micropolitical and/or signifying practices (i.e., strategies of exorbitation and supplementation) incapable of formulating their own autonomous teleology. In other words, these strategies, in their attempts to realize themselves as radical and interventionary perspectives, are still caught up, in a reactive mode, with the canonicity of the given metropolitan text. Instead of signifying on an "alien" text, should they not be signifying on their own texts? But then, on the other hand, doesn't the very nature of "signifying" turn inside-out the proper differentiation between "one's own" and the "other's?"

A Third World Utopia

In a moving essay Ashis Nandy makes a concerted effort at realizing the third world both as perspective and as the possibility of a different vision and content: "Thus, no utopia can be without an implicit or explicit theory of suffering. This is especially so in the peripheries of the world, euphemistically called the third world."[16] Nandy goes on to say that "to have a meaningful life in the minds of men, such a utopia must start with the issue of man-made suffering, which has given the third world both its name and uniqueness."[17] Nandy affirms that his essay is

> guided by the belief that the only way the third world can transcend the sloganeering of its well-wishers is, first, by becoming a collective representation of the victims of man-made suffering everywhere in the world and in all past times;

second, by internalizing or owning up to the outside forces of oppression and then, coping with them as inner vectors; and third, by recognizing the oppressed or marginalized selves of the first and the second worlds as civilizational allies in the battle against institutionalized suffering.[18]

Nandy's essay dares to use the much-maligned term "utopia" with theoretical rigor and ethico-political conviction. It enacts a creative tension between the desired placelessness of utopia and the perspectival specificity of the location from which utopia is being visualized. A similar move is made by Amitav Ghosh in his novel *The Shadow Lines* (more of that novel a little later in this chapter).

Another feature of Nandy's contribution is that it boldly espouses "content" as the basis on which third world utopias may be differentiated from other utopias. The content term that Nandy goes for is not "development," "progress," "emancipation," or "industrialization". The key word for him is "suffering." And with that word Nandy strikes an ethical register unequivocally.[19]

Rather than invoke the pathos inherent in suffering, Nandy seeks to ground suffering as a powerful intrasubjective, intersubjective, and cognitive category. Unlike technological and developmental/positivist utopianism that seeks to negate suffering, consolidate gains already made on the basis of a zero-sum, winner-take-all model, and thereby perpetuate the terrain of imbalance and inequity,[20] the ethical appeal of Nandy's utopianism is directed at the human conscience in all its inter-civilizational and intra-civilizational complexity. In conceptualizing suffering as that perspectival category from which utopia is to be envisioned, Nandy opens up a vital relationship between self-centered imaginings and other-oriented commitments.[21] In endowing epistemology with an authority that is coevally but differentially ethical, Nandy in effect limits and renders the self-centered economy of the political abidingly vulnerable to the ubiquitous demands of alterity.

Two points need to be made to differentiate Nandy's conceptualization of suffering from a pathos-based and/or victim-centered articulation of suffering.

First, in Nandy's discourse, suffering is realized simultaneously as experiential and proactively agential. Out of suffering comes critical knowledge, which in turn empowers the voice of suffering to make its own cognitive–epistemological intervention by envisioning its own utopia, rather than accepting an assigned position within amelioratory schemes proposed by the dominant discourse. Secondly, suffering, though exemplified in a certain way by the third world, is thought through as a universal and omni-locational phenomenon that cuts across rigid and overdetermined self–other oppositions. No one or no one position has a monopoly on suffering, and furthermore, it would be quite unethical to participate in what Angela Davis has memorably termed "an Olympics of suffering." Suffering as such demands exotopic and trans-local modes of understanding and diagnosis.[22] Unlike the call of dominance that incites mindless emulation on the part of the slave to desire the place of the master,[23] the empathy that suffering generates makes possible a decentered mode of cognition that is deconstructive of the politics of binarity – of normative insides and outsides. Nandy's rhetoric also establishes a vital connection that typically remains occluded in most political discussions: the connection between the affective and the cognitive.

It is only on the basis of such an epistemology of suffering that the third world perspective on utopia can be actualized as a perspective of persuasion. Not unlike the project of ethicizing subalternity, which liberates "subaltern as perspective"[24] from subaltern as merely teleological, Nandy's rhetoric of advocacy seeks to realize the third world perspective as the ethics of the permanent revolution. Just as it is the objective of subalternity as perspective not to get rid of subalternity as ethico-political force and category, it is Nandy's objective to keep alive "suffering" as a point of view even as he attempts to coordinate a global project to eradicate suffering in all its protean manifestations. It is in this spirit that Nandy's rhetoric on behalf of the third world and therefore the entire world seeks to "transcend the sloganeering of its well wishers."

It is vital to notice that the crucial trope here is that of transcendence: a transcendence of the merely political and the opportunistic in the name of a multilateral, universal, ethical accountability. In an ironic way, much in the vein of a Foucault who would relentlessly question the smugness as well as the fakery of ready-made answers, Nandy questions the process of disingenuous politicization that reduces a thoughtful response to suffering into mere sloganeering and shibboleth-making. For not only is sloganeering superficial and unself-reflexive, it is also sanctimonious in its dogmatic self-righteousness.

Implicit in Nandy's ironic problematization of the political as knee-jerk response is a critique (a) of a vulgar and axiomatic insiderism that assumes that the third world is recognizable through ideological posturings of defensive and paranoid rectitude; and (b) of a tendency to treat the third world as a ghettoizable zone rather than as a universalizable perspective with the potential for a trans-local jurisdiction with transformative powers of persuasion. Nandy's discourse deconstructs the putative opposition between past and present, between the West and the Rest, and Nandy's intention of course is to galvanize ethical accountability as a persuasive universal imperative.

Just as Edward Said would insist that ethico-political projects need to be imagined across and beyond existing asymmetries, and that generalizations need to be made audaciously precisely when they seem least probable, so Nandy enlists the first world, what used to be the second world, and the third world as civilizational allies in the fight against institutional suffering. I would also like to point out how astutely Nandy uses the third world as imaginative topos (and not merely as location, which results in the impasse of relativism and the freezing of location into a non-negotiable form of difference and specificity) to bring about reciprocal recognition between vectors of oppression that are external and those that are internal. Nandy seems to be suggesting that insides and outsides are never given as absolute *a priori* points of and for orientation, but are indeed constituted and produced as transactional functions of inter-historical, intra-historical, and civilizational influence and dialogue.

This critical stance of Nandy's is particularly valuable in the context of the third world, or the non-West, which is typically forced to "choose to be one or the other,"[25] or is constitutively caught up in the profoundly counterproductive task of drawing dogmatic lines and boundaries between insides and outsides. Just as he had argued in *The Intimate Enemy* that colonialism inflicts deep wounds on the colonizer and the colonized, here too Nandy tries to imagine therapeutic spaces of reciprocal rehabilitation and healing. It is precisely by avowing the ubiquitous nature of oppression and suffering, and by acknowledging ongoing collusions between so-called insides and outsides in the perpetuation of oppression and suffering, that a utopian transcendence may be imagined in a multilateral mode.

Nandy offers us three assumptions on which his aspirations are based: (1) no civilization has a monopoly over good or right ethics; (2) the purpose of any civilization is to critically alter its own self-awareness; (3) any utopian imagination is unavoidably caught up in the contradictions and imperfections of its own particular historical situation. In Nandy's words, "imperfect societies produce imperfect remedies of their imperfections."[26] It is this last assumption that I wish to elaborate some more in the context of the current euphoric drive towards globalization. My point is that techno-capital blueprints for globalization are in fact tacit and ideologically disavowed utopian blueprints as well: globalization as a natural panacea for all human ills.

As I have already stated at the beginning of this chapter, it is exactly by delinking the ethico-political and the ideological from the economic, and the theoretical–critical from the descriptive, and the politics of representation from simulacral phenomenology, that the rhetoric of globalization has been able to conceal the fact that globalization is intended as a utopian resolution of the problems of the world: utopia sans politics, sans ethics, and sans ideological content. It has become possible, thanks to techno-capital, to embody utopia as a form of seductive immanence, of the here-and-now, and bracket away once and for all questions of representation and ideological perspectivism.

In a post-communist post-socialist world where "politics" and "ideology" are dirty words, techno-capital has become the undisputed motor of history

that decides descriptively "what is to be done." The difference between an ethically inflected utopianism and the utopianism of techno-capital is that the
latter, blessed with historical amnesia, can afford to be unself-reflexive toward
its own practices and assumptions: its very rootedness in an imperfect world.
In denying the necessary dialectical tension between the far from perfect perspective from which utopia is being imagined, i.e., in being brashly positivist
as against being deconstructive or hermeneutic (the latter model would insist
on the need for a double session that refuses to sever the connection between
the affirmative and the auto-critical, between the act of producing counter-
mnemonically, as it were, a better future and the ethico-political obligation to
redress the injustices of the past, between going forward as a break and the
politics of recursive thinking), the dream of globalization ossifies or degenerates into the literalism of a fulfilled utopia.[27]

The point of view that authorizes the utopian vision is dramatically purged,
to use Foucault's language, of its own unreasonable history and genealogy. The
ruse of techno-capital is that it creates an illusion that its perspective is already
immaculately endowed with the semantic content of the utopia-to-be. Instead
of utopia as multilaterally imagined and utopia as an ongoing radical difference from itself, we now entertain utopia as the unipolar uniperspectival
valorization of the temporality of "techno-capital." If the creation of violent
dystopias during times when Marxism–communism degenerated into
Stalinist statism had to do with the brutalization of the present in the name
of the future and the violation of the ethics of the means in the name of the
ends of politics, the current rhetoric of utopian globalization offers a somewhat different scenario.

Having discovered that the means will always defer, complicate, and reroute
the authority of the ends, the current globalist discourse, in all its spectacular
implosive brilliance, creates the magical impression that the realm of the means
has been exorcized altogether. The "means" are the magical body of the Real.
The networks, the flows, the border busting, the trashing of national sovereignties, etc., are not means instrumentalized towards a specific end; instead,
they are phenomena that are part of the Real: the elusive Lacanian real has now
been mediatized and made available as pure and formal expressivity across the
international division of labor.

Imagining with Precision

What sense does the world make and from what point of view? How is it that
point of view is both transcended and preserved, as it were, in its cognitive

access to the alterity of the world as real? If all that we are talking about is point of view and its sublation through transcendence, how is one to distinguish and adjudicate among the legitimacies of different points of view? Upon what criteria is one point of view deemed invasive, colonizing of reality, and preemptive of other perspectives on the real, and another point of view recognized as generous, and solicitous of reality on behalf of every perspectival desire and longing? Amitav Ghosh raises this question with memorable brilliance in his novel, *The Shadow Lines*:

> One could never know anything except through desire, real desire, which was not the same thing as greed or lust: a pure, painful and primitive desire, a longing for everything that was not in oneself, a torment of the flesh, that carried one beyond the limits of one's mind to other times and other places, and even, if one was lucky, to a place where there was no border between oneself and one's image in the mirror.[28]

Before I undertake an analysis of this statement of real desire, it might be useful to add that this novel begins with the following definition of the value of human relationality and connectedness: "I could not bring myself to believe that their worth in my eyes could be reduced to something as arbitrary and unimportant as a blood relationship."[29] If going global means acknowledging a certain connectedness, what is the basis for such a connectedness? The narrator in the novel asserts unambiguously that the order of affiliation is of greater significance than the merely given but arbitrarily consecrated order of filiation.[30] Filial is arbitrary whereas affiliation is the result of agential choice and elaboration. Blood relationships tend to be tautologous, banal, repressive, and even racist in their militant exclusivity that gets naturalized in the name of natalism/nativism.

Throughout the novel, Ghosh ambiguates and denaturalizes the ontological status of blood and its putative capacity to build and cement solidarities such as nationhood. Is blood, to echo Derrida's famous reading of Lévi-Strauss, nature or culture? If blood is what unites all of humanity, then all human beings are one large oceanic and undifferentiated family.[31] Blood is indisputably coextensive with all human life. But on the other hand, contradictorily, blood does not get ideologized as national blood unless and until it is shed in a certain cause, within the structure of a certain antagonism: blood against blood in denominational fury, blood shed passionately for one group and in hatred of another, both bloods divided but semanticized as "official and national bloods." It is in the historical reality of being spilt that blood becomes meaningful as a filiative category and construct. When the English and the French are at war as nations, they demonstrate themselves as national universals at the very moment when the nationalness of each repudiates the universal in the other. It is of course undeniably true that the shedding of blood by colonized peoples in their struggle against colonialism is of a different ethico-political order than the blood shed between two "equal nations": my point is that the necessary "shedding of blood" is ritualistically sacralized as the foundation of a collective and yet exclusionary identity.

It is this undecidability of blood as it straddles the filiative and the affiliative orders that has rendered all nationalisms a scandal. Within the aporetic figurality of nationalism, the affiliative (i.e., those bonds that were created in historical and secular struggle), is valorized as a form of filiation and naturalized. Such naturalization militarizes borders, and inaugurates a politics of immurement that guarantees that there will be perpetual outsiders. But what would it take to value affiliation radically, so that solidarities and recognitions will always take place in an open space rather than within exclusionary regimes? Time now to revisit *The Shadow Lines* on the nature of desire.

What is real desire that is painful and primitive (a dangerous anthropological term being used so positively by a third world writer and intellectual?) and how is it to be known apart from lust and greed? What is the object of real desire and what is the object of lust? How is the alterity of the Real honored by real desire, but traduced by lust? "The longing for everything that is not in oneself": isn't that a kind of exoticism/Orientals that finds in the other, by way of a prescription for the incompleteness of the self, that mystique that will cure and complete the lack in one's self? Didn't colonialist desire dress up its determinate lack as universal and symbolic Lack and thereby justify its appetitive objectification of "the colony"? Didn't colonialist desire find itself narcissistically in the very lack that was nothing but the object of the colonial gaze?[32] In what way is the postcolonial, third world desire for loss of self anything other than a mimetic recuperation of the anthropological impulse? Within the dyadic structure of desire and lack, which term fixes the other so that the desire–lack game can be set in motion? Within this dyadic game, can the gaze be returned, its direction reversed, so that the roles get mutually reversible? If the desire of man fixes woman as "his" lack, and the desire of the West fixes the East as "its" lack, can woman and the East realize man and the West as their respective "lacks?" How can reciprocity of the gaze be achieved without the objective alterity of a third term? Transactions between self and other need to take place simultaneously on two registers: one, where the self is negotiating with the alterity of the world, and the second, the register where different selves are negotiating with one another as one another's self and other. Both registers are getting played out at the same time with implications for each other. Now to apply this model in the context of the location of desire and its object in Ghosh's text.

How is the alterity of the world as Real invoked differently by the subaltern gaze and the dominant gaze? I would like to suggest that the very alterity of the world-as-real is neither a given, nor is it single. It is only within the specificity of an epistemological model or gaze that the alterity of the Object is announced and recognized. And, since there are several perspectival gazes oriented to the Object, there are as many alterities as Object as there are gazes. It is in this sense that one asks: what is the subaltern world like compared to the dominant world, even though there is only one subtending reality that relates the subaltern to the dominant? The ability of each gaze or perspective to realize the alterity (symbolic authority) of the Object is perennially interrupted by the perspectivism of every other gaze, each engaged in realizing its own symbolic authority. The very alterity of the world-as-real is pluriform and contested, and the eventual "worlding" of the world depends on the extent to which the different gazes negotiate with each other on the basis of the strength of their symbolic currency. It is both a matter of contestation and persuasion.

On the register of the political, the subaltern political imaginary has to produce its own symbolic authority in opposition to and with the intention of unseating the symbolic authority of the dominant discourse.[33] On the ethical register of persuasion, however, the subaltern task is that of convincing the dominant discourse that in a world of shifting significations, it is wiser, truer, freer, and more just to relate to the world-as-real on the basis of the subaltern symbolic than on the basis of the dominant symbolic, that the subaltern representation of the Real is more valuable and worthwhile for all concerned than the dominant representation.[34] The difference as well as the distance between "what the world looks like" and "what the world should look like" (i.e., the difference between the actual and the ideal, the "is" and "the ought to be") is best expressed as a function of ongoing multilateral transactions among perspectives committed to the task of reciprocal transcendence in the name of the One world in the making.

To put all this in the context of the politics of globalization, it matters from whose perspective the world is being realized as One. It also matters in what or whose currency the world is being "worlded" and within the symbolics of whose language the pros and cons of globalization are being discussed. As I have tried to argue by way of Ghosh's novel, there are good and bad instances of transcendence. "Eating the Other" is certainly not an example of ethical transcendence.[35] Lusty or greedy transcendence would be one in which one point of view preying on another establishes a binding and normative relationship with the Real on behalf of all perspectives. It is a logic whereby I say that I don't have the responsibility of proving the benevolence and the legitimacy of my God so long as I have the ability and the power to desecrate or destabilize the authority of your God. What makes my perspective axiomatic and universally binding is not the justice or the fairness of its vision but its power to destroy or depoliticize other perspectives. The lust of the dominant desire is posited on the objectification of the other and the nihilation of the right to pleasure of the other. It is through this process of nihilation that the dominant participants name their desire as the Real of the encounter, and their lack as the semantic body of the Real. The other in this experiential nexus ceases to have the right to name the experience and interpret it. The ultimate trope of such an encounter is of course rape, where the other is both implicated and silenced in the dominant self's experience.

But I still haven't answered the question how is real desire different from lust. How does the economy of real transcendence create a balance between what is lost and what is gained, and who is gaining and who is losing? For starters, real desire is non-egocentric and derives from the notion of a radical "lack" that impoverishes every ego that would seek to sign for plenitude in its own name. Transcendence is intended as a qualitative movement that acknowledges the specificity of the location that inaugurates the transcendence, while at the same time marking that very location or state of being as one to be left behind. At the other end of the arc of transcendence is the other as activated and eroticized by the desire of the self. Is the other as self violated by the desire of the self undertaking the transcendence? Why should the "other self" be available for transcendence at all unless the transcendence is mutually effected? I do not mind being the object or terminus of your transcendence so long as you consent to being the object and terminus of my transcendence. It is only within such a context of reciprocal transcendence and the ethical obligation that it entails that the question of freedom can even begin to be posed contrapuntally against the reality of objectification. Are relationships unthinkable outside the law of mutual objectification? Is freedom conceivable as a proactive project undertaken in multiple solidarities rather than as a game of mutual negations and objectifications? In other words, can you and I ground our freedom in the universality of the One rather than make freedom the function of the following formula: my freedom is in my right to objectify you and yours in your right to objectify me?

As I have argued, the issue of freedom as a transcendental function among and between perspectives can only be part of a more basic accountability to the alterity of the big O: the alterity of the One World as Real that is perennially both pregiven and available for realization by the heterogeneity of multiple perspectives.[36] To return to the dynamics of transcendence as proposed by Amitav Ghosh: one of the chief preoccupations in that novel is how to realize a critical and mutually transformative relationship between "mirrors" and "windows." Under what conditions do mirrors that reflect the self back to itself become windows that open out to the others outside, and when do windows that provide a vision "outside" for the self become surfaces of self-recognition?[37] Indeed, if such a transformation is possible, what would be the nature of globality that underlies such a possibility?

If the world has indeed gone global, within such a cartography is it possible for a village in India to look itself in the mirror and as a result see the metropolitan reality of Paris? When London looks through the window at Lagos, does it see a critical reflection of itself? The reasons for transcendence that Ghosh offers us are similar to Nandy's: no one culture or civilization is complete in itself and the only way to deal with incompleteness is to radically "dialogize" possibilities of knowledge and cognition (i.e., in-mix self-centered perceptions with other-oriented perceptions and in the process actualize a different world, script a different historiography). Wonderful as all this sounds in a utopian vein, a cautionary note needs to be sounded. Who is seeking completion and who is undertaking the pilgrimage of losing self in the other? Even given the unavoidable incompleteness of any civilization, are some incomplete civilizations more dominant and deemed less incomplete than others? To put it more concretely, in a world structured in dominance between East and West, between developing and developed nations, is the longing of the West for completion from the East somehow considered not as drastic as the longing of the East for completion by the West? Let us say (using fairly stereotypical characterizations just to make a point), the West is looking for spiritual enhancement and enrichment by the East and the East is looking to the West for technological advancement. Which of these two needs for completion would be considered more dire? In a world-historical situation where materialism and technology are valorized more than spirituality and matters "interior," it is inevitable that Oriental dependency would position itself in a weaker position within the global structure, whereas the West will not come off all that badly after all, despite its dependency.

There is a further problem with the ontology of the transcendence model, considered in a utopian framework. What is the nature of the tension between the egocentric "one" seeking transcendence and the pre-personal One without whom transcendence loses all meaning? Between the initial egocentric "one" that is the protagonist of transcendence (the Indian one, the American one, the Somalian one, the female one, the ethnic one, etc.) and the figurality of transcendence there lies a gap, and it is worthwhile to ensure that the project of transcendence is not betrayed into a mere act of surrender to a dominant discourse. This danger is particularly endemic in the context of postcolonial transcendence, as envisioned by Ghosh, since postcolonial realities can never be sure that they have succeeded in persuading the metropolis to play the same game that they are interested in playing. In other words, unless the ethical imperative honored by both parties is the same, there is every possibility that transcendence might have the effect of depoliticizing postcolonial interest and agency.

This dangerous possibility can easily be understood in the context of a game in which one jumps and the other catches. What if the other, midway through the game, sensing superior control, intends differently and chooses not to catch? Within the symbolic alterity of the utopian horizon, there must be some way of making sure that no one participating political imaginary suddenly decides to own the horizon in its own name and thereby claim that its mirror be unilaterally legitimated as the window for all. The commitment to the utopian horizon has to find a way to keep the space of the Real open, so that the globality of the world does not become just another name for Westernization or Americanization.

The problem, both theoretical and methodological, with utopian spatiality is that of coordination and synchronization. How to deal simultaneously with the here and now and the long haul? How to think into reality the qualitative placelessness of utopia as a function and consequence of a critical thinking through of the problems of the here and now? How to entertain passionately and postpone in rigorous critique the utopian horizon in the name of present history? In Ghosh's terms, how to go beyond the "shadow lines" of nationally demarcated identity regimes, not by denying the historical reality of the shadow lines, but by working deconstructively through the lines so that their authority may be rendered insubstantial, substanceless, and shadowy? If utopia is the imaginary multilateral answer to the problem of unequal perspectives and uneven temporalities, then such a resolution, to be legitimate, has to work its way through the agonistic field of perspectivism, redress wrongs and injustices en route, and not make a clean break from the politics of perspectives.

Ghosh offers us the practice of what a character in his novel calls "imagining with precision." Though all realities are imagined or invented and not natural, it is important that people invent their own realities rather than dwell passively and reactively in realities invented by others. The point here is that it is a good thing to be othered in general by the process of epistemology, but within such a general alienation, there is still a place for political agency.[38] But the real and intricate challenge is how to imagine one's reality, not in egocentric isolation, but relationally with other imaginings.

One of the cardinal points that Ghosh makes through his inventive and transgressive reading of cartography is that places in the world that are considered far and remote from one another are in fact closer. Often, a place in another nation is closer to one's location than another place within one's own country. It is in the context of a creative and diasporan rethinking of the politics of proximity and distance that Ghosh uses the phrase "imagine with precision." The phrase dramatizes a valuable tension between the freedom to be different, heterogeneous, non-normative, and subjective as realized in the word "imagine," and the rigor invoked by the term "precision," which denotes a certain representational fidelity as well as accountability. Here, by precision, Ghosh does not mean the facticity of empiricism, or the propositional rectitude of positivism, or the egocentric drive towards self-adequation. In Ghosh's text, precision does not inhere in any one location. Precision is a thoroughly exotopic and ek-static concept whereby the correctness of any one location can be determined only with reference to the precision with which it invokes its relationship to all other locations, and thereby the correctness of every other location. Precision operates as a form of global accountability as well as connectedness that functions as the ethical *a priori* that sanctions the attempt of every location to name and understand itself. Precision becomes the ethic as well as the narrative aesthetic whereby the story of every self is committed, but not to violate the story of the other. Precision is honored as that radical alterity without which the narrative of humanity degenerates into the history of warring nations, militarized boundaries, and homes that reek with hatred of the other. It may not be a bad idea to submit globality to such imaginative precision.

4
Derivative Discourses and the Problem of Signification

There is a bitter-sweet moment in Amitav Ghosh's *The Shadow Lines*,[1] when Tridib, the utopian-cosmopolitan Bengali intellectual, and May Price, his beloved from England, meet in Calcutta in front of the august Victoria Memorial that sits right in the middle of the city, directing and shaping the traffic swirling all around it. Ghosh simultaneously stages the event and makes it happen almost fortuitously: there is a sense both of a narrative "happening" and a texture of meta-fictional, theoretical self-consciousness about the passage. It is as though Ghosh wants to show and tell at the same time. The emotional *frissons* of the moment would not be intelligible without the histories that have brought the lovers together. There are two registers of relationship operating in this scene. One register is that of interpersonal heterosexual eroticism that does not necessarily pose the question of collective or representative identity. In other words, Tridib and May are attracted to each other as a male and a female within the libidinal economy of heterosexual desire, and that should suffice. It should not matter if he is from an ex-colonized culture and she from an ex-colonizer's culture. Their intersubjective reality as individuals in love brackets the historical density of where each of them comes from: all that matters is the history of the present, its immanence.[2] The second register is where the immanence of the experience is articulated as a problem or as a mystery that has to be understood in terms of historical traces and genealogies. In other words, the lovers will have to work to produce a legitimate counter-memory. Any attempt at universalizing or allegorizing the meaning of their love will have to pass through the gauntlet of political and historical unevenness and asymmetry. Interpellated differentially by colonial modernity, each of them has to compile an inventory of his/her traces before she/he makes sense of their relationship.[3]

Throughout the novel, Amitav Ghosh acknowledges and problematizes the authority of the past, as each of his characters attempts to elaborate his or her freedom, both as collective and uniquely individual, as a function of a theoretical understanding of what it means to be in history. The Victoria Memorial in Calcutta marks the *longue durée* of colonialism well into the period of independent postcoloniality. May's response to the monument is one of horror, disgust, and a visceral sensation of *mea culpa*. The memorial stands for what "we" have done to "you," and she would rather have the monument erased into oblivion. Tridib's reaction, however, is quite affirmative. He avers that the monument is as much "ours" as it is "yours," and this statement is intended both substantively and ironically. From within the double consciousness of postcolonial emergence, Tridib claims the Victoria Memorial as his own in the context of independent India.[4] In addition, he claims it as "our" common postcolonial ruin: a ruin vivified and claimed on behalf of both by his ex-colonized imagination. What takes place here is an act of subversive signification. If May thinks of the monument in terms of its provenance, Tridib is focused more on the consequences of the travel of the so-called origin.[5] His ideological stance is that of Chinua Achebe, who argued *contra* Ngugi wa Thiong'O that precisely because modernity is constitutively colonial in nature, it does not belong exclusively to the colonizer.[6] Achebe reserves to himself the right to heterogenize, hybridize, and relativize the authority of modernity and that of the English language, just as he imposes on English and the West the onus of accountability to postcolonial and post-Western significations. Both the Victoria Memorial and the English language as master signifiers are stripped of their colonial dominance and reterritorialized in response to the postcolonial will to hegemony.

In an influential essay, Edward Said underscores the reality that though the ex-colonizer and the ex-colonized share a common history, each of them remembers it differently, asymmetrically.[7] Said's objective, of course, is not to monumentalize the asymmetry as a form of non-negotiable incommensurability.[8] On the contrary, Said's impulse is to work through and beyond what he eloquently calls "the politics of blame and guilt." This task could well be termed the production of a relational postcolonial universal space. And the haunting problem is this: from what perspective or political position is such a space to be imagined? Both in Said's rhetoric and in Ghosh's fictive strategy there is a marked tendency to downplay what is conflictual and antagonistic in postcoloniality and to focus instead on possibilities of persuasion and understanding across and beyond boundaries. Take, for example, Said's use of "contrapuntal reading" in his *Culture and Imperialism*.[9] For Said, the counterpoint is the most useful and inclusive way of understanding the significance of any text, any historical event. Said tries to cover both bases: on the one hand, the resistance and the antagonism implied in the prefix "counter-"; on the other hand, the aesthetic precontainment of antagonism within the figurality of the counterpoint as musical value. Both the point and the counterpoint, despite their discrete trajectories, are made part of an overarching structural synchronicity. What is problematic about the practice of counterpoint is that it is not clear if it is representational or post-representational. In other words, who or which historical subject is speaking and who is being spoken for by the contrapuntal arrangement? In the context of Tridib and May's encounter, the immanence of the contrapuntal figuration is ostensible and not real. What makes the reciprocity of the counterpoint even imaginable in the first place is the symbolic authority of the Victoria Memorial, which interpellates the counterpoint into being. In the context of Amitav Ghosh's diasporically disseminated postcolonial cartography, East and West, Asia and Europe are always-already mutually imbricated. It goes without saying that in an obvious way the two are indeed mutually imbricated, but the question has to do, not with the facticity of such an imbrication, but rather with its implications for a postcolonial world.[10] The question I would like to pose is this: how and under what conditions does Europe, a post-Eurocentric Europe, remain germane to postcoloniality?[11] If postcoloniality is a term to be shared globally and not to be used as a substitute for third world, or anglophone, or francophone, what are the criteria that will help us adjudicate among different claims on the postcolonial condition? Simply put, is it really the case that England, too, like India, is postcolonial after August 15, 1947? Is France postcolonial just like Algeria? In the context of what Edward Said imaginatively calls "the voyage within,"[12] in the aftermath of colonialism and the prolific emergence of diasporic Asian and African communities within the metropolis, postcoloniality becomes a global and mobile space that moves beyond the sovereignties of national states and the orthodoxies of places of origin. Thus, the current controversy in England about the legitimacy or otherwise of mandating England as a multicultural nation is anathema to hardcore Anglo-Saxons mainly because it constrains them to remember and narrativize England in ways "other" than those that they have been used to.[13] The postcolonial disturbance or eruption within the metropolis threatens to Asianize or Africanize European citizenship: diasporas threaten the so-called purity of nationalisms.[14] Still, the notion of the "voyage within" privileges the West as the site of postcolonial transformations, just as in the case of Tridib and May's tryst it is the Western memorial that is privileged as the agent of historical cathexis. What if the building had been a Muslim mosque, a Hindu temple, or an indigenous precolonial site? What if the traces to be remembered were to go beyond the aegis of the colonial regime?

Touched by Space

In Ghosh's novel as well as in Said's theory, even though Western metropolitan authority is thoroughly problematized, internally heterogenized, and rendered inescapably vulnerable to "the other within," the West retains its central position as epistemic space, as the necessary cosmopolitan threshold that has to be achieved by the entire world if a utopian future is to be imaginable at all.[15] Cosmopolitanism in its very de-rootedness or multi-rootedness demonstrates the exemplarity of Western spaces and locations. Just as national modernity was deemed organic to the history of the West, and alien or derivative when applied to the East, the cosmopolitan imagination is conceived as the natural extension of a Western mode of radical "non- or multi-belonging."[16] The utopian dreaming subject has to be touched by the West in a certain way before it can envision a cosmopolitan universality. My point is that although Ghosh's novel aspires towards a transgressive cartography of unprecedented distances and proximities, it continues to operate on the assumption that "Europe" is indispensable for the project of the universalization of the parochial and the trans-localization of the local.

One of the central tensions in the novel has to do with the ideologies of nationalism. Nationalism is simultaneously acknowledged and read against the grain in the novel. The "shadow lines" of nationalism are both avowed and disavowed, and Ghosh's point is that the only way to transcend nationalism is by going through nationalism in a certain way. It is from the point of view of such an ethic that Ghosh, through his narrative strategies, promotes mobility between "here" and "there," between "home" and "location," and between "coming" and "going."[17] If Tridib, the postcolonial visionary, is able to imagine the world with real transcendent, non-egocentric desire, it is because he has been touched by the West in a certain way. The issue is how to make that touch "one's own," how *not* to wear that touch as a mark of derivativeness.

Postmodern discourses of spatiality have found a way to substitute a historically dense and fraught sense of place with a simulacral sense of place that is devoid of representational specificity.[18] Thus, Europe is a geopolitically stable and determinate place, an epistemological condition, a state of mind, and a potential for movement that calls into question the proper name and the accreditations that go with the proper name. It is the ability of Europe to have influenced the whole world on the basis of colonial modernity that empowers it to function simultaneously as a place and non-place. The cosmopolitan imagination builds on the advantages and privileges shored-up by colonial modernity rather than functions as a break from it. One of the recurrent motifs in *The Shadow Lines* is that knowledge about places needs to be imagined, and that the invention of such knowledge has nothing to do with the notion of inherence in a place. If anything, Ghosh tries to promulgate the conviction that places can be known proximally and remotely, endo-locationally and exo-locationally. As the narrator puts it, "her practical, bustling London was no less invented than mine."[19] A local Londoner *ipso facto* is no more in possession of the truth about London than is an outsider. It all depends who has taken the trouble to produce London into knowledge by "imagining it with precision."[20] Is such a way of imagining postcolonial, or postmodern, or both? Is it cosmo-politan, subaltern, or both? Whatever the answer, one thing is clear, and that is the ineluctability of postcolonial double consciousness. How should the narrative honor the reality of double consciousness and at the same time generate this double consciousness perspectivally and agentially?

The strategy of reading locality as an epistemic or cognitive effect inde-pendent of physical location has all kinds of possibilities: some politically prob-lematic, and others perhaps not. To use Walter Mignolo's locution, "If one is where one thinks," how then does one decide if "where one thinks" is a good place or not?[21] Should "who one is" dictate "where one should think" in the name of filial piety, or should "where one thinks" play with the ostensible ontology of "who one is"? If postcolonial double consciousness produces an aporia between ontological conviction and epistemological practice, how and in whose or what name is such an aporia to be broken open? To frame this question in the context of the role of Europe in postcoloniality: when Europe or, for that matter, modernity becomes a floating signifier, what happens to the Europe of Eurocentrism? What makes Europe float as a signifier? Is it possible that Europe floats on the basis of the subaltern imagination? Is it conceivable that the subaltern, in using the master's tools to dismantle the master's house, could have succeeded in inaugurating a different direction towards the future? If during the period of colonialism "Europe" is *what the colonized had to know*, during postcoloniality "Europe" is *what the non-West knows*. To borrow from one of Salman Rushdie's characters in *The Satanic Verses*, "What do the English know of their history? It happened overseas."[22] Within the binarity of the master–slave, colonizer–colonized configuration, the ethical as well as the epis-temological imperative of the postcolonial subject is to demonstrate that it "knows" as much as the colonizer and "more," and the "more" is as much a matter of substance as it is of perspective. In other words, the knowledge and the truth claims of the colonized, born as they are in conflict and resistance, are of a higher order of ethico-political persuasion than those of the colonizer. Not satisfied with the mere adversarial enactment of the structural necessity of binarity, whereby the slave's desire for freedom is identified terminally as the slave's desire to occupy the position of the master, the subaltern subject has to create what I call "a new ethics of knowing" that is not reducible to mere political pragmatism or opportunism.[23]

One of the fascinating features of *The Shadow Lines* is the deft and nuanced dramatization of the tension between the radical nowhereness of utopian idealism and the irreducible localizability of the perspective from which the utopian imagination is inaugurated.[24] Thus, Tridib, while being an intense inhabitant of Calcutta and its social *addas*,[25] envisions a cartography that destabilizes all regnant regimes and bureaucracies of identity – most notably that of nationalism. If London and Paris and Shakespeare and Beethoven and Wagner are available to the subaltern imagination, they are available only on the basis of a reinvented cartography and not on the basis of a literal colonial modernity. It is only on the assumption of a radical misrecognition of the world *as it is* that the subaltern imagination opens up a different space for a new and emerging kind of cathexis between desire and the object of desire: a space for unprecedented coalitions and solidarities. Now, why does Europe have to be the floating signifier in this entire process of the utopianization of the political–cultural imagination? Why not Asia, why not Africa? Why does Tridib, in his efforts to universalize his love for May Price, resort to Tristan and Isolde and not to Shakuntala and Dushyanta, or Laila and Majnu?

The ongoing work of the Indian subaltern historian Dipesh Chakrabarty is of great relevance in this area.[26] Chakrabarty raises a question that concerns the very category of "history" as envisioned by postcolonial historiography. Who is this history for, and in whose reading or understanding is this history to be valorized?[27] If the non-West fails to produce a history that is not recognizable as history in the gaze of the West, does it mean then that the non-West has no history? And even more fundamentally, what about the very category called "history," and the compulsion to produce history? Is "history" itself a Western form of interpellation and the compulsion to produce history no more than an invitation to mimicry and a glorified derivativeness? How can the postcolonial subject afford to forget that it is out of a sense of shame and "emasculation" that it is being moved to produce its own articulation *à la* the colonizer? Had *we* been like *them*, despite our vaunted ancient culture and civilization, we would not have been colonized. As the powerful but anguish-torn grandmother argues virulently in *The Shadow Lines*, we need to construct our national identity *here*, just like they (the English) constructed theirs *there*. In her plangent insistence she is supremely unaware of the latent irony in her situation. She is in effect arguing against herself, for it is precisely because India has imitated the nationalism of the West that she finds herself sundered from her place of birth, which is now in Bangladesh and once was in East Pakistan. Not having read Partha Chatterjee on "nationalism as a problem,"[28] she is unaware that her existential attachment to her "native place" has been violated once and for all in the name of the shadow lines of nationalism and that the very form of her political clamor is in fact underwritten by the epistemology of Western Reason. She may be decolonized politically, but not epistemologically.[29]

If one were to pursue this line of thought, one would have to conclude that postcolonial historians should cease historicizing altogether in the name of a radical problematization of the category of history as such. Either that, or invent new modes of writing anchored in one's own epistemology. How to find a way out of the double bind of double consciousness, and out of the ignominy of derivativeness? I guess the answer ought to be through the production of one's own narratology in alignment with one's own history and identity. The "one's own" as a category is characterized by an unavoidable ambiguity: on the one hand, it would seem to operate as an *a priori*, on the other hand as the *a posteriori* effect of an act of production. Through processes of critical and relevant significations it would indeed be possible to think up alternative, alterior, heterogeneous, hybrid, and polycentric modernities. Either that, or a thorough and definitive break with the modern altogether, whatever and however that may mean.

What is a Derivative?

I have always been vaguely titillated and intrigued by the barely discernible interrogative sign that punctuates the subtitle of Partha Chatterjee's classic text, *Nationalism and Postcolonial Thought: A Derivative Discourse?* Is the question mark intentional, an afterthought, conscious or unconscious? Does the syntactic but non-semantic marker of interrogation function as that "dangerous Derridean supplement" and question the status of derivative discourses, and of derivativeness in general? And what would it mean to question a derivative discourse: from within, from without? What is the connection between the postcolonial instance of derivativeness, and derivativeness in general? If it is indeed the case that there is nothing that is not derivative, why should postcoloniality alone be made to carry derivativeness as a stigma? Is derivativeness as such being interrogated in the name of postcolonial derivativeness, or is postcolonial derivativeness being instrumentalized in the allegorical deconstruction of derivativeness as such?

Why should derivativeness be such a hot issue to start with? To follow up on Chatterjee's diagnosis, does derivativeness hurt because it is political, epistemological, or both? The acuity of Chatterjee's thesis lies in the fact that it points out that the very moment of political independence may be symptomatic of a deeper thralldom: that epistemology cannot be reduced to the merely political.[30] But then, why is epistemology such an urgent issue for the postcolonial/subaltern subject? Why should the subaltern subject want to anchor its political hegemony in its own epistemology or worldview? Is the relationship between the political and the epistemological in general (i.e., non-subaltern instances) always organic? Isn't it always the case, as Marx has argued, that even the most radical revolutions are not born with their appropriate apparatus made to order; they have to use whatever is there in the form of available history and use it to their own ends?

It is not surprising that to the ex-colonized subject epistemological deriva-tiveness would be particularly offensive and demeaning, since it was at the level of epistemology that colonization achieved its lasting psychic effect. In the aftermath of colonial degradation, how should the postcolonial subject align its ontology with its epistemology, its pedagogy (to use Homi Bhabha's locu-tion) with its performative practice?[31] And in all this, what is the role played by representation and what are the recognitions and misrecognitions engen-dered by postcolonial self-representation? Does representation go wrong in the hands of postcolonial agency, but not when motored by the dominant agency? Is the dominant discourse any more the master of its own representational processes than subaltern discourse? Can representation as process be really owned by any discourse, however hegemonic or dominant? Is it the potential for ownership of discourse that separates the subaltern from the dominant? How, indeed, is the general/theoretical truth about the nature of representa-tion to be thematized in a world that is structured in dominance? In other words, in a world where some representations are more powerful and influen-tial and dominant than others, how should theory deal with the basic cogni-tive failure of all representation?

Time now to take a quick look at Gayatri Chakravorty Spivak's powerful intervention in the cultural politics of the subaltern school of historians. Until Spivak's entry onto the stage, the subalternists were not particularly invested in the poststructuralist problematic. Surely, Guha and Chatterjee, and Chakrabarty and Pandey, knew their Derrida and their Foucault as well as they knew their Marx, Gramsci, and the discourses of British colonialism and Indian nationalism. However, the poststructuralist dimension did not in any way modify or re-identify their subaltern agenda. With Spivak's entry, the subaltern school goes through a radical change in self-consciousness. In addition to the introduction of gender and sexuality to the subaltern program, a subtle but all-important theoretical shift occurs. If, in a sense, the subaltern school was already double-conscious, Spivak's poststructuralization of subalternity con-solidates this double consciousness and renders it fundamental to subaltern subjectivity. Here is Spivak's classic presentation of her politics: to be part of the subaltern solidarity *and* read subalternity against the grain, engage in hegemonic representational practices in the interests of political scrupulosity *and* undertake a radical and indeterminate deconstruction of representation as such; rigorously mark out the historical terrain of subalternity for all to see *and* realize subalternity as the allegorical vanishing point of representation as such.[32] By way of legitimating her poststructuralization of subalternity, Spivak maintains that there always was a poststructuralist "unconscious" lurking beneath subaltern positivism, and all that she is doing is making explicit what was latent all along. In other words, poststructuralism is not alien to subaltern practice. Within the double consciousness of subaltern self-consciousness, Spivak hyphenates a connection between the project of shaking up the axiomatics of Eurocentric theory and the task of achieving subaltern hegemony. Hence her famous double reading of "alienation": on the one hand, alienation as corrigible in the name of political disalienated practice, and on the other hand, alienation as fundamental and incorrigible even in and particularly in the subaltern instance. The task of the subaltern is to thematize alienation "double-consciously" and to commit to the practice of representation post-representationally.

We cannot afford to forget that the same Spivak who introjected poststructuralist theory into subalternity also vigorously critiqued Foucault and Deleuze for their cavalier dismissal of representation.[33] It is only within the double-conscious contingencies of postcoloniality that one can make sense of Spivak's contradictory intervention: a poststructuralist demystification of subaltern positivism hand in hand with a subaltern castigation of poststructuralist avant-gardism. Spivak's critique of Foucault and Deleuze is directed at their nonchalant post-representational move, all in the name of experiential spontaneism and the phenomenology of the present. She is also annoyed by their lack of awareness of their own intellectual complicity with the logics of capitalism and the international division of labor. In maintaining a kind of epiphanic trance that reality is happening in factories, schools, asylums, and prisons, Foucault and Deleuze end up discrediting the reality of the uneven relationship between theory and practice, between the leaders and the led.[34] They also assume that a deconstruction of representation in theory is also a deconstruction of the historical practice of representation. It is in the name of a representative and representational solidarity that Spivak takes the poststructuralist intellectual to task, even as she feels compelled to critique subaltern positivity by way of a poststructuralist critique. Even if representation were suspect for theoretical reasons, the interrogation of representation as such ought not to be delinked from the political critique of a world structured in dominance. Spivak's intervention serves to open up the space of asymmetry between the first and the third worlds for rigorous critical interrogation, without at the same time foreclosing possibilities of transactional coalitions. In instrumentalizing poststructuralism, derivatively perhaps, and making it part of the subaltern agenda, and by insisting on the accountability of European theory to non-Western realities, Spivak ends up reformulating the very meaning of the term "constituency."

To connect this discussion more directly to my presentation of postcolonial derivativeness, when Foucault and Deleuze are carried away by the immediacy of lived life and theorize their enthusiasm in the name of poststructuralist epistemology, they are in effect guilty of ontologizing epistemology. They *are* poststructuralists in much the same way that someone else *is* a Latino, an African-American, or a third world subject. If the postcolonial anxiety about derivativeness was two-pronged – the fear of being ridiculed for being "essentialist," or a sense of shame about not being able to convert ontology into epistemology – Spivak's critique of Foucault and Deleuze points out that even avant-garde Western theory is guilty of conflating epistemology with ontology. In contrast, the political practice of subalternity informed by poststructuralist theory opens up the space of the "in between" that cannot be domesticated in the name either of subaltern affirmation or theoretical critique. The third world subject is no more a victim of derivativeness than the first world subject is a master of representation. In much the same spirit in which Fanon exclaimed "The Negro is not. Any more than the white man,"[35] the third world is no less epistemological than the first world is apolitical. In all the grand excitement about "lived life," the important insight that is overlooked is the reality that what cannot be owned is "the process of representation," neither by the dominant nor by the subaltern subject. But to arrive at such an insight is to pay attention to "representation" and not to make it disappear altogether in the name of theoretical profundity. The reference to Fanon is by no means coincidental, for wasn't it Fanon who envisioned the creation of a new humanism from within the implacable contradictions of colonialism? Ashis Nandy makes a similar point when he maintains that all imaginings of utopia are bound to be marked by the imperfections of the historical moment, and Nietzsche, the supreme anti-axiologist, considers the transvaluation of all values.

Empowering Ambivalence

If postcoloniality has to find a way out of the curse of "derivativeness," it can do so only on the basis of a double strategy: redeem itself specifically from the mark of derivativeness by signifying on modernity and the West in a certain way, and engage itself in the multilateral demonstration that there is nothing that is not derivative. Postcolonial thought has to open up a space for articulation between the multilateral project of de-stigmatizing derivativeness universally and the immediate task on hand of finding a cure for its own determinate derivativeness. It is inevitable that the privilege as well as the burden of undertaking this double task should fall on the postcolonial/subaltern subject: the task of opening up the hyphen that connects the ethical to the political. If political teleology insists on the need for "one's own hegemony" and the necessity of owning one's own representation definitively, the ethical imperative seeks to find the other within the hegemonic moment of representation in the name of a multilateral and universal alterity. It is from within the determinate indeterminacy of the space of the hyphen that postcolonial epistemology speaks.

I would like to think that one of Amitav Ghosh's chief concerns in *The Shadow Lines* is to open up a space for such a theoretical knowledge: a space between the clamor of language and the stillness of silence, between the determinacy of names and the unnamable, between the endless task of making an inventory of one's traces and the project of finding one's freedom, shuttling perennially and homelessly between freedom as decolonization and freedom as proactive affirmation, between freedom as political prerogative and freedom as political accountability. In the novel, Tridib makes a point that is close to Judith Butler's formulation of "contingent foundations": that all realities are nothing but inventions, and yet it is crucial to invent one's own realities, for if one didn't, one would become the prisoner/object of someone else's invention. What takes place here is a double movement: the de-ontologization of reality and the perspectival legitimation of epistemology. As I argued in chapter 2, the pronoun "one" functions pronominally, both to refer ostensively to a determinate presence and to defer it in the name of the unnamable One. Ghosh's novel takes on the theme of naming and unnaming, representation and the interrogation of representation on two levels: the political and the erotic. If the political critique in the novel induces a vertiginous remapping and recognition of the world and opens up regimes of identity to an underlying phenomenological groundlessness, the theme of love plays with the reality of names. Love is the site where names are used, but only to thematize the utter arbitrariness of all names. Names are arbitrary in the Saussurean sense of the signifier, but the arbitrariness moves in a different direction as well. From within the constructed and differential arbitrariness of language, which is to say, without the backing of a foundational ontology, the arbitrariness of love also seeks to discover universality through the contingent, the allegorical by way of the historical.

The invocation by Tridib of Tristan and Isolde addresses two vital issues that challenge postcolonial subjectivity: one is that of engendering universal possibility on the basis of a rigorous and critical exercise of perspectivism, and the other is the problem of realizing freedom through the practice of representation. How should love as a dialogic exchange of intersubjectivity transcend the trap of binarity, the endless repetition of reciprocal objectification? How is the specificity of any situation to be embodied in a way such that the specificity of the name may function as an opening up to the universal? If the access of the specific to the universal is mediated by the representational logic of names, then the propriety of names is simultaneously affirmed and deconstructed. It does not really matter if the mythological lovers invoked are Radha and Krishna, or Laila and Majnu, or Tristan and Isolde. All we want from the names is a universal potential; the names as such do not matter. There is a problem here, however, for once a name is used, it takes on a prescriptive specificity that is preemptive of other specificities. At the very least, the name that is used assumes an exemplarity that is kept from the other possible names that were not actually employed. Thus, it would be both churlish and legitimate to demand, "Why Tristan and Isolde, and not Shakuntala and Dushyanta, or even Orpheus and Eurydice (the latter pair would be an intracultural variation)?" It does and does not matter, as value ascends from singularity to exemplarity, from regionality to universality. To insist on justice and representation at the level of the "name" could be construed either as an act of begging the question of the universal, or as a necessary act of critical vigilance to ensure that universality is not hijacked in the name of the dominant culture.

The second problem could be characterized thus: why should Tridib, just because his skin is brown, be constrained to use an example from "his own culture" rather than indulge in the freedom to roam worldwide to find his example? Is this expectation not similar to our expectation that an African-American scholar should be organically attached to African-American subjects, and the postcolonial intellectual from India should be naturally committed to themes that are South Asian? How does one draw the line between "one's own" as a free domain and "one's own" as a single-conscious ghetto or limitation? If Shakespeare sings as much to Du Bois as he does to a European reader, why should Du Bois, in the name of either authenticity or political organicity, be constrained to *exclusively refer to the black spiritual*?[36] Isn't critical double consciousness supposed to be a way out of such ruinous either/or choices? If the category "one's own" were really "one's own," wouldn't one then have the power and the right to choose "what one's own" is really all about, rather than be forced to follow an immaculate line of filial correctness? Isn't it also true freedom for one to disavow "one's own" in a spirit autonomy and self-figuration? Wouldn't it also be a fulfillment of anthropological fantasy to condemn the native to some indigenous or autochthonous content and in the process deny her the formal or fictive freedom to invent her own realities, affiliations, and narrative trajectories? To state it directly in the context of my discussion of derivativeness, why would it be more natural and less derivative for May Price to make a reference to Tristan and Isolde than it should be for her brown lover? After all, isn't it the goal of an ethically inflected epistemology to question all modes of proprietary ownership of knowledge, so that knowledge can become the domain of all and not the fiefdom of the few? In that sense, then, is it not a contradiction in terms to insist that knowledge be identified as exclusive and exclusionary possession of any "one," whichever "the one?"

I can only hope that by now I have made it clear that the meaning of terms like "one's own" and "derivative," and the relationship between the two, are quite ambiguous. To "be one's own" means different things depending on whether the issue is posed politically, ethically, or epistemologically. It may indeed be impossible to be one's own epistemologically and ethically, whereas it may be legitimate and even necessary to be strategically interested in a kind of political "one's-own-ness." Unless and until the relationship among ethics, epistemology, and politics is critically thought through, it is impossible to adjudicate in any meaningful way between derivativeness and originality/authenticity/integrity.

To conclude, then, with one of the most moving, and by that very token, one of the most suspect passages in *The Shadow Lines*, where the narrator tries to make a distinction between real desire and mere lust, between a real desire to lose oneself in alterity and a concupiscent hankering after otherness:

> He said to me once that one could never know anything except through desire, real desire, which was not the same thing as greed or lust: a pure, painful and primitive desire, a desire for everything that was not in oneself, a torment of the flesh, that carried one beyond the limits of one's mind to other times and places, and even, if one was lucky, to a place where there was no border between oneself and one's image in the mirror.[37]

One does not have to be an erudite Lacanian to see through this passage. It is moving precisely because it acknowledges the Real as the big O to which there is no "other." But alas, the path to the big O has to be historically mediated through determinate exchanges between a particular self and a particular other, both of whom are acting out in a world that is structured in dominance: a world that occludes the big O and seeks to possess the Real in the name of dominance. The political is too much with us, but unfortunately any gesturing towards the Real that bypasses the political can only be a pseudo-gesture.

The only way to transcend the sovereignty of the shadow lines is to work from within deconstructively, double-consciously. The attempt to shore-up one's self in the imaginary of the mirror may well be pre-symbolic or pre-theoretical *naïveté*, but the self-conscious invocation of the mirror, along with the reference to "borders," could well be a powerful attempt to interrogate the tyranny of the Symbolic, especially when it turns into dogma, or into an orthodoxy that prevents the Real from irrupting transgressively into the normal, the regnant, the regime of the status quo.

As Jacques Derrida puts it in his inimitably enigmatic way, "We only ever speak one language. We never speak just one language."[38] It is our very attachment to a proper monolingualism that makes monolingualism untenable, and it is our inevitable contamination by the Other that makes us mindful of our monolingual performativity. With typical finesse, Derrida is seeking a differential out of binarity by stepping into it in a certain way. Neither speaking for the "multi-," nor speaking the One, language is a mode of shuttling between "the prosthesis of origin" and the inimitability of derivativeness.

5
Theory in an Uneven World

Says Who?

The phrase "politics of location" was used some time ago by Adrienne Rich, and to this day it carries extraordinary polemical and philosophical resonance.[1] It will be recalled that Rich used the phrase to mark a particularly fraught and rich moment in the history of Western feminism. It was a moment of rigorous self-reflexivity on the part of Rich, as she attempted to historicize Western feminism both in terms of itself and as part of a more inclusive epistemic paradigm known as European or Enlightenment rationality.[2] Who can speak for whom and from what location? Is universality possible, thinkable, even desirable, and from what point of view? If universality were indeed perspectival, would such a realization be the death knell of universality as such? If feminism was an attempt to generate solidarities among women from all over the world, to what extent was such a call in itself marked by the hegemonic will to power of the white or first world feminist? Is it conceivable that the location of the first world feminist, subaltern in the context of first world patriarchy, is ineluctably dominant *vis-à-vis* women of color, both in the West and the rest of the world?[3] If feminism were indeed divided and contradictory within itself, how then can it speak without at the same time silencing a range of others within? These questions clearly invoke both the necessity as well as the flawed nature of all representations – of all attempts to universalize "speaking" as a "speaking for" in the name of all constituencies. What was also at stake was the very meaning of the term "constituency," its shifting and often treacherous parameters.

It is far from coincidental that Adrienne Rich's interlocutor in her essay was none other than Virginia Woolf, who had proclaimed that woman knows no national boundaries. Subsequent to Woolf's statement there has been a spate of scholarship the world over focusing on the troubled but necessary relationship between feminisms and nationalisms.[4] If indeed the objective is to produce universality inclusively, what category, feminism or nationalism, would be the most appropriate and legitimate vehicle for such a production? What Rich does early on in her essay is to declare her location in antagonistic solidarity with the ideological stance of Virginia Woolf. The antagonism has to do with the following issues and concerns: (1) Woolf does not seem aware of her position as a white Western woman. (2) She is not mindful of her own classed complicity with the macro-politics of British colonial modernity/nationalism. (3) Her attempt at universality in the name of all women does not deconstruct the very category of "in the name of" and therefore blandly affirms a universal possibility without paying critical attention to the formal–epistemological conditions under which the affirmation is being made. Once location is denaturalized and weaned away from an unquestioned universalist ontology, critical or deconstructive self-reflexivity becomes an integral part of all affirmative politics. To put it in Derridean terms, politics is invented and imagined in the chiasmatic relationship of the affirmative to the deconstructive. Rich's strategy is close to what Gayatri Chakravorty Spivak has since called "unlearning one's privilege as loss." As we connect such a radical unlearning with the critical practice of self-reflexivity, a question begins to loom on the horizon. Is the concern for deconstruction and self-reflexivity exclusively that of dominant discourses, or is it to be required of all locations: subaltern, dominant, or hegemonic? If the answer is that it is *de rigueur* for all constituencies, then how is subaltern self-reflexivity to be differentiated from the dominant or the hegemonic version? I shall return to this theme when I examine "universality" as a category in the context of the unevenness that obtains between the first and the third worlds.

Can self-reflexivity induce a paralysis of the capacity of an affirmative politics? Who is to decide, and why and how, under what conditions the affirmative and the deconstructive trajectories are to be collocated as an organic constituency? Is there a lurking danger that deconstructive politics, given its dominant or *hegemonic* provenance, will find a way somehow to perpetuate the *longue durée* of the master's discourse and thereby neutralize the affirmative agenda as envisioned perspectivally by the subaltern subject of praxis?[5] To put it bluntly, will deconstructive epistemology dominate global discourse in the form of a negative ontology?

As we begin to ponder these questions, it would be worthwhile to put some pressure on the category of "self-reflexivity." For example, in her critique of

Woolf's dominant universalism, is Rich proposing self-reflexivity in the name of a radical politics of difference, whereby a lesbian, middle-class, American, Jewish woman cannot by epistemological fiat speak for the working-class woman of color from Antigua? Or is she advocating self-reflexivity as a way of recovering a coeval and multilateral universality? One way to ask the question is as follows: what is the ultimate purpose or ethic of self-reflexivity: the perpetuation of a moral and political relativism, or the recovery of coeval historical praxis based on multilateralism?

There is a remarkably powerful scene in Nadine Gordimer's *Burger's Daughter* that dramatizes this very ethical problematic. Rosa Burger, the Afrikaner protagonist of the novel, is the daughter of Lionel Burger, an impassioned anti-apartheid communist activist–intellectual who has affiliatively made the black cause his own.[6] The only reality that Rosa Burger has known all her life is that of political activism. Being Lionel Burger's daughter, she cannot but be politically motivated and correct. It is through the transcendence and the sublation of her personal life by politics that she is forced to find meaning for her existence. Instrumentalized obsessively and often brutally by her father's messianic political passion, Rosa Burger loses her autonomy and resents being "Burger's daughter." She may well indeed accept the rectitude of her father's ethico-political position, but she needs to arrive at that truth in her own way, from her own embodied perspective, and not have her father's ideology preside over her life in the form of a coercive teleology.[7]

On the one hand, Rosa is engaged in the battle of giving birth to herself in a spirit of patricidal ontogenetic transgression. On the other hand, she is also involved in the critical narratological task of understanding her own truth against the grain in the macro-political context of racial apartheid.[8] The place or the location she occupies ("I am the place in which something has occurred" is an epigraph from Lévi-Strauss that Gordimer uses at the very beginning of her book) marks the intersection of the inter- and the intra- dimensions of identity politics and the politics of representation. As her black half-brother Baasie/Zwel-in-zima demonstrates explosively towards the end of the novel, Rosa is neither one of "them" (the blacks) affiliatively speaking, nor one of "us" (the whites). Sure enough, her father has ensured, by way of ideological indoctrination, her affiliation with the black cause, but this enforced doctrinaire affiliation has had the double negative effect of (a) alienating her filiatively and (b) foisting on her a political temporality and a way of being that is not a production of her own critical consciousness. As a member of the dominant Afrikaner group she has the power to represent, but such a "speaking for" would be deeply unethical, and hence her aversion to representation. As a subaltern dominated daughter, however, she is the victim or prisoner of representation and is looking for authentic self-expression. Within the same consciousness Rosa experiences herself as ambivalence: subaltern and dominant, but each in a different context. Gordimer's narrative technique does all it can to render Rosa's double consciousness full justice. The split narrative presents Rosa as "seeing" and as "being scene," as gaze and as spectacle.

In the scene in question Rosa is traveling in the countryside of South Africa and is suddenly confronted with a black African man whipping his donkey madly, deliriously. Now what is Rosa to do? The tension here is between "what can be said" and "who is saying it."[9] It is impossible for Rosa to act spontaneously, without submitting the very possibility for action to a prior politics of deconstructive self-reflexivity. She is fully aware that as a white woman she could intervene easily and without any cost. Her hegemonic intervention would be immediately effective and the black man would be in trouble right away. What freezes Rosa ethically at that moment, despite the perceived need for political action or intervention, is the nauseating realization that her action would be effective, not as a function of ethical legitimacy, but as an effect of power and privilege. It would have been unearned. If she spoke, she would be listened to, and at once her "speaking" would acquire the historico-political density of "speaking for" and of "representation." Whereas if the black man spoke in defense of himself his articulation would remain sub-political: no effect of representation there. The immediate "correctness" of intervening on behalf of the hapless animal is always already contaminated by the ethico-political enormity of her location as dominant white. Furthermore, her judgment of the situation would be supremely a-contextual and dominant–universal in nature, since she has no way of understanding where the black man is coming from. She would be judging from an Olympian height. Moreover, her very ability to speak and act in consonance with that judgment would in fact be a form of free choice not available to her black African compatriots. She, Rosa Burger, has the luxury to autonomize the ethical moment as quandary and as dilemma and abstract it analytically and existentially from its organic embeddedness in the macro-political situation. In contrast, the black African subject under apartheid would have experienced the situation quite differently: no room here for such ethical luxury or for the reification of praxis to make room for the suspended temporality of thought against itself in ethical deferral of agency.

Should Rosa then not bother about her "intra-identitarian" moral impasse and just go ahead and act politically without ethical sanction? Or should she postpone programmatic action until her interior dilemma is resolved rigorously and authentically? Within a chiasmatic double bind, Rosa's political agency gets "ethicized," while her interior ethical tussle is publicly "politicized."[10] For most of the novel Rosa dwells uncomfortably within the hyphen that differentially conjoins the ethical and the political. Politics becomes ethics and ethics politics in a conjuncture that will not be broken open through some gesture of transcendence. It is from within the suffocating immanence of the hyphen that Rosa has to produce her narrative.

Gordimer focuses on this moment as a way of theorizing the problem of representation, both historically and allegorically. In capturing the embodied historical specificity of Rosa's predicament, Gordimer also tries to allegorize and thereby universalize "what is ethical" in Rosa's particular condition. Any attempt at producing allegorical verities on the basis of historical finitude runs into the problem of perspectivism. Why should the allegorical move be contemplated from that particular historical vantage point rather than from some other perspective? Is allegory indeed so cheap that it can be produced from every conceivable point of view? Are there as many allegories as there are points of view? Isn't it all too natural that the point of view that "imagines" allegorically should end up making its particular "content" the driving form of the vision? Allegorical truth is seductive precisely because it succeeds in burying its historical traces in the name of a transcendent insight. Also, when allegorical truth is narrativized into existence, it automatically takes on a certain magisterial–universal valence that makes it singular and dominantly representative.[11] Isn't it conceivable that the allegory could have been penned from the point of view of the donkey-flogging black African male? If Rosa's allegorical experience enjoins her not to speak, act, or represent, then does it automatically mean that no one else can speak, act, or represent either?

After this traumatizing episode Rosa Burger finds living in "her/Lionel's country" totally unbearable. She has to leave her father and her country as a necessary prolegomenon for her self-discovery. Now, in resorting to the allegorical mode on behalf of her character, could Gordimer be accused of a certain bad consciousness? Is the invocation of the allegorical mode an effort to thematize the omni-historical – to borrow from Althusser – reality of suffering and of what human beings do to one another under different regimes? Or is it nothing more than a sophisticated ploy to assuage and/or exculpate the dominant consciousness in the name of a subtle and refined ethical sensitivity? Should Rosa be given any special credit (and this credit is precisely what her half-black brother would angrily contest)? Why credit Rosa Burger, and by extension Gordimer herself, for her practice of ethical askesis in the face of political responsibility, when by the same token she could easily be critiqued for choosing not to "represent" and for resorting to allegorical indeterminacy? In other words, in unlearning her privilege as loss at the level of determinate history, could she not be deemed guilty (consciously or unconsciously) of arrogating to herself the privilege of suspending the political in the name of a higher ethical value; guilty, too, of practicing an aporetic ethics of post-representation in the context of an urgent reality screaming out for representation? Could she also not be found fault with for forfeiting a lesser good so that she can garner the kudos for going after a rarer and purer virtue?

After all, who can afford the luxury of suspending a political commitment for the sake of highlighting and bringing into crisis an interior ethical ambivalence except someone from a dominant constituency? If, in a certain sense, Rosa Burger has earned nothing but the highest honors for trying to pry open the space of the hyphen between the "ethical" and the "political," then in another sense could Rosa not be admonished for purchasing ethical capital at the expense of the political? The Burger family could choose to be politically correct and garner kudos for their exceptional behavior, whereas thousands of black families struggled choicelessly and anonymously, colonized by the immanence of the present history of apartheid and without the comfort of the ethical pause in the very heat of the moment. My point is that it is extremely difficult to anticipate the historical effects of the politics of self-reflexivity, or be able to adjudicate when and where such a politics degenerates into precious posturing and an aggrandizement of ethical subjectivity into an absolute commitment, and when it leads into a transformative politics beyond the rigidities of self and other.[12]

Gordimer is extremely careful in the way in which she presents the scene. It would be all too easy and self-serving to condemn the black African for his brutality, as though this characteristic were essential to his personality. On the contrary, Gordimer has Rosa ponder over how little she knows about his reality and where he comes from. Even as she presents that scene almost as an epiphanic slice of a timeless present in Rosa's consciousness, Gordimer at the same time demonstrates the limitations of Rosa's existential–temporal horizon. To bring Johannes Fabian usefully into the discussion, Gordimer's problem as a novelist is how to narrativize "coevalness" while inhabiting a single chronotope.[13] How can she represent Rosa's temporal location coevally with that of the black man without resorting to the violence of representation? The challenge is that coevalness is profoundly relational in nature and as such is not available to monologic representation; and an omniscient narrator is out of the question. Rosa Burger then has to understand "where the black man is coming from" without letting such an understanding take the place of condoning his action. Judge after all she must; she cannot simulate innocence of history or attempt a Christ-like gesture that absolves guilt, since there is no one who is not guilty. That kind of right to forgive is reserved for the subalterns, as demonstrated through the Truth and Reconciliation Commission. Just as the abdication of the ethical in the name of a transparent politics of action is inadmissible, so is the avoidance of contamination by politics in the name of ethical purity. What is required of Rosa is a double vision that will honor the "elsewhereness" of the ethical and at the same time valorize the ethical position in tension with the all too "hereness" of the political conjuncture.[14] At any rate what is not admissible is the use of the ethical pause as an excuse for political inaction.

It all comes back to self-reflexivity and the uses of self-reflexivity. Let us say that Woolf had passed the self-reflexivity test prescribed by Rich. Would self-reflexivity on Woolf's part necessarily result in the recantation of the claim that a woman has no nationality? In being preciously self-reflexive, will Woolf then not be guilty of throwing away the macro-political wisdom of "a woman having no nationality" all for the sake of an inner dilemma? My main point in this entire discussion is that any evaluation of the politics of self-reflexivity has to be aligned, coordinated, and "synchronized in difference" with a historical and theoretical awareness of the "objective" macro-political asymmetry of a world structured in dominance. Lest I be misconstrued as being overly harsh and unappreciative of Rosa Burger and her unconscionable predicament, let me clarify. It is precisely because Rosa brackets the history phenomenologically that she is able to usher in the ethical that is often occluded by the demands of the political imperative. To the black South African under apartheid, the differentiation of the ethical from the political might seem precious and unwarranted, for, to the subaltern, in her particular historical situation, the ethical and the political might well speak for each other without any sliding or slippage. It is in this particular sense that all locations have something to learn from "dominance in deconstruction": the dominant or the hegemonic discourse in the act of what Gordimer calls "self-consciencization"[15] thematizes the ethical in a way that is not automatically available to emergent formations whose "correct" political ideology subsumes ethical imperatives, often without sufficient examination or critique. To paraphrase the Tamil novelist Jayakanthan in a preface to his short stories: ethics or morality comes into its own, not in the good acts of the Samaritan, but at that moment when the wrongdoer weeps his/her eyes out in self-understanding and prepares for atonement and self-transformation. That moment of tears is also the moment when all the putative "right doers" recognize themselves potentially with "wrong doing" and in doing so prepare themselves rigorously for guarding against dominance in the development of their respective teleologies: the agent of "wrongdoing," allegorically speaking, could well have been me, you, him, or her. It was precisely in this spirit that Mohandas Gandhi empathized with the colonists even as he fought their colonialism uncompromisingly.

What is at stake here in Rosa's situation *vis-à-vis* the donkey and its tormentor is the genuineness of empathy.[16] One of the features of the scene that astonishes Rosa is the utter silence and non-resistance of the animal as it flails its body around in ineffable agony.[17] Its resistance is its muteness. The untenability of the animal's situation is analogous to that of the blacks under apartheid in her country, in her father's country. In both situations the iron grid of binarity rules. It is only through the empathy of analogy that Rosa understands the doubleness of her location: that she is occupying two contradictory positions, empowered and bereft of representation. Rosa's project is to align her moral sensibility with the political imperative, coordinate her embodied subjectivity with the given and objective macro-political situation, and learn how to act and participate in the struggle without in any way "speaking" for the black consciousness (i.e., unlearn her privilege as loss). It is only through understanding her situation as "marginally organic" that she can contribute to the political struggle in good faith. And, in fact, when Rosa returns to her father's country after her escape to Europe, that precisely is what she does. Now to the scene:

> I didn't see the whip. I saw agony. Agony that came from some terrible Centre seized within the group of donkey, cart, driver and people behind him. They made a single object that contracted itself in the desperation of a hideous final energy. Not seeing the whip, I saw the infliction of pain broken away from the will that creates it; broken lose, a force existing of itself, ravishment without the ravisher, torture without the torturer, rampage, pure cruelty gone beyond control of the humans who have spent thousands of years devising it. The entire ingenuity from thumbscrew and rack to electric shock, the infinite variety and gradation of suffering, by lash, by hunger, by solitary confinement – the camps, concentration, labour, resettlement, the Siberias of snow or sun, the lives of Mandela, Sisulu, Mbeki, Kathrada, Kgosana, gull-picked on the Island . . .[18]

Now, what exactly does Rosa see or not see in that scene such that the history is transformed into an allegorical vision and a political impasse turns into a purely ethical dilemma? What Rosa chooses to see or not to see, what Rosa chooses to exorcize or occult into visibility should help the reader determine if her objective is self-exculpation or the elevation of ethical accountability as a higher calling than that of the merely political. As Rosa sees the whip descend over and over again onto the body of the donkey, this is what she sees: the whip operating by itself, delinked from all determinate or determinable agency. She realizes that this same insane and unconscionable exercise of domination, this exercise of humanity dehumanizing itself, has been going on for ever and ever, omni-historically, under different roles, masks, and guises, and with different instruments of torture. In one sense, then, it is vital to see, recognize, and identify the hand holding the whip and the body that is being subjected to the blows; crucial to name the oppressor and the oppressed; but in another sense, it is equally vital to recognize the deed namelessly and allegorically. The actual scene is historical and political, whereas the imagined scene is allegorical and ethical. To activate the ethical vision, one (Rosa) has to suspend the present, see beneath or beyond the actual spectacle, and this way of seeing can only be allegorical. And the allegorical gaze sees a certain absence: that which is materially and circumstantially absent in the actual historical spectacle. This active absence could be seen as the unconscious of the political[19] or as a surplus that has to be produced through an act of ethical interpretation and transcendence.

Is it possible to have a double vision of an act: one with agency and the other without? Rosa is guilty of ethical hallucination – of seeing what is actually not there by overseeing what is there, or to put it differently, of transcending the visible in the name of the invisible and of valorizing the visible in terms of the invisible.[20] This dialectical interplay of opposites in her gaze points to the "presence in absence" of the ethical within the machiavellian clamor of political immanence. The ethical is the radical and unnamable absence in the moment that has to be perceived into reality, both with the help and against the grain of the visible. When the whip operates by itself in autonomization of the action sans agency, what Rosa is enabled to see is the predicament of the "human One" concealed behind the agony of a "specific human one."[21] Seeing the "One" in the "one" could be termed the allegorical "oversight" of history. If historical specificity became the only obsessive concern it would become virtually impossible to understand the diachronic trials and tribulations of history as the effects and functions of an underlying systemic synchronicity. The occultation of the insensible or the supersensible into the scopic regime of the political could be loosely interpreted as the irruption of the Lacanian Real and as the fleeting phantasmatic corporealization of the ethical unconscious within the hegemonic body of the symbolic order. But is such an allegorization of history a little too felicitous, a little too friction-free? Does the allegorization as undertaken from a dominant point of view in deconstruction of its authority amount to a denial of the specificity of history? Similarly, does the focus on ethics simplify or de-prioritize the obligation to the political? As I have argued in chapter 2, the ethical register gestures towards alterity as such, whereas the political mode is a constant reminder of a world structured in dominance. It is within the unevenness of such a dilemma that theory as epistemology has to invent itself as an ongoing tension between the ethical and the political. Given my analysis of Rosa Burger's troublesome location, it is inevitable that we conclude that there is a universal or at least an omni-historical lesson to be learned from the politics of self-reflexivity as it emanates from the dominant discourse.

Who is in the Language?

If so far I have been focusing on the manner in which location complicates and enables the politics of representation, now I would like to turn towards another concept that in the last couple of decades has influenced the articulation of the political: the concept of the "subject position." If "location" fragments the plenitude of representation, subject positionality eviscerates "representation" in the name of language. The ontological person "enoncing" the articulation and the "enonce" within language are not identical with each other. The rigorous observance of subject positionality results in a different practice of self-reflexivity. If the macro-politics of location dealt with ontological–existential predications of the sort, "I am Jewish," I am working-class Latino," "I am an Asian-American lesbian," and so on, the micro-political self-situating of subject positionality results in predicative–discursive formations such as "I am a poststructuralist," "I am a New Historicist," "I am a post-Marxist of the postmodern persuasion," or broadly speaking, "I speak from within a certain language or discourse that in the very act of letting me speak has me subjected and constituted in a certain unavoidable way."[22] In other words, epistemological and discursive positions get played out as critical ontological markers, such that an Asian-American who practices poststructuralism is now constrained to practice two forms of self-reflexivity: one vis-à-vis her Asian-American constituency and the other with reference to her chosen methodological/epistemological discourse. One's epistemological practice is not just an ornamental epiphenomenal nuance: it is indeed constitutive of one's "identity" as well as politics of representation.

Before I get into an extended discussion of the politics of self-reflexivity based on subject positionality it would be useful to rehearse critically the semantics of the term "subject position." As we pay heed to Foucault's famous declaration that subject positions are assigned and not chosen in freedom, we also need to keep in mind that unlike "location" the "subject position" is discursively or linguistically constituted: a possibility enabled by the famous Saussurean "linguistic turn." With the autonomization of language as "the language of language" (an extreme demonstration of this trend being the nerve-wracking analysis of Baudelaire's poem "Cats" by Jakobson and Lévi-Strauss, where the materiality of language renders semantic meaning virtually impossible), all forms of knowledge are constrained to consider their particular form of rhetoricity as constitutive of their truth claims: expertise is not to be transcended as thrown away in the name of an open, transcendent, and perhaps transparent "wordliness." In understanding as experts how meaning works through the materiality of the signifier, specialists in a way abandon the primacy of meaning, choosing instead to inhabit what Foucault would term "regimes of truth" and discursive spaces that do not constitute the truth, but instead dwell "dans le vrai," i.e., "within the true." Truth, then, is discursively spatialized as an area where some things are "sayable." We thus have Foucault, in *The Archaeology of Knowledge*, patiently accounting for the ways in which truths are rendered sayable. In other words, in this maddeningly hermetic book, Foucault seems to speak from within discourse: no alternatives or "outsides" here to discourse. The sayable is the true: that is all "ye" need to know. Archeology offers no room for activism or for rubbing history against the grain, or for legitimating or valorizing "subjugated knowledges." It is through genealogy that Foucault recovers possibilities for questioning official history.

The self-reflexive sensitivity of the specialist intellectual could either be construed as a self-serving narcissistic commitment to professionalism, or lauded as a rigorous ethical sensibility that disallows the comfort of an easy worldly politics uncontaminated by professional complications. If I am a poststructuralist by training and by professional conviction and commitment, I cannot, except in bad faith, take time off from my poststructuralism to be able to see the world in some easier and organic way. To be a poststructuralist is a full-time activity, and from such a point of view, the way to political credibility is to exercise the constitutive double bind of the academic professional to *realpolitik*. If, to Rosa Burger, the political becomes ethical only when she is able to read her particular embodied locational valence in relationship to the givenness of macro-political reality, to the subject-positional intellectual, the only reputable point of entry into the worldliness of the world is on the basis of the micro-political worldliness of her professional discourse.

The two theorists of our own times who, each in his/her own way, have addressed and in a way embodied the complex and non-totalizable relationship of the macro-political to the micro-political are Edward Said and Gayatri Chakravorty Spivak. By and large, it would be fair to say that Said prefers a critical praxis that privileges "worldliness" over the exactions of micro-political professional commitment, whereas Spivak's ethical rigor works its way from within the micro-politics of subject positionality out into "the world," hoping in the process to call into question the axiomatic outsideness of the world and the insideness of academic discourse. It is no coincidence that the title of one of her books is *Outside in the Teaching Machine*: a title that coordinates a Mobius strip-like relationship between outsides and insides.[23] It is precisely by being in the teaching machine that Spivak hopes to be outside in the real world. To put it differently, the quality of her worldliness is directly proportional to the quality of her self-reflexivity as a subject positional professional intellectual. In Spivak's scenario, even though interpellation by the world is in a sense primary and given, and interpellation by Marxism, post-structuralism, and deconstruction is secondary, in true Derridean fashion, the secondary discourse interrupts the given authority of the primary by rendering it contingent on the procedures of the secondary. "What is your politics as a poststructuralist, Marxist-deconstructivist?" is her question, whereas Said's question is "How do you critically apprehend the world in spite of and/or beyond your allegiance to your particular epistemological model?" Said, it must be remembered, after *Orientalism*, and with *The World, the Text, the Critic*, made a conscious agential choice to avoid the practice of what he calls "wall to wall discourse," and perform instead as a traveling secular critic "between culture and system." Not bothering to call himself a Foucauldian or a Marxist or a Gramscian, Said makes himself vulnerable to charges that his theoretical models are not tight and that his use of theorists and theories is impressionistic and not systematic enough. Said perhaps would respond, if he chose, with a "There! I rest my case. If that is what it takes to be a worldly critic, so be it."

So it all comes back to self-reflexivity and the truth claims that can be made on its behalf. The question here, just as it was in the case of Rosa Burger's politics of location, is when is the politics of self-reflexivity no more than a glorified act of navel-gazing, and when is it productive of genuine transformations and persuasions against the grain? Both Said and Spivak insist on the importance of critical consciousness, but they mediate it differently. It is partly a means and ends problem. Should the model be instrumentally discarded (and this would be Said's preference) in the name of a higher and more real value (i.e., the worldliness of the world), or should the ethic of the intellectual take the form of an irreducible–immanent commitment to the model as an unavoidable precondition to the "worlding of the world?"[24] The latter would be Spivak's choice. The all-important theoretical question is what is self-reflexivity all "about," or what is its referential or representational credentials? If Rosa's self-reflexivity were only all about herself, then in a real sense the world is lost at the altar of a fierce and romantic subjectivism. If, on the other hand, the world were gained at the expense of Rosa's subjectivity or in a cavalier transcendence of it, then is the world worth winning at all? Analogously, in the case of an academic intellectual who is a citizen both of the world and his/her world, how are the two worlds to be sustained and honored with reference to each other non-hierarchically, and without recourse to the privilege of ontological priority? Much of what Spivak calls "affirmative deconstruction" is in principle compatible with Said's secular oppositional politics. Where the two part company is in the context of the politics of "in the name of." Whereas Said's political and cultural interventions are in the name of the world, Spivak's critical agency is "gestured" or addressed to the world in the name of poststructuralism, deconstruction, and subaltern feminism. Said is convinced that extreme methodological integrity, rather than opening up the world, results in the occlusion of the world. It is in this context that he talks about "professing" (*à la* Emerson one might add) degenerating into mere self-serving meritocratic professionalism and a self-absorbed and insular specialization: almost a kind of amoral mercenary activity.

In the name of the world and not in the name of theory or system or methodology: that is Said's motivation. I will not get into the question of whether this makes Said an old fashioned humanist as political activist or whether his lack of system does not by itself constitute a methodology in its own right, however "traveling," eclectic, and impressionistic.[25] To me, what makes Said interesting as a thinker and intellectual is the fact that he is full of productive contradictions. He is not the purveyor of a grand and synchronic theory that systematically resolves every contradiction, both at the local and the general levels. Much in the spirit of Adorno, who insisted that a real thought is one that could think contradiction, Said's thinking does not run away from contradictions in the name of pure monothetic resolutions. Thus Said, the forever oppositional intellectual, is also a pro-Palestinian advocate and agitator. Said, who often sounds Foucauldian in his advocacy of post-representational possibilities for the entire world, contextually guards the separation between "who is speaking" and "what is being said." Said the indefatigable opponent and critic of nationalism of every sort and kind is a champion of subaltern Palestinian nationalism. Said, who is often called by his enemies the professor of terror, is in fact a great lover of ambiguity, ambivalence, and contrapuntal possibilities learned from high European/Western culture. There is a reason why I am mapping Said's agency in terms of what it is for and what it is against. The two do not add up into one coherent, seamless, indivisible sense of constituency or belonging. There is no reductive or formulaically or programmatically derivable relationship between what Said is for and what he is against. What we get instead is a non-totalizable, non-absolute labor of ambivalence in search of an open-ended politics. Said does not attempt through theory or critical consciousness to master "our" highly contradictory, overdetermined, and uneven global situation; rather, in the very act of assuming agency proactively, he submits himself to symptomatization by the historical circumstances he is living and working under.

Now to Spivak and the contradictions and ambivalences that constitute her cultural and intellectual politics. To begin with, and at the expense of repeating myself, Spivak styles herself a deconstructionist and poststructuralist as much as she identifies herself as a third world subaltern Marxist feminist. In the relationship between ontology and epistemology, it is indeed possible to stake one's ontological claims as epistemological, and vice versa. In Spivak's self-styling, ontology and epistemology address each other differentially, and to use one of Spivak's own favorite locutions, transactionally. To Spivak, epistemology (and here I use the term interchangeably with the notion of a "theoretical model") and ontology are reciprocally textual without the benefit of an ultimate ontological anchorage.[26] If Said is concerned that academic professionalism would evacuate the world of its worldliness, Spivak is bothered that in the name of a "world out there" the professional subject positionality one occupies would be voided of its political valence, and one's "cognitive appropriation of reality," to use Althusser's phrase, simplified into an essential and unmediated experience of the world. What differentiates the two, both methodologically and temperamentally, is the way they invest in theory. Said wears theory almost invisibly, almost to the point of making it transparent through instrumentalization, whereas Spivak wears it prominently as a badge.

Dharma as Dilemma/Dilemma as Dharma

I am no expert on the concept of dharma (loosely translated as the "right code of conduct" to be arrived at both through gnosis and praxis) as propounded in Hindu thought and philosophy. Yet I cannot resist a dilettantish digression into the concept of "swa-dharma" (one's particular obligation) to illustrate some of the points I have been making in the context of Said and Spivak. Dharma is no one's possession; however, it is a binding universal obligation made available subject positionally. One is constrained to find it existentially for oneself, in one's own terms. Anything other would be fake, meretricious. But what if one's own terms are erroneous, wildly off the mark, distorted horribly *vis-à-vis* objective reality? The expectation is that one should be true to one's self and practice dharma creatively, transformatively. There is no dharma except by way of swa-dharma (roughly translatable as one's own specific accountability as warrior, priest, king, husband, friend, wife, etc.). In other words, dharma is an objective and absolute command or interpellation, while swa-dharma could be seen as subjective exemplarity. Between the unavoidable immanence of swa-dharma and the absolute objectivity of dharma, histories and human lives take shape. The practice of dharma on one's own basis thus represents an uncomfortable straddle between the performative contingency of swa-dharma and the pedagogical demand of dharma as such. The actualization of dharma as such in violation of one's swa-dharma is ethically as inadmissible as the narcissistic practice of swa-dharma without reference to dharma as such. Here, according to the *Bhagavad Gita*, is the double bind: one has to transform oneself, but only on the basis of oneself, and the "one" in "oneself" is both the "one" to be cultivated and the "one" to be left behind in the name of duty, right conduct, dharma as such. Dharma is both an *a priori* and the result of embodied action. In the term "swa-dharma," dharma is both the pedagogical *telos* in whose name "the self or swa" has to be practiced, and a performative obligation through which the self becomes the self. The term "dharma sankata" refers to that unbearable moment of existential dilemma when a person has difficulty in choosing which particular dharma to uphold and which one to reject. This model obviously allows for irreducible and non-negotiable contradictions among different dharmas: as a warrior, as a father, as a citizen, as a wife, as a guru, and so on. A number of characters in the *Ramayana* and the *Mahabharatha* resort to one of two strategies to break the dilemma: some characters (Vibhishana in the *Ramayana* is a good example) resort to a hierarchical calculus that helps them decide which of the dharmas is the higher of the two or three, and that is the way they choose. Certain other characters (Kumbhakarna, Vibhishana's brother in the *Ramayana*, comes to mind) choose to remain trapped in the immanence of one specific obligation and forgo the way out offered by the hierarchical–transcendent model. And in choosing his path, one of the brothers goes against God, and the other, with. These are agonizingly conscious choices, since they know that in their choice they are both right and wrong. For the most part, the ones who perish are those that refuse transcendence. Thus, when Krishna exhorts Arjuna in the battle-field of Kurukshetra to do his duty, he theorizes the notion of nishkamya karma (i.e., non-teleological or non-desiring agency): a kind of purposeless purposiveness.[27] He also tells Arjuna, his disciple (we cannot afford to forget that this is a supreme pedagogical moment), to act and leave all responsibility to him, i.e., God. The category of "in the name of" is thus simultaneously honored and abandoned through the figurality of sublation. The irreducible immanence of Arjuna's subject position as a warrior who now has to kill his cousins, and teachers, and elders, is acknowledged not as an end in itself, but as a necessary starting point to the realization of an objective and absolute "beyond" that cannot be understood except through action. Arjuna's agency is both asserted and surrendered to a pure alterity (in this case God) through a kind of leap of faith. Arjuna then may be said to have practiced subject-positional self-reflexivity, *à la* a theist existentialist protagonist, with the comfort of divine assistance (i.e., the solace of faith), whereas a character like Karna goes through a similar exercise, but rather like a Sartrean existentialist who refuses to take the leap of faith. And it is interesting that both protagonists are lauded in the Hindu tradition.

This excursion into the *Mahabharatha* by way of the concept of dharma was just to put some meta-theoretical pressure on the concept of self-reflexivity. As

I have attempted to show, there is a macro-political self-reflexivity based on what I would like to term "ontological location," and a discursive self-reflexivity based on the subject position. How do the two work together in tandem, or perhaps in contradiction, perhaps incommensurably? Thus, when we evaluate Spivak's poststructuralist intervention in the politics of subalternity, for example, when she talks about transactional readings between Barthesian semiotropy and the subaltern realities of a Naxalite village, by what normative expectations are we hoping to motor our verdict? Is poststructuralism intrinsically irrelevant in the context of subalternity? What is so wrong about a subaltern subject traveling with poststructuralist theory and in the process signifying a different inflection on it? Is poststructuralism off bounds to the authentic subaltern, and who says so? A similar debate is taking place in the development of Asian-American Studies in the United States. Is poststructuralism or postmodernism integral or inimical to the self-recognition of Asian-American studies?[28] How should any constituency defined as location go about choosing its discursive parameters? Are some parameters intrinsically wrong *vis-à-vis* certain locations, or is the negotiation between location and subject positionality contingent and open ended? Take Spivak, for example. On the one hand, we have her macro-political reprimand, in "Can the Subaltern Speak?" of Foucault and Deleuze for their over-hasty celebration of the death of representation; on the other hand, there is her masterly poststructuralization of subalternity in her essay "Deconstructing Historiography," where her pedagogical interest is to make the subalternists aware of their "theoretical unconscious": an unconscious they have suppressed in the name of political interest. In addition to enfranchising the subaltern woman (gender and sexuality had indeed been an egregious absence in the work of the Indian subaltern historians), Spivak's intervention serves to make poststructuralist theory an organic part of the subaltern project. Spivak's is a double-conscious commitment. From within this double consciousness she activates both location and subject position transactionally in a way that is not conducive to the task of finding one's constituency definitively and terminally. Spivak's rationale for rejecting the nonchalance of poststructuralist theory and her reasons for theorizing subalternity via poststructuralism do not add up to one unified constituency. The two rationales together can only symptomatically express the form of a double consciousness. In making avant-garde European theory aware of the macro-political realities of a world structured in dominance, Spivak asserts her agency as subaltern/postcolonial, and when the same Spivak reads subalternity against the grain but in solidarity, she complicates the politics of subaltern affirmation by way of the micro-politics of theory. The Europe–Other divide is both acknowledged and deconstructed in this model.

Spivak is certainly open to the criticism that she is trying to have the best of both worlds: both deal with the West as a fixed political category that dominates the Rest, and entertain the West as a moving epistemic location thoroughly available to postcolonial double consciousness. So which one is it? We could perhaps give Spivak the benefit of the doubt (possible if one believes in the reality of double consciousness) and suggest that her formulation of the subaltern predicament is both a symptom of an unavoidable asymmetry and an attempt to instrumentalize the asymmetry by way of a performative double consciousness.[29] I will return to Spivak a little later in the chapter when I discuss the ethical dilemma of the postcolonial intellectual.

The reality that underpins both kinds of self-reflexivity is that of unevenness.[30] To recall Rosa Burger's predicament briefly, self-reflexivity is enjoined both as a subjective or intra-identitarian imperative and as an objective or inter-identitarian imperative. Both imperatives are subtended by the uneven reality that obtains between whites and blacks in Lionel's country. My point is that self-reflexivity by itself does not a politics make unless it is also addressed simultaneously to the unevenness of a world that is structured in dominance. To put it in Jesse Jackson's words to Michael Dukakis, "Even though we are now on the same boat, we came on different ships." Rosa Burger's problem is how to understand and act on the coevalness that obtains between her situation and that of her black brothers. Alas! If only the scene could be understood in a purely objective and non-perspectival way! The problem is that reality is taking place both out there and within Rosa's subjectivity. As I have already argued at length, the chronotope of the historical–allegorical introduces something hallucinatory and phantasmatic to the scene that derails perception. The scene is taking place "in between," which is the temporality of the coeval that is relational through and through. It is only within the aegis of coevalness that is not bound to any one history or temporality that genuine action becomes possible, i.e., action that is viable both ethically and politically. It is altogether understandable why Gordimer consistently spatializes time in her novel. Gordimer is effectively steering her narrative and her protagonist's consciousness away from the teleology of historicism and its unilinearity that is dismissive of the spatial dispersion of time into heterogeneous locations. The experiential humanism of the "I" is maintained in erasure as the "I" becomes the space where events take place; and the spatialized "I" is unmoored from the fixity of a single temporal marking.

I attempt now to interweave some of the questions that I have been trying to unpack:

1   How is self-reflexivity to be exercised, not narcissistically, but as a form of openness to the world's coevalness?

2   How is the self-reflexivity based on ontological considerations of identity different from the self-reflexivity that derives from epistemological models of self-understanding?
3   To what extent can epistemological self-identifications such as "I am a post-structuralist, post-Marxist," etc. be perceived as ontological recognitions, and conversely, do ontological markers such as "I am Indian" function as epistemological models?

What would be a category that could pass both as ontological and as epistemological; furthermore, a category that has universal purchase despite all the global asymmetry and unevenness? I can't think of a better candidate than secularism.

Secularism Between Worlds

One is secular and one practices secularism as an epistemology. Surely, one is Hindu/Christian/Jewish/Muslim and one practices these religions. But is the "givenness" of secularism somehow different from the filiative–natal givenness of the latter? Secularism pertains both to identity and to knowledge production valorized as a coherent worldview. Furthermore, secularism fits the description, since it is born in the "West" as the brainchild of the Enlightenment and travels invasively to the non-West on the wings of colonialism. It is therefore symptomatic of a putative universal sovereignty structured in dominance. It would be interesting to analyze how secularism has fared across the uneven divide of colonizer–colonized, West and the Rest. My references as I go along would be Edward Said, Rustom Bharucha, Partha Chatterjee, and William Connolly. My polemical strategy here is to position secularism as a phenomenon that both divides and connects the two worlds. Though the common point of reference is indeed secularism, proponents and critics of secularism from the two sides of the divide are saying different things and employing different arguments on the basis of their differential relationships to secularism. Secularism thus functions both as a nameless philosophy with no provenance and as a determinate ideology complicit with colonial modernity. Consequently, though in some important ways Rustom Bharucha and William Connolly's dissatisfaction with secularism can be politicized on a common platform, their specific reasons for their disaffection warrant a differentiation within the identification.

Take the following identity statements: "I am a Sikh," "I am a Punjabi," "I am a Hindu," and then the statement "I am secular." Which of these statements are ontological and which epistemological? Are the two interchangeable? Most crucially, how do these identifications enter the field of representation: with the categorical authority of an *a priori*, or contingently, i.e., open and vulnerable to the performative contingencies of the process of representation? Or to use Said's useful distinction, which of these identifications are filiative and which affiliative? Which natal, which adopted? Which primary, which acquired? Is one born any less secular than one is born Jewish or female or Brahmin?[31] Or does one become as much Arab or Hindu as one becomes secular? Are the accountabilities of "becoming" more or less or equally binding as "natal" or "native" accountabilities? Is "becoming" a decentered and non-identical repetition of origins, or is it a binding axiomatization of the origin? When I say "I am secular" what exactly am I describing and claiming: an identity, a mode of representation, a card-carrying normative adherence to a particular way of looking at the world, or a native presence? To put the question in popular terms, what are the roots of secularism? Can they be existential? If the mandate of secularism is to call into question and deterritorialize certain preexisting identities and modes, what about its own claim to truth? Is its appeal to reason, affect, or being? Is secularism, to use that nifty phrase from none other than T. S. Eliot, "autotelic"? Does it carry within itself its *raison d'être*, and any more so than other modes of identification?

Before I get too abstract, let me take a look at secularism as viewed by Said. Broadly speaking, for Said, secularism is historical through and through. It is recursively, self-constitutively historical. Secularism in principle is opposed to ideas of absolute origins and the notion of primordiality. Under the aegis of secularism, no one history can trump another in the name of its primordiality. Secularism does not admit a transhistorical ground of origin; on the contrary, it is profoundly vulnerable to non-identical repetitions.[32] Most crucially, to Said, secularism has everything to do with the politics of representation and very little to do with identity politics. To speak and to speak for in the context of Saidian secularism is not to own an immutable identity or to claim axiomatically a normative one-to-one relationship between "who is saying" and "what is being said." In other words, when someone is saying, the reality of that "one" is perspectival and not ontological. The "one" of ontology does not precede the "one" who discovers oneself through the perspectival action of "saying."

Perspectives, then, are sharable across filiations, across native and genetic determinations. Under secularism, for Said, the politics of representation is philosophically ungrounded even though politically it is directed and interested. So I would argue, and I am sure to Said's dismay and chagrin, that in many ways his position is closer to Foucault's than Chomsky's. One's own proximal ontology does not take the place of one's truth by bypassing the politics of representation. In the act of representing "oneself" the one is politically charged but not ontologically secure. Said insists time and again and in the same breath where he is partisan that he does not believe in the exclusive representation of Arabs by Arabs, Jews by Jews, and women by women. If anything, it is in the heart of partisanship that Said would wish to parse the meaning of solidarity affiliatively, and not filiatively. Said as the "border intellectual" deals with borderliness both as a lay individual and as a practicing critical intellectual invested in perennial oppositionality.[33] It would be interesting to examine how secularism as theoretical or epistemological practice informs and underwrites Said's resolve to inhabit "betweenness" as a mobile set of coordinates that will not reach home.[34] Now, to what extent does secularism practice what it professes, particularly in the context of the West–Rest asymmetry or unevenness?

There is no question that secularism has considerable representative and representational range, but what are the limits to that range? Is secularism aware of its own limitations? If so, how does it make sure it does not make any truth claims where it has no say or expertise? To invoke Shakespeare in an offhanded way, if it is true that there are more things in the world than are dreamt of in anyone's philosophy, how does secularism deal with its "others," its "outsides?" How does secularism situate itself *vis-à-vis* universality? The peculiar characteristic of secularist claims is that they are made in the name of Reason itself. If that is the case, either Reason must be coextensive with everything that "is," or else those phenomena that do not fall within Reason must be adjudicated out of hand as extant but "unreasonable" – as phenomena whose ontological essence is their "unreasonableness."[35] As one historicizes secularism (something that Said does not do), one has to come to terms with not just what is good/beautiful and bad/ugly about secularism, but the very conditions of its propagation globally. As heir and consummation of Enlightenment Reason,[36] secularism does a twofold job: it presents itself as the exemplary form of rational community, and demystifies or problematizes earlier forms of belonging. In other words, the strength of its operation has to do with the fact that it operates as a critique, and its being is polemical through and through. And as a critique speaking in the name of Reason itself, it conceals its own provinciality, its own tradition of indigeny, and thereby vanquishes "earlier" modes of thought and belonging in the name of developmental historicism. But where is the point where the "being" of secularism intersects with its "rationale?" If *raison d'être* is what we are thinking of in the context of the Cartesian *cogito*, then, to echo Foucault somewhat, is the existence of reason the same thing as the reasonableness of existence? Is community rational/possible? Is it rational to be communal? Which forms of the communal are rational, and which ones irrational and "primitive?"[37] To avail ourselves of Partha Chatterjee's work, the reality is that of a world structured in dominance, a world divided into two zones: one where rationality and being would seem to come together, and the other where the two are seemingly at odds.

It is significant that the term "communal" has always been double coded. On the one hand, it evokes togetherness, solidarity, social cohesion, and a healthy communitarian transcendence of the self, the individual, and the ego. On the other hand, it is associated with an irrational, fierce, and primitive attachment to provincialism, insularity, a bloody and visceral and essentialist sense of self and belonging that is inimical to progress, movement, and transformations by reason. For example, communal violence is always to be feared as a dark form of nescience, but state violence is to be interpreted and understood by Reason. Analogously, violence by the State of Israel is meaningful, but violence practiced by Palestinian "hordes" that have no state is pathological. Secularism as the epistemological product of Reason had the mandate to resolve this chronic ambivalence at the very heart of "community," but has secularism been successful in transcending the split between the existential copula and the thinking self? As Partha Chatterjee has demonstrated memorably in *Nationalist Thought and the Colonial World*, European reason in the form of secular modernity needed to maintain a clear distinction between an "us" capable of evolving naturally and organically into Reason, and a "them" who need to have Reason thrust upon them (i.e., those who can embody Reason only in the form of a cognitive dissidence). Chatterjee's inter-historical rereading of secular modernity as colonial modernity finds great resonance with a number of "Occidental" or intra-historical critiques of secularism (more of this later when I discuss William Connolly) – critiques that focus on the incompleteness and the unacknowledged contingency of secular discourse.

Let me take up the problem of incomplete predication as it confronts the truth claims of secularism. By incomplete predication I mean statements such as "I am male," "I am Hindu Brahmin," "I am a lesbian Catholic" – statements that as predications gesture towards a certain kind of regional plenitude (predications that universalize from a regional perspective), but do so only as an expression of an underlying incompleteness, since the fullness of the being making these predications requires other predications as well. To put it simply, none of these predications represent the entire person, unless the "identity" that comes after as the copula succeeds in hegemonizing itself as a core value, in which case it begins to speak for the entire being. Thus, for a core Catholic, it is impossible to sustain herself as gay, so the predication of "being gay," for lack of valorization/legitimation within the Catholic core, drops out of (or is practiced in a closet form) of the identity register altogether, or remains valueless and unparsed within that syntax. Thus it is a question not only of incomplete predication, but also a problem concerning contradiction and alterity. What does an orthodox Catholic do with gay sensibilities, or a staunch secu-

larist with spirituality? The only way any of these worldviews work is hegemonically, in Gramsci's sense of the term. Thus, if one is secular, and secularism is a combinatory of different beliefs, values, and convictions, then some
values take on the centrality of "core" values and on the basis of that hegemony
they begin to speak for all the other issues and themes that constitute the bloc.
Hegemonic representation becomes the norm of representation as such, with
the result that some values within the bloc remain dependent on the hegemonic core values, not to speak of the many other trajectories and perspectives that do not find a place in the bloc. A Catholic, for example, understands
and comes to terms with her sexuality on the basis of religious faith, and a secularist uses her core values to make sense both of her model of the world and
the world that such a model speaks for. We have now run into the problem of
"in the name of."

It is not coincidental that Rustom Bharucha's brief but powerful book is
entitled *In the Name of the Secular*. The problem is that since no category is
coextensive with all of life and its protean experiential flows and patterns, the
only way the locution "in the name of" can work is ideologically, and not
merely descriptively. In other words, when a secularist speaks "in the name of"
secularism, he or she is actually speaking "in the name of the world itself": the
blank or the namelessness (see chapter 2) that follows "in the name of" has
been filled by the ideology of secularism. This is true of "in the name of
Hinduism/Christianity/Islam," etc. Here is the theoretical dilemma: if any discourse or theoretical model is to speak intransitively in its own name and in
the name of the world, it has to have persuasion, jurisdiction, and theoretical
purchase along different axes, and across other and different theoretical
models. It is as though the other theoretical models or epistemologies have
agreed to regionalize themselves (i.e., consented not to push their own specific
claims to universality "in the name of" their specific names), and have conceded to the one successful model to establish its relationship to universality
as the one and only relationship to universality as such. But why would they
do that unless they have been effectively "inferiorized," persuaded that their
philosophies do not deserve hegemonization? Here, too, I am using "hegemonization" in Gramsci's sense. To Gramsci, the hegemonic classes were those that
were successful in establishing a representative connection between civil society
and the modern nation-state, which is to say that hegemonic groups could
make sure that their internal values could be translated, represented, and
recoded as the values of the state as well, whereas the internal values and truth
claims of the non-hegemonic groups are privatized – they are valuable, but not
to the state. Hegemonic groups have direct access to the currency of the state,
whereas the non-hegemonic groups lack such direct access. The separation
of church and state and the consensus among different groups as to what

constitutes "minimal rationality" follow a similar path. The things that really matter and cause discord among the different participants are shelved as chronic disagreements, and the common ground that is articulated is as vapid as it is exiguous. To quote from Rustom Bharucha:

> The aura of neutrality and impartiality informing these clauses endow the State with a quintessential power rising above religion. Understandably, in the multi-religious context of India, this affirmation of *dharmanirapeksata* is almost always substituted, if not superseded by the more familiar rhetoric of *sarva dharma sama bhava*, in which Gandhi had placed so much faith. Today, we are seeing the abuse of both principles – *dharmanirapeksata* is attacked by the Hindu Right as a disguised means of appeasing minority communities, while *sarva dharma sama bhava* has become not so much a philosophy advocating "reverence for all *dharma*," but a clarion call for a single *dharma: Hindu dharma eka bhava.*[38]

Secularism could be translated as Dharmanirapeksha (impartiality to religion) or as Sarva dharma sama bhava (equal respect for all religions). Bharucha points out that the former maxim is perceived by the Hindus in India as a slight to religion, and the latter hijacked by the Hindus in their name. What must be noted here is that the secular state, by way of following in the footsteps of Enlightenment Reason, is monomaniacal in its insistence on the production of the One out of the many (the *pluribus unum* thesis). Since the One is privileged and the "many" not, there is a mad and frenetic rush on the part of the several constituencies that make up the "many" to speak "in the name of" the One. But by definition the only "one" that can speak in the name of the One is the state; and hence the frustration experienced by Hinduism, and Islam, Christianity, and Sikhism, who are now dramatically introduced to the regime of the One, but in the capacity of lowly interpellated subjects. Whereas the secular "one" can become the One, such a privilege does not await the destiny of the "other" ones.

The two formulations quoted above are as complex as they are ambiguous. In "Sarva dharma" who is the "sarva" or the "all?" Is the "all" an instantiation of the "one" or is the "one" an instantiation of the "all?" Is it because "all" religions are to be regarded dispassionately, that any "one" religion is also being viewed dispassionately? Where does the ostensive denotation begin: with the one or with the all? If "I" am everyman, then who is "every man?"[39] What is at work here is a process of denominalization that works from a safe remove. For any one religion, say Islam or Hinduism (and this certainly has to do with majoritarianism and minoritarianism), to be treated "the same" as "all" other religions, it has to be reduced to a general instance of religion as such, whatever that means. In other words, it has to be negated as Islam. Simply put, Islam is neither all religions, nor is it a religion, but to its practitioners it is *the* religion. So it is only by way of the essentialization of "religion as such" and the dubiously non-ostensive taxonomy of the "all" and the "one" that the two formulations operate as the working manifesto of secularism. Where does the sweeping inclusiveness of the secularist discourse come from? Clearly, from a point of power that is "without": a point that Bharucha astutely recognizes as the coordinates of the state. There is no "all" except from the point of view of a certain official gaze that in a "governmental" move interpellates the all and the one.[40]

In order to understand how the two statements work in tandem it is important to analyze their rhetoricity as well as their mode of address. Now, who is making the exhortation of impartiality and equal respect, and to whom is it addressed? If one were to argue that this is a plea or a command issuing from the heart of secularism and addressed to the heart of the non-secular, does this mean automatically that impartiality and respect for all religions cannot be practiced from within Hindu, Islamic, and Christian spaces? To put it differently, is secularism one of the players in the conversation/conflict, or is it purely an impartial facilitator from the outside who is forced to intervene only because the participants in the conflict have proven their inability to resolve the dispute? If the impartiality of secularism is a mere function of its "indifference" (as an outsider as arbiter) to the dispute on hand, isn't such impartiality merely procedural, sans substance, sans content? Would it not be much more worthwhile and significant for the parties concerned to generate a space for impartiality from within their entrenched positions as disputants? If, on the other hand, the claim is that secularism is not merely procedural but that it has chosen to participate in the fray substantively and maintain its role as potential arbiter, then secularism is constrained to show all its cards. Secularism cannot hide its polemical investment in the debate any more: it will have to lay bare the connections between its formation as a theory/philosophy/epistemology and its colonial–modern political project. The way secularism has solved this problem in practice is by taking for granted its privileged position as the upholder of universal Reason. Having arrogated to itself this important and world-making privilege, secularism parades itself as pure knowledge and on that basis aligns itself with impartiality.

To be impartial and judge on matters where the judge has no expertise or jurisdiction – that is what it comes down to. In a debate about the intricacies of Hindu law or the Shariat, secularism has nothing to say: it is an outsider, a non-expert and non participant, and yet by a sweeping formalism of hegemonic sovereignty it will still adjudicate, and as happened in the Shabano case, quite disastrously. It is difficult to maintain a dialogic relationship between the secular and the non-secular, or to have any meaningful debate, when it is assumed always-already that the two bodies of doctrine (secularism no less than Islam, say) are incommensurable, and despite this incommensurability, one of them (secularism) is the superior and the more evolved. The customary way to ease tensions is to resort to the principle of minimal rationality: a public sphere is created and semanticized with a limited lexicon, and whatever falls outside this lexicon then belongs to the inner life of the religious doctrines. The assumption, of course, is that secularism, the discourse that dictates minimal morality, is all out of the closet. It has nothing to hide: pure transparency, inside and outside coincident as the immaculate figurality of reason itself. What such an arrangement overlooks entirely is that prior to the advent of secularism, the indigenous religious doctrines did not see themselves as fragmented, compartmentalized bits and pieces of insight lacking in a center. They perceived themselves, rightly or wrongly, as holistic worldviews on all kinds of themes and issues. I as a feminist–secularist of the male gender wholeheartedly condemn the pope *qua* having a papal position on sexuality. But that is neither here nor there. A Muslim Sufi or a Hindu mystic will turn around and say, rightly so, that secularism should have no opinion on the realities of unmediated knowledge and revelations. Here there are two unresolvable issues: (1) who decides what is viable and demonstrable as a domain of knowledge (and here we could think about the denial of scientific status to ayurveda medicine by the Western medical establishment) and (2) who and by what authority decides what is public and what is private? Of great concern to the non-secular constituencies is the fact that those themes and concerns that they consider to be "the heart of the matter" are declared non-public by the secular state. There is the duplicity of maintaining the liberal stance of "defending the other's right to speak despite one's disagreement with the other," on the one hand, and the non-dialogic and unilateral determination of what constitutes the political and what constitutes the personal, on the other. It ensures that certain lines will never be crossed and certain kinds of trans-communal, trans-identitarian, and trans-epistemic dialogues, disagreements, and evaluations will never ever be initiated.

Take, for example, the consecrated principle of the separation of church and state. A necessary separation indeed, but when it becomes the kind of separation, based not on the relative autonomy of each within a common totality, but on an iron-clad division that makes a conversation between the two impossible, especially on matters that generate great passion and vehemence on either side, what we get as a result is a community poised precariously on layers of resentment and frustration ready to burst into flames at the slightest provocation. No "one" is hearing the "other."

Just to play devil's advocate, let me briefly but polemically negotiate with the American custom of having the national anthem sung before a ball game.

To me this practice constitutes an ugly and egregious violation of the separation of the public and the private, the political and the personal. I would find
it equally objectionable if the song sung were from the Rig Veda, or the Bible,
the Koran, or the Zend Avesta. Why should a multitude of people who are
about to have the private pleasure of watching a ball game be suddenly and
solemnly interpellated by the call of the nation, unless that call is interpreted
duplicitously as natural? It is assumed that it is natural to be national, and being
natural goes beyond all divides: inner–outer, private–public, personal–
political. The imagined community of the national is after all natural. Furthermore, what then happens to those segments among the spectators who are
non-citizens, H1 visa holders, illegal and legal aliens, and dissenting minority
and hyphenated, diasporic Americans who do not believe in all-America?
Should such people walk out, excuse themselves, or just be submitted without
recourse to this profoundly ideological ritual? One glib way out of this untenable scenario would be to maintain that in a world structured as a community
of nation-states, what indeed could be more of a felicitous common currency
than the national anthem – any national anthem, the national anthem of the
mightiest country of the world; and surely this anthem will speak to and for
the entire world? Well, tell that to the Palestinians. Or why not play the national
anthem of South Korea, or Nigeria, or Iraq, for they too are coeval nations?
Why not honor the evil states within the transcendent temporality of the
nation-state? It was quite amusing and quite symptomatic that Bush after 9/11
exhorted the leaders of all the free nations of the world to synchronize their
watches and clocks and boldly unfurl their flags at that very moment when the
first plane struck the first tower. What if Saddam Hussein and the Taliban
regime had heeded the call and unfurled their flags? All the hilarious and plangent ironies of such a situation escape the attention of a non-hybrid, univocal,
unilateral secular modernism.

The strength as well as the vulnerability of secularism in its colonial and
postcolonial context is that it seeks to operate as pure critique without a body
or an interiority of its own. Of course, as Gauri Viswanathan has demonstrated
in the context of British education and the politics of conversion, English or
colonial politics has a body of its own, both in the mother country as well as
in the colony, but the colonial effect would have us believe that reason and
modernity reach the colony in an always-already state of immaculate perfec-
tion: no genealogies of the "becoming" of modernity by way of colonialism.[41]
One's ontology is already secular since one is the legitimate heir of Reason, and
therefore when the "one" practices secularism performatively and epistemologically, all one is doing is repeating ontology as epistemology.

It should be clear by now that what I am doing here is similar to, and
indebted to, Partha Chatterjee's nuanced analysis of the colonial and

postcolonial difference within modernity. Secularism does not have to secu-larize itself, whereas Hinduism and Islam need to be secularized. I will not get into the contradictory and overdetermined relationship between Judaeo-Christian values and Western secularism (I will touch on it in my discussion of William Connolly, who does claim that secularism inherits its umbrella structure of legitimation from Judaeo-Christianity that it seeks to replace). Suffice it to say for my purposes here that in the colonial and the postcolonial context secularism succeeds in selling itself as an effective insider precisely because it is a gifted and unexceptionable outsider.

The logic that the colonized internalize is this: why worry about the prove-nance of the answer so long as it works? Let us make the answer our own, deriv-atively, to borrow from Partha Chatterjee. The questions that are suppressed in the process are: is the answer really appropriate and is there really a dearth of answers "within"? Also, given the enormity of the claims made by secular-ism, is it not conceivable that secularism could be as fundamentalist as any of the religions that are condemned, deservedly, for their fundamentalisms? In the colonial and the postcolonial context, secularism is hypersaturated with political rationality and sovereignty, whereas it is hyposaturated with histori-cal and existential density. If anything, the hypersaturation is the direct effect of the hyposaturation. As I have already tried to show, because of its hegemonic relationship to the modern state, secularism has already determined which values are political and which private. In a manner that resembles the high-handed logical positivist dismissal of all phenomenological thinking from phi-losophy, secularism minimizes and stacks the ante, and wins.[42] The non-secular philosophies have to live in a state of schizophrenic tension, i.e., continue to participate in a political process that systematically disallows dialogue on a range of issues that matter to them, but only privately. Secular authority func-tions much like "the center" that Derrida deconstructs: the center that in being "elsewhere" inaugurates and authorizes "play" without ever getting caught up in the play.[43]

I hope my discussion so far makes it unambiguously clear as to where I stand *vis-à-vis* secularism. Like Dipesh Chakrabarty, who in his book *Provin-cializing Europe* has no problems acknowledging the beneficial effects of the Enlightenment (even as he reads the Enlightenment as symptomatic of a Eurocentrism that will not allow reciprocity of influence between the West and the Rest), I endorse secularism politically without abandoning the project of a genealogical study of secularism. Given the ascendancy of Hindu fundamen-talism in India as well as in the Indian diasporas all over the world, not being secular is not even an option. But my point is that the political advocacy and practice of secularism in the context of a Muslim-hating Hindu fundamental-ism is not mutually exclusive of an epistemological interrogation, say *à la* Ashis

Nandy, of secularism. Nor is secularism the secure and desirable terminus of world-historical processes. Indeed, as William Connolly demonstrates in his critique of secularism in the West, secularism is deeply fissured. My objective is to open up secularism to its own contradictions and its problematic colonial–modern provenance. In what follows, my focus will be on secularism as a mode of being and secularism as a mode of knowing, and secularism as a critical practice that allows for a certain relationship between the two modes of knowing and being. How is a secular community more rational than any other community? If the answer is that secularism acts fundamentally as a critique and as a demystification of earlier modes of knowing and being, does this mean (a) that these other modes of being are incapable of auto-critique, and (b) that secularism is a disembodied and unencumbered critique that has somehow successfully solved the problem of its own embodiment and materiality (in other words, it has earned the privilege of being pure rational agent without history or baggage)? Neither of these claims deserves any serious consideration or refutation. There really is no way, except through the gratuitous force of dominance, to prove that any one community is rational than any other. Perhaps all communities are irrational, or each community is rational in its own way; but there is no exemplary community that has sublated community into reason and embodied reason as community.

The crucial question to ask, it seems to me, is what is the relationship between the critique and its "object"? As both Said and Derrida would insist, each in his own way, the critique or the critical consciousness should be heterogeneous with its object for it to be "oppositional." Indeed, so it should; but should the heterogeneity be so radical that the critique loses solidarity with its object? Said does not answer this question theoretically, but instead he demonstrates solidarity through his actions and political writings, thus making himself vulnerable to charges of contradictoriness and inconsistency. Derrida, on the other hand, rarely ventures into any politics except the politics of theory and so he merely theorizes the relationship of heterogeneity without risking it in any way. The only site where it does acquire vulnerability is in the context of the politics of the university; but this site is already formalized as a place where thought can think itself intransitively and thus the world in a sense has been strategically de-referentialized. My concern is with how one can think solidarity with critique within the same thought. To put it in the context of a debate prevalent in postmodern literary theory a couple of decades ago: how should the same work of narrative work as fiction and meta-fiction, i.e., both as elaboration of experience and a relevant problematization of that very experience? In the postcolonial context of "derivativeness" it is often too easily conceded that the story is one's own but the theory is "theirs," and we need their theory to alienate ourselves into ourselves. Could there be internal critiques that are secular with reference to themselves, i.e., secular without the need for deregionalization or universalization in the name of the West?

The Indigenous Critique

To unpack this question, I go to a story by Jayakanthan, an outstanding contemporary Tamil writer and intellectual (the kind of writer of whom Salman Rushdie would know nothing and would choose to know nothing, and yet proceed on the basis of this self-sanctioned ignorance to pontificate about the state of contemporary literature in Indian languages). Years ago, Jayakanthan asked me with some asperity, "Radhakrishnan, saar, you ask me, 'Have you read Sartre?' and I ask you, 'Has Sartre read Jayakanthan?'"

Jayakanthan's story *Suya Darisanam* roughly translates as "Self-vision" or "Self-staging or revelation."[44] Its protagonist is an ugly and misshapen Brahmin man, the unworthy son of a renowned Vedantic scholar and teacher. He is an embarrassment to his father, son, and daughter-in-law. Naive, unerudite, uncomplex, and intellectually unremarkable, he is only a Brahmin by birth, and not by performance or eminence. He is an affront to the tradition of the "Brahmin," who should be perpetually engaged in the gnostic quest of self-actualization in the form of "That thou art." Jayakanthan plays here with the received notion of who a Brahmin is in Hindu tradition and renders it undecidable. On the one hand, one is a "Brahmin" natally and thus participates in the apartheid of the caste system, but philosophically speaking, anybody could be a "Brahmin" on the basis of his (not her) achievements. The ontology of Brahminhood is affiliative and acquired ideally and intellectually speaking, but historicized filiatively by way of *varnashramadharma* (by way of caste positioning that locks one into the caste one is born into). Jayakanthan is also raising the question about the truth of Hinduism: which Hinduism, the one that legitimated the caste system, or the one that dared to think non-denominationally?[45] Ganapathi Sastrigal is a performative failure: merely a "given" Brahman but not an effective Brahman. Even though he knows the mantras by rote, he does not understand them. Here Jayakanthan is initiating a serious critique of a Brahmanism that has ossified into meaningless ritual uninformed by scholarship and insight. By contrast, there is his guru brother (guru brother is a sibling by virtue of having shared the same teacher: more nuances here in terms of filiation, affiliation, and the genealogical transmission of knowledge), who is brilliant, learned, articulate, and quite the Brahmin.

One random evening, there is an awkward meeting between the two on the steps of the local temple pond. There are onlookers in the form of an active public. The guru brother humiliates Ganapathi Sastrigal for his ignorance, for his not "knowing that he is a Brahmin." Ganapathi Sastrigal is utterly demoralized, even deontologized (for who is he if he is not a Brahmin?) by this onslaught in public. Rendered naked both within himself and in front of the public, he has nowhere to go but he leaves the village, and this he does without giving anyone any notice. Months later, his son receives a letter of explanation from his nomadic father. The letter is indeed the narrative of Ganapathi Sastrigal's "self-revelation" in exile: his "secular" critical understanding of himself. The son and the daughter-in-law read the letter with tears in their eyes, amazed beyond belief that their idiot father/father-in-law could be capable of such poignant profundities. What is so remarkable about this story is that Jayakanthan explores the "Who am I?" question simultaneously on two registers: the historical and the allegorical or metaphysical. In this story, "being Brahmin" is both filiative and affiliative. It is also macro-politically locational (the native or natal location) and micro-politically subject positional (discursive position). To Jayakanthan's immense credit, he does not shun writing from the location of a Brahmin: a position that is after all politically incorrect and socially retrogressive. Truths can be produced from a variety of perspectives simply because truth is a matter of rigorous and conscientious performance and not the pious endorsement of a pregiven teleology: hence, too, the existential(ist) dimension of the story. It is interesting to note here that Jayakanthan, who is not a Brahmin by birth, has always claimed that the reality that he knows best is that of the upper lower/middle class South Indian Tamil Brahmin family. In this story, Jayakanthan does a deconstructive number on Brahmanism, both as location and as subject position. Just as Rosa Burger has to postpone her pedagogical sense of self to make room for performative failures and detours, here too, Ganapathi Sastrigal has to invest in himself locationally and subject positionally before he can relate to the Real. His location as well as his subject position act like the *pharmakon*, poison and remedy all at once.[46]

The "Who am I?" question in all its generality is articulated in profound tension with the more historically determinate question "Who am I as a Brahmin?" In other words, the allegorical frame does not eliminate the specificity of the historical frame, but works with it, in tension. Neither question is askable without the other. There is a relationship of organic difference between the two registers. In his letter to his son, Ganapathi Sastrigal declares that he is totally and utterly lost, lost in a surplus of being that overflows identity codes, denominational registers, and analytic procedures. It is as though Sastrigal has found himself in a spirit of rapturous Nietzschean nihilism: a nihilism that Nietzsche claimed as the ultimate embodied affirmation of life in opposition to the philosopher's sclerotic negation of life. Ganapathi Sastrigal's self-revelation takes place in a theater that has very little to do with vedantic meta-physics or Brahmanic orthodoxy and canonicity. He is in a state of critical epiphany (a subtle combination of nay-saying and aye-saying) that has seen through the empty pieties of anthropological role playing. Not that he is insensitive to history. If anything, he now finds himself in a different part of India where the people and their language are different, as are their historical legacies.

We could say that Ganapathi Sastrigal has secularized himself on the basis of his location and his subject positionality. The oceanic surge of Being (or what Heidegger might call the being of Being) that Sastrigal experiences is the result of hard theoretical work: work that both alienates and reintegrates. The theoretical or epistemological component is simultaneously affective and cognitive and develops organically from the predicament of the character, with no awkward borrowings from the West. All of Jayakanthan's works create their own epistemological terrain that could be termed, for want of a better word, "indigenous," or home-spun, to borrow from Mohandas Gandhi. I say this not to suggest that writers like Jayakanthan have been untouched by the West (there is no such possibility), but merely to argue *contra* Rushdie that Indian literature has been theorizing itself in ways that are not necessarily connected to secular modernism. Unlike Jayakanthan, there are other and equally important Tamil writers and playwrights whose works sound like transliterations into Tamil of a Western sensibility: stories constructed so artificially and convolutedly that it is obvious that the author is using the Tamil form tendentiously to prove to the world at large that he or she is conversant with, say, the Oedipus complex and Freudian psychology. But in stories such as *Rishimoolam* (The Origin of Saints) and *Aadum Naarkkaligal Aadukindrana* (The Rocking Chairs Keep Rocking), Jayakanthan freely and daringly probes sexual repression and incest without the help of Western theoretical apparatus. Of course, references to Freud are inevitable and enriching, but the stories are not dependent on these references. In all these narratives, the fiction and the meta-fiction move and work together in alienation and the theory is embedded in the aesthetic existence of the work. Jayakanthan is not attempting programmatically to eschew Western influences. He just does not need the West to do what he is doing.

It is presumable that Rushdie, should he read Jayakanthan, might still find him parochial and incurably local, mainly because Jayakanthan's protagonist has to ask "Who am I as a Brahmin?" as a necessary counterpart to the cosmic question, "Who am I?" But one wonders if Rushdie's aesthetic modality is all that different after all. Indeed, Rushdie, along with others, has crafted the new ontology of hybridity, but isn't this ontology based on a certain migrant–ethnic–diasporic condition that is shot through with history? The problem here (and this is not Rushdie's personal problem) is systemic and inscribed into the very being of secular modernism and therefore secular post-modernism and cosmopolitanism. Secular modernism assumes that certain historical states of being have been left behind, pre-historicized in the name of progress. For example, Rushdie claims audaciously that so much of Indian literature written in the "vernaculars" has not even reached the twentieth century. So what is the twentieth century and whose is it? There is an assumption that the twentieth century has been exhausted, normatively spoken for, and left behind. Honestly, if these literatures are not in the twentieth century, where does Rushdie think they are? Just as secularism disavows the reality of its historical body and pretends to be all reason and thought, so too does Rushdie's normativity disavow its specific sedimented historical "content." It is ironic (and in a way quite sad) that Rushdie, who has done so much through style and grammatology to enable hybridity to speak and speak for, would deny the same right to a different location or content to represent its ontology through artistic representation. Instead, his charge is that it is all "tractor art," or outdated realism without stylistic self-consciousness. Whereas metropolitan hybridity enjoys itself as "authentic" and vibrant epistemology, realities of the so-called vernacular are immediately diagnosed as backward "identity conditions," as prehistorical modes of being that have long ago been left behind by Western narratives.[47] What Rushdie does in effect to his literary brothers and sisters of Indian vernaculars is identical to what Achebe claims Conrad has done to the African human being: I call it "the little brotherization" of the African male by the European man.

My point is simply this. Despite all its claims of eclecticism, tolerance for difference, and universal solidarity, secularism can be obsessively monovocal and normative: accepting of certain configurations, certain forms of hybridity and not others. Examples and stories help, and here is an incident from my life. Years ago, two passionate young undergraduate intellectuals, my friend and I, were traveling by train from Bombay to Madras, now Chennai. Both of us, filial young, Brahmin-born, were going through a rigorous and searing process of secularization and de-Brahminization. Fierce atheists, heavily influenced by Bertrand Russell on the one hand and Jean-Paul Sartre on the other, we were holding forth vehemently on religion and obscurantism, religion and authoritarianism, and the intellectual backwardness of religion in general, and Hinduism in particular. Suddenly, in the middle of the conversation, my friend noticed that the rhythm of the train had changed, and of course it had, for we were crossing the River Narmada. My friend stopped mid-sentence, exclaimed "Oh my God! It is the Narmada," searched frantically in his pockets for some loose change, found the coins, and flung them into the river with a rapt look on his face: all done just in time before the river and the bridge were "over" and the train got back to its other rhythm. And sure enough, my friend rejoined his syntax just where he had left off. Now, this affective behavior was an interruption in what was going on prior to the river. Is my friend's behavior irrational? Is it compatible with rationality, as a hybridized, deviant version of it? Will the discourse of rational secularism make room for this affective/aesthetic/superstitious gesture? In my friend's ambivalent and/or schizophrenic behavior, what is the epistemic status of "having flung the coins into the river?" Could his affective/aesthetic endorsement of the river coexist with secularism? Was his secularism flawed as a result of his recidivism into a primitive mode of relating to the world? Europeans throw coins into wishing wells, don't they? The moment of throwing the coin is a profoundly political one that challenges secular representation. If the ritualistic behavior is not worthy of representation, then clearly it is not political. And if it is not political, it speaks, but not "for" that other worldview of which it is a metonymic expression. In other words, my friend's behavior was meaningful but not rational or reasonable. Secularism as the champion of the One frame is not tolerant of odd juxtapositions unless it can control the structure of the composition.

I find myself wondering, after all these years, what if the act of coin-throwing had happened in its own temporality, or in a different confluence of discourses, and not as an interruption of the discourse of Reason? How would that gesture have found its meaning? Would it have been conspicuous? Or to turn tables, what if the temporality of the coin throw had been on stage already and secular discourse had been the interloper; and indeed, wasn't secularism the interloper? I am reminded here of the Wallace Stevens poem "The Anecdote of the Jar," where the wilderness is literally anabaptized into meaning by the sovereignty of the jar. The wilderness "no longer wild" is committed forever to its binary relationship to the jar: a relationship secured in dominance. Just as in the poem it is difficult to read the representation of the jar from the point of view of the wilderness, here too, it is not easy to read the secular discourse of modernity from the aesthetic–affective (and cognitive) point of view of the ritual coin throw. Could we not with equal legitimacy read the secular dismissal of the ineffable sacredness of rivers as an ugly, unaesthetic, and unrefined response to the sublimity of nature? Secularism comes down heavily against any form of double consciousness, forgetting all the while that by definition secular modernity as colonial modernity is already double conscious, contaminated in its very being by the other. I will just mention in passing a recent debate in the Turkish parliament, where secular reason prohibited the wearing of traditional headgear in parliament (too traditional to be assimilated by the modern) since it would constitute a violation of the principle of the separation of mosque and state.

In juxtaposing Jayakanthan's theorization of his fiction and the necessary double consciousness negated by dominant secularism, I hope I have argued persuasively that postcoloniality can take shape differentially and heterogeneously under different conditions and that writers and thinkers act out on the basis of their given locations and positions. No one location or position is better or purer than any other.

Time now to turn to Spivak and her mode of double consciousness as it works across and between locationality and positionality in ever-shifting combinations and nuances. As briefly discussed earlier in this chapter, both Edward Said and Gayatri Spivak would admit to double consciousness. Both are mindful of the politics of location, with Spivak being the more rigorously subject positional of the two, and Said privileging the world over the micro-political exactions of academic discourse. For my purposes here I would like to focus on Spivak mainly because it is in her theory that the "cross-hatchings" (to use one of her favorite locutions) between the macro-political and the micro-political are most visible. Also, within her mode of transactional (rather than say traveling or contrapuntal) reading, special attention is drawn to the ongoing and never totally predictable relationship between ontology and epistemology: a relationship mediated by the politics of representation.

"Ubiquitizing" Ethics: The Subaltern Speaks

Spivak is an overtly political theorist. She is also an academically grounded theorist: third world, subaltern, feminist, Marxist, and poststructuralist–affirmative–deconstructionist. Which is she primarily, and which secondarily? Which is her epistemological stance and which one her ontology? Could it be her intention (discursive, of course) to find the political in the undecidable space that opens up between ontology and epistemology: a space where neither speaks for the other, but speaking goes on? As a politically charged intellectual she seeks specific solidarities which put her "inside" in a way, but her insistence on rubbing even solidarities "against the grain" lets her "out." Like Said, whose insistence on oppositionality is as substantive and primary as his call for solidarity, Spivak "doubles," but in a different way. I am particularly interested in how Spivak's interventionist agency speaks for and within the asymmetry of a world structured in dominance, and at the same time seeks a way out of this asymmetry. I would like to juxtapose two specific instances where Spivak's interventions made a big difference in the fields of subaltern and postcolonial studies. One is her celebrated admonition of Foucault and Deleuze for their high-handed dismissal of representation, in her essay "Can the Subaltern Speak?" The other is her pedagogically intended poststructuralization of subaltern studies in "Deconstructing Historiography."[48] When one puts these essays together and tries to sum them up within a single axis, it just does not work. They work together, but against each other within the bind of double consciousness. What is at work here is not a unified or a total politics, not even a unified or unifiable constituency. The questions that always come up, sometimes frivolously and at other times quite gravely, in the context of Spivak, are: where is she? Where does she stand on this issue and where is she speaking from? Is she somewhere else than where we thought we had fixed her? Detractors of Spivak love to find fault with her for her incorrigible theoretical mobility or her unrepresentable slipperiness – speaking from one location now, exercising a different subject position there. Unlike Edward Said, Spivak's worldliness cannot be at the expense of her discursive subject positionality.

In "Can the Subaltern Speak?" Spivak invokes the macro-political realities of colonialism and the international division of labor to remind the post-structuralist theorist that it is altogether callous and unprincipled to declare that representation no longer exists on the assumption that reality speaks for itself, as do the people. She chides them, despite their theoretical virtuosity, for not being mindful of their own intellectual imbrications with macro-politics.[49] In asserting that representation no longer exists, they are in fact guilty of making a representation in the name of the avant-gardism of theory. It is my contention that she catches them red-handed in the act of ontologizing high theory. Is it possible that, to them, being poststructuralist is an irreducible ontological commitment? Spivak points out that in their theoretical haste they conflate the two meanings of representation, one cognitive and the other political, they dismantle the distinction between "who is saying it" and "what is being said." Are they then rebels without a cause exoticizing Maoism as a form of phenomenological spontaneism? In this entire polemic organized around the crucial issue of representation, Spivak (who is otherwise as poststructuralist as Deleuze and Foucault) critiques poststructuralism from a location that is subaltern.

In her essay on the work of Ranajit Guha and the subaltern collective, Spivak takes on a benevolent pedagogical role and brings the collective up to par, theoretically speaking. Declaring her macro-political solidarity with the subaltern collective, Spivak goes on to read them against the grain. Here, in this context, it is her micro-political and subject positional expertise that lends credentials to her pedagogy. If Foucault and Deleuze's lack of self-reflexivity is the function of their blindness to macro-politics, the lack of self-reflexivity of Guha and others is the result of their political oversight of theoretical issues. In the first case, too much theory overlooks the world, and in the latter case, an exclusively political commitment overlooks theory. Spivak (who is implicated in both constituencies) makes her pedagogy cut both ways. I would argue that once double consciousness is accepted and not pathologized, Spivak's mode of intervention should not raise too many eyebrows. Spivak not only introduces poststructuralism to subalternity, but also insists that poststructuralism should not be merely instrumental in the subaltern cause. In other words, subalternity and poststructuralism are implicated together in a coordinated (as against a subordinated) relationship. Spivak's double-conscious attitude is really quite in keeping with the initial Gramscian formulation itself; did not Gramsci in his six-point narrativization of the subaltern agenda envision a plan of action whereby the subaltern would signify its intention on the body of the dominant discourse before it really becomes subaltern?[50] And in Spivak's case it only makes sense to befriend poststructuralism and deconstruction, since what they are all about is the interrogation of Eurocentrism and the Enlightenment from "within."

If the derivativeness of the subaltern condition is both political and epistemological or psychic, it is only appropriate that the subaltern project should address both issues upon a common platform.[51] Poststructuralism is lacking in macro-political density, whereas an exclusively politically oriented subalternity fails to address itself symptomatically. It is important to note that Spivak maintains that poststructuralist theory/deconstruction is already lurking in the unconscious of the subaltern program. All that she is doing is letting the unconscious surface and breathe. Spivak makes no bones about what she calls "the strategic essentialism"(it could also be termed variably as "strategic positivism") practiced by the subaltern collective: a certain suppression of theory is taking place in the interests of political scrupulosity, and this is not a bad thing in the short run. But in the long run – now that is a different matter. Typically, the short term is political and machiavellian, in the sense in which Gramsci used it; and the long term is ethical and epistemological. That is where the means can be evaluated ethically and not just with reference to effectiveness and functionalism. In integrating poststructuralism with subalternity, Spivak could be perceived in one of two ways: either as contaminating or weakening subaltern agency, or as empowering and de-ghettoizing (deregionalizing) subalternity. Much depends on the meaning and the territoriality we give to the term "the West." To Spivak, the issue is clear. When asked in an interview about the ontological status of the "indigenous" as well as its retrievability, she makes it clear that there is no pure way back to the indigenous or the precolonial except through double consciousness.[52] We have all been touched by the West. The important question is not about ontological purity, but about strategies of using the West against itself in conjunction with finding one's own "voice." The affirmative deconstruction, an agenda that Spivak elaborates, is not always-already there in Derrida. Spivak's position is that "we are both where we are and where we think," and if in a sense, as a result of colonialism, "where we think" is the West as well, it is quixotic to deny it. The way out is bricolage, transactional readings based on bilateralism, and multiple non-totalizable interruptions. To put it cryptically, her path has more in common with Achebe's choice to write in English than with Ngugi's choice to eschew English altogether.

The debate that comes up when Spivak (or, for that matter, Chantal Mouffe and Ernesto Laclau) is evaluated as a subaltern theorist is whether her articulations are a dire misrecognition of Gramsci's originary subaltern program. There are two ways of responding to this. The first is to be aggressively belligerent and ask, who cares? So long as the post-Gramscian elaborations are interesting and complex in themselves and are productive of new formations, solidarities, and nodes of thought, how does it really matter whether the elaborations honor the originary intention or not. For God's sake, doesn't "Always historicize" also signify "sometimes dehistoricize"? Gramsci's historical context was both enabling and restrictive; keeping Gramsci alive is not a matter of keeping the original "intentionality" transcendentally alive. I have often had debates with fellow theorists and friends of the purist persuasion who find the very idea of "reading against the grain" arrogant and insolent. Their insistence is "first read the text and then read against the grain." If it is a question of scholarly integrity and adequacy, I quite agree. But the matter is more serious than that. Reading is also a matter of perspective and it is amusing that those Gramscian critics who profess to know their Gramsci better than the late-coming poststructuralist Gramscians conveniently forget the fact that their reading is not neutral; it is indeed a reading *with the grain*. The only difference is that readings with the grain remain unmarked as readings, whereas readings against the grain are marked right away as unnatural, maverick, and incorrect.

The debate is not whether one is getting Gramsci right in an attitude of neutral piety to the text, but rather a polemical contention about what to do with Gramsci. The projects of Stuart Hall, Chantal Mouffe, and Spivak are indeed different from those of the strictly Marxist political–economic Gramscians. The second response, more sober, is that indeed there is enough in Gramsci that gestures towards a poststructuralist turn. There is, in Gramsci, the notion of the intellectual as "permanent persuader" and this notion is as ethical as it is political. Even though through his strategic machiavellianism of praxis Gramsci closes up the gap between the ethical and the political in the name of political urgency, we can discern in his six-point program an ambivalent mix of affirmation and negation, as well as an ambivalent perspective on the possibilities of a totally disalienated political practice. Will the subaltern ever arrive at "itself" is a question that Gramsci poses on two registers: the political and the ethical, the practical and the theoretical, but his immediate contextual responses and solutions are more overtly political and practical. Gramsci does indeed ponder the possibility of going beyond the economic–corporate sphere and dreams of a post-representational episteme where there will be no division between the leaders and the led. But "that" time is not "now." The question for Gramsci has always been how to historicize the "utopian" in and through the contradictions of what Foucault would call "the history of the present." Should the subaltern program attend to the political first and then deal with the cultural and the ethical, or should the program take on, asynchronously, multiple determinations all together? On a different plane, and consistent with one of the leitmotifs of this entire chapter, should the history of subalternity be narrated simultaneously with the allegory of subalternity? This is the suppressed question that Spivak brings to the surface. Spivak's discourse is partly of the Internationalist Marxism of Gramsci and partly of the anti-colonial political struggle recodable as anti-Eurocentrism: a dimension lacking in Gramsci and in most of Western Marxism.

Indeed, poststructuralism can be an ally of the postcolonial and the subaltern (I realize that as academic formations the two are not interchangeable) provided this coalition also acknowledges the asymmetry that links the two partners. I would indeed say that the direction that Spivak's subject positional or micro-political practice takes is quite compatible with Edward Said's moving and memorable call for cooperative projects and solidarities across the asymmetry, for a relational politics that goes beyond guilt and blame. Spivak's work, at its best (as in the two essays cited above), brings about a reciprocal recognition between poststructuralism and subalternity that enables a different articulation between theory and history than the usual. A poststructuralized subalternity would attempt to address the political as in the here and now and address the ethical understood as a perennial preoccupation that is always in excess (and not in negation) of the political. As a politically motivated subalternity and an epistemologically oriented poststructuralism begin to negotiate with each other, a different and challenging role opens up for theory: not just the good old theory–praxis nexus, and not the formulaic opposition between the good folk who always historicize and the bad and self-indulgent ones who only theorize.

Let us take a look at how Spivak deals with the theme of alienation in her essay "Deconstructing Historiography." She opens up a space between two meanings of alienation and this space cannot be spoken for by an act of representation. There is alienation in the political Marxist sense of the term, whereby it is not a desirable state of affairs. The movement should be towards the eradication of alienation through agential revolutions. And there is the philosophical meaning of alienation, worked out from Hegel, to Derrida, to Lacan, and in this tradition alienation is constitutive of knowledge itself and is therefore incorrigible. To want to get rid of alienation on this register would be tantamount to a desire to get rid of alterity altogether in the name of positivistic knowledge. The ethic of theory is not to close off the gap between these two registers in the name of full representation, but to activate the gap itself as a form of accountability that is not fully reducible either to the political or the ethical. The lightning rod for all these transactions is the theme of representation. While Spivak resolutely argues for a politics of representation in her critique of high theoretical avant-gardism, it is representation itself that she dangles in the abyss during her deconstructive theorization of subalternity. Paradoxically, the very historical occasion when the subaltern represents itself and inscribes itself into history is also the moment when representation as such is problematized, and the agent doing the problematization is the subaltern subject.

If the subaltern is constrained to use the methods of dominance to achieve its own hegemony in the scrupulosity of political interest, what then about its ethical imperative to change the very apparatus of representation? Should subalternity, in the act of achieving victory, also not transform the very nature of representation? This is the difference between identifying the subaltern positivistically as a teleology-driven "content," and the subaltern conceptualized as "perspective."[53] This, too, is the difference between subalternity thought through as a mono-conscious plan of action and subalternity envisioned as double conscious. When understood as double conscious, subalternity also takes on the charge of subalternizing the very apparatus of representation. Subalternity as "content" or "state of affairs" is to be remedied and transcended through hegemonization, but subalternity as perspective has to be kept alive; and that indeed is the subaltern difference as ethical possibility.

Just as Rosa Burger had to hallucinate the ethical into perceptual reality (from her dominant–deconstructive location), so it is through a certain generosity that the subaltern subject goes beyond the political and gestures powerfully towards the ethical. As Walter Benjamin would have it, the subaltern desire is to win a weak victory, or better still, in the very act of winning, to deconstruct the zero-sum, winner-take-all model of historical struggle.[54] Critics of poststructuralized subalternity are utterly credulous of the politics of representation. To them, representation is the political (and if by that they mean "no politics, no representation," then who would disagree with that?), and there is no more to be said. But what they forget is that, more than any other bloc or constituency, it is the subaltern and the marginal and the minoritized constituencies who need to be most wary of representation, even as they resort to it strategically and cautiously. The history of representation is hardly a clean history, and in this sense Foucault and Deleuze are right on, but where they go "wrong" is in their appropriation of that insight. A subaltern interrogation of representation is not co-valent with a metropolitan interrogation of representation. It is by protecting its ethical difference from the totalizing sovereignty of representation that the subaltern subject seeks not to repeat the history of the same. This perhaps could be termed empty, idealistic, or (worse still) utopian politics, and I would take all those characterizations as terms of praise.

Ethical politics cannot afford to be full, or merely pragmatic, or be opportunistically presentist. The allegorization of the subaltern project is necessary so long as (a) the allegorization is undertaken agentially from the point of view of the subaltern and (b) the allegorical register is in a relationship of ongoing tension with the historical. By "ethical" here I also mean the kind of insight that is occluded by political triumphalism: the insight that something precious is lost in the moment of victory.[55] Mohandas Gandhi's satyagraha is an outstanding model that combines the politics of resistance with an introverted ethics of self-styling or askesis. Never for a moment willing to sever the utopian from the imminent, Gandhi's ethical vision did not make any exception for the location of the oppressed and the colonized. The political legitimacy of their cause still had to be submitted to rigorous ethical self-interrogation. Needless to say, the ethical will not and cannot emerge into visibility unless the political itself is posed as a question and as a dilemma. Theory, in my analysis, is that third term that operates in the hyphen that forms the basis of the differential relationship of the political to the ethical. Theory, not a mere catalyst, but an active and vulnerable participant in the triangular nexus (as I shall try to demonstrate in the next few paragraphs), creates multiple and nontotalizable forms of critical practice that are accountable both to the relative autonomies of ethics, politics, and epistemology, and to the relational totality that the three registers constitute.

When Spivak, for example, brings into play the notion of strategic essentialism, she is trying, on behalf of the subaltern subject, to have it both ways: neither the pure contingency of nothing but strategy without the comfort of identity effect; nor a naive essentialism that believes in itself – strategic essentialism understood as such in the scrupulosity of political interest. There is here a guarded exoneration of "the political," since politics somehow has to be done the old-fashioned way and it really cannot afford to give itself up to the radicality of theory. Also, politics being politics, it is only all-too appropriate that it should be instrumental, opportunistic, and machiavellian (in the Gramscian sense of the term) and more concerned with the ends than with the purity of the means. And what is politics if not "interested"? Then comes this strange juxtaposition of the ethically charged term scrupulosity with political interest. The ethical moment is being invited into the heart of political interestedness. There is a way in which one can think of the ethical as a neutral ombudsperson who performs officially and blows the whistle on the political from the outside.[56] However, if this outside becomes absolute, then the ethical steps out of its hyphenated connection with the political. If the integrity of the hyphen is to be maintained, so that the ethical dimension is not rarefied into a vaporous discourse of primordiality, the ethical has to be both inside and outside the political moment. In fact, it has to deconstruct the figurality of in and out. There is a double movement in the deconstructive logic. First, there is the insistence on the ethic of epistemology that persuades the positivistic agenda of subalternity to get in touch with its unconscious. In this movement, the political is transcended in the name of an ethic realized as epistemology or theory. The second movement is where a certain polemical or political imma-nence is legitimated in the name of scrupulosity, i.e., the ethical. Here the message is clear and simple. It would be unethical for the subaltern not to be political. In this movement the political mode is being acknowledged as its own swadharma. It has its own internal–immanent ethic. In this model ethics itself is doubled: both transcendent and situationally fraught. All these movements, let us not forget, are taking place in the performative theater of representation, where ethics, politics, and epistemology play roles that overlap and intersect.

I am not sure if Spivak herself intends her theory to work this way, but here is my explanation. Ethics animates her theory transactionally and I would even say that it is the active agent and promoter of these transactions. Ethics, in Spivak's discourse, is not an *a priori* in-itself, but a contingent for-itself that acts on specific domains and occasions to "ethicize" whatever is taking place there. Thus, in "Can the Subaltern Speak?" the ethical speaks in the name of the political to problematize the unquestioned avant-gardism of theory. In "Deconstructing Historiography" the ethical works in the name of theory/epis-temology to call into question the myopic opportunism of political positivism. And in the endorsement of a strategic essentialism in the interests of political scrupulosity, it is in the name of the ethical that politics and epistemology/ theory meet in a relationship of critical interruption with neither granting the other its absolute claims. Within this model the ethical is literally ubiquitous, all over the place, not as idea or category or an essential truth, but as a rela-tionship of accountability that works in the name of "in the name of" without giving it a determinate name. Neither politics nor epistemology is capable of performing this task namelessly. It is only in the name of the ethical, which is to say, namelessly, that the interests of the historical–political one and the tran-scendent accountability to the objective "One" can be dialogized perennially. There is then no need to make Ethics (with a capital E) an absolute authority, a categorical imperative that is of a different order from politics and episte-mology. In this newly triangulated relationship, the ethical gets distributed, cir-culated, and generalized as a form and a horizon of accountability within a relationality without recourse.

There has been a long-standing debate over the real nature of deconstruc-tion: whether it is a politics, or an axiology, a new ideology or a new worldview; or whether it is a mere textual form of virtuosity, perhaps no more than a form of mercenary exercise open to all kinds of takeover. In the kind of affirmative deconstruction that Spivak develops, deconstruction finds itself as an ethical practice that is not reducible either to the political or the theoretical/ epistemological; neither a primary domain interested in securing its sovereignty, nor a hapless appendix dispensable in its very materiality, but an active in-betweenness that makes all the difference by attempting to achieve representation, but in the name of the "post-" that comes after.

The problem with Spivak's model, for a number of theorists, is that it seeks to realize a non-localizable mobility as a legitimate form of constituency: a project that is doomed from the start. But is it necessarily doomed just because it refuses to sum up heterogeneous impulses and directions into one axis and to iron out contradictions in the name of a transcendent macro-politics? Another concern is that perhaps in an attempt to actualize a cultural politics of "the in-between," Spivak ends up with an apotheosis of theory that becomes pure constituency by itself. It depends on how one defines "constituency," as open ended or as definitively given. In my own critical practice, from a diasporan location, and along with a number of similar-minded thinkers and theorists to whom I owe a great deal, I have tried to conceptualize constituency as a question and not as an answer. It is in the asking of the question "Who are we?" that constituency takes shape and not in the neutralization of the question with an immediate ready-made answer: "We are Latinos, Asian-Americans, Marxist–feminists of color." Surely, we are all that and much more, but my insistence is on something else, something other. Those declarations of axiology, belonging, and political and historical rootedness do not automatically generate an open-ended politics unless they are integrated with the hesitant contingency of "Who are we?" asked in all ethical earnestness. I can perhaps anticipate the objection that the insistence on the question form is so predictably metropolitan–diasporan. Such an objection is really disingenuous, for no one is (at least I am not) making the claim that a theoretically charged diaspora has a monopoly on the question, or even that the question "Who are we?" is a luxury organic to a few privileged high-theoretical diasporan locations. Nothing is more universal than that question (as I have tried to demonstrate through Rosa Burger and Ganapathi Sastrigal). The tragedy is that in the name of the urgency of political closure and clarity, the question is never raised in the very heat of the political moment and its exciting proximity to teleological arrival. I would even say that there is no better moment to ask the ethically inflected question "Who are we?" than the moment when a hard-won political hegemony seems to have found the answer. Hegemonic political discourse has a way of rendering ethical concerns (as also, *mutatis mutandis*, aesthetic concerns) precious, pious, self-indulgent, and redundant, even luxuriant.

But this is a violent repression of the ethical as well as the theoretical, and I only hope that in my abiding advocacy of the ethical and the allegorical I have made it somewhat clear that my commitment is not at the expense of the political (or the allegorical at the expense of the political), but rather to the double-conscious modality of the hyphen and its highly determinable indeterminacy.

Differentiating the "West"

I wish to engage with the head-and- heart-felt contributions of William Connolly to political thought, and in particular, some of his positions in his book, *Why I am not a Secularist.*[57] Like Ashis Nandy, Connolly has found a rigorous and theoretically engaging way in which to deal with cognitive issues in politics affectively, and issues of affect with cognitive complexity and clarity. One of the points I was trying to make in my critical discussion of secularism is that often, in the third world and increasingly in the first world, secularism is perceived in a relationship of disjunction with matters of the heart and matters of faith. Often, secularism wins out either by declaring certain anxieties off limits or by compartmentalizing the lived totality of life in a way that makes it easy for reason to choose certain areas and registers and neglect others. Alternatively, reason, as in a moment of judgment, will not let you see the affective reality of the criminal or the so-called terrorist who is profiled, criminalized, and pathologized with utter disregard to her humanity. I would like to mention in passing that it is just in refutation of such a regime of dealing with the affective side of existence that Ashis Nandy undertook a compassionate and empathic analysis of an actual hijacking incident.[58] Nandy, like Connolly, is vitally interested in processes of "becoming" that far exceed the conceptual parameters provided by secularism. Connolly's critical engagement with secularism, however, emerges from the "Occidental" side of the asymmetry. I say this by way of reiterating my emphasis throughout this chapter on the relationship between place as ontological–historical and perspectival, and place as epistemological–theoretical and universal. Thus, secularism both unites and differentiates: on the one hand, it does matter if the secularism is Nigerian, Indian, or American; on the other hand, it would seem not to matter at all.

Here, for example, is Connolly, in a rhetorical mode *à la* Ashis Nandy (I discuss Nandy's rhetoric in chapter 3), making a poignant plea for the integration of the affective and the visceral with the cognitive practices of Reason.

> The visceral register of subjectivity and intersubjectivity, as I will call it, is at once part of thinking, indispensable to more conceptually refined thinking, a periodic

spur to creative thinking, and a potential impediment to rethinking. The visceral register, however, can be drawn upon to thicken an intersubjective ethos of generous engagement between diverse constituencies or to harden strife between partisans. It can be and do all these things, and others besides. And yet modern secularism – in the main and for the most part – either ignores this register or disparages it. It does so in the name of a public sphere in which reason, morality, and tolerance flourish. By doing so it forfeits some of the very resources needed to foster a generous pluralism.[59]

Connolly's reading is that secularism succeeds only by leaving behind its formative and informing hinterland in a spirit of urban or metropolitan avant-gardism. Reason has nothing to learn from those registers. I am reminded of Mohandas Gandhi's injunction, on his return from South Africa, to a whole cadre of urban English speakers (including Mohammed Ali Jinnah), that they go to the villages of India and learn from them rather than presume to teach the people. He reverses the direction of pedagogy. As Chatterjee argues in *Nationalist Thought and the Colonial World*, Gandhi's political pedagogy was conveniently forgotten and left behind once independence was achieved and India inexorably launched into the teleology of urban and scientific modernity. I will comment in passing how Connolly's rhetoric – in the very act of making secularism sensitive to its "other" – ends up repeating and revalorizing that very split. For example, the visceral register in Connolly's discourse is ambivalent: it could be productive of good or bad consequences, it could be rational or irrational. But could it constitute a mediated language of its own? This question is unaskable from within the grid of binarity. If these registers are a periodic impetus to creativity, where then does one find them during those periods when they do not surface as periodic spurs to the creativity of reason refashioning and updating itself? Does it require a crisis to achieve the enfranchisement of those registers? Should the enfranchisement not be holistic and perennial? In this sense, then, Connolly remains prisoner to what Foucault would call the ratio of the Word that establishes the logos as a primordial scission within itself and then speaks for itself and the silence of "un-reason": what Foucault called "the monologue of Reason," or madness as "the absence of work."[60] My concern is twofold: (1) in keeping with the thematics of this chapter, how beneficial and transformative can self-reflexivity be in this context? (2) Why can the visceral not speak for the cognitive, or better still, why can reason not be double voiced, double historical, double conscious, and double registered? Why insist, as I think Connolly does, on the dialectical resolution of oppositions in the context of the visceral register (I have visions of reason fattening itself in the process), rather than a differential and dyadic playing out of these antagonistic tensions? Why the necessary appeal to a third term, for that raises the question of how and to whom and to which particular invocation the third term is responsive to?

Here I am basing my question on an interesting and far-reaching insight that Dipesh Chakrabarty offers in his discussion of "vernacular translations."[61] It is worth keeping in mind that Chakrabarty is comparing and contrasting two kinds of translations: one from English to a vernacular, and the other between two vernaculars. In other words, within the ideological world where there are "vernaculars" and "non-vernaculars," Chakrabarty is attempting to calibrate different registers of the "alienness" of languages. There is of course the "alienness of all languages or of language as such," as theorized by Walter Benjamin,[62] and there are the more discretely measurable differences within alienation as it is negotiated by translation both allegorically and historically, both inter-historically and intra-historically. The point that Chakrabarty makes is that vernacular or indigenous translations – say, from Bengali to Tamil – do not often seem to require a conceptual or symbolic grounding in a third term. The translation works dyadically through the logic of substitution, without the necessity to produce a theoretical language of the meta-kind. The same point had been made, on a macro level if you will, both by Antonio Gramsci and Ranajit Guha regarding the nature of subaltern historiography. According to Gramsci, subaltern histories remain discontinuous and episodic, and are therefore unable to represent themselves hegemonically. Such a representation has to be the function of representing oneself to and in the eyes of the state – the state that is initially nationalist even in Marxist thought. Guha, in his earlier writing, is a bit more ambivalent than Gramsci regarding the episodic and the discontinuous. More aware than Gramsci of the Eurocentrism that underwrites even a Marxist modernity, Guha remains solicitous of the episodic and the discontinuous even as he remains incapable of making the claim that the subaltern *qua* subaltern has spoken. The pharmakon here (the blessing and the curse, the poison as well as the remedy) is nationalism. Subaltern historiographies have to be nationalized, and if they are it will indeed be a pyrrhic victory for the subaltern. How necessary are modernism/secular reason/nationalism? If they are necessary, how open are they to "indigenous" signification, assuming in the first place that there are no indigenous alternatives at all?

When Connolly (at least, in my recoding) resorts to the visceral as though it were the forgotten and misrecognized hinterland, a kind of raw material (and I use the term particularly to invoke the figure of the Industrial Revolution and colonial modernity), it is not clear how aware he is of the reality that what he would term the visceral register within the West was indeed "all of the East." The "dominant One's designated other" was none other than the total Self of the Orient, the non-West. It is because secularism, as well as colonial modernity, took shape in and between two worlds to elaborate a relationship structured in dominance, that any globally responsible critique of secularism has to identify the effects of secularism along two axes or registers. For example, it is not enough for Connolly to identify and then empower the discarded and counter-valorized visceral dimension within the "West." He must take that recognition one step further by acknowledging that colonial modernity essentialized and ontologized the colonies as the natural–primordial home of the visceral, the irrational, of unreason.

I must say that as a longtime reader and fan of Connolly's work, I was quite surprised and even dismayed when I saw the title, *Why I am not a Secularist*. I even checked twice to see if it was William Connolly and not some other Connolly. Has the postmodern political theorist of difference suddenly turned spiritual and/or fundamentalist? Has he decided to take the leap of faith simply because realities have become unbearable, what with the unbridgeable chasm between utopian theory and ugly recalcitrant reality? Is he on his way to becoming an eclectic guru? Might he be, could he be, saying things in the book that would find some far-fetched resonance with, say, the BJP or the Viswa Hindu Parishad? These were my disconcerting thoughts. It just goes to prove what a stranglehold secularism has over our collective reason, such that any breaking of rank from secularism immediately sounds like atavism, a freefall back into chaos, primitivism, communal frenzy, and God knows what else. This also reminds me of that other contemporary scenario: any criticism of the Israeli state is immediately construed as anti-Semitism, which of course has taken on an unshakable exemplarity on behalf of all oppressed groups and constituencies. Not wanting to be secular gets instantly parsed as wanting to be the binary opposite of secularism.

As one who has believed in secularism all his life, albeit by way of colonial modernity, I must in all honesty confess to a particular bias. As a middle-class South Indian Tamil male Brahmin (the current sociological rubric for such a person now is Tam-brahm) who grew up in India, I had seen nothing worthwhile, revolutionary, progressive, pro-subaltern, feminist, or emancipatory in the Brahmin ethos.[63] It was indeed by way of Bertrand Russell and Sartre (to recall again the railway incident) and a whole range of secular atheist–agnostic Western thinkers that I had fought my bitter battles against Hindu Brahmin orthodoxy. And to this day I do not see what there is to defend in that worldview except perhaps to grant it the benefit of doubt, within a class-action category, as one of those structures to be damaged by colonial modernity. This baggage was indeed so intense that when I encountered forms of African-American spirituality in the vanguard of profound and outstanding political revolutions, I had difficulty accepting them. I found myself wishing that Martin Luther King were a non-believer, an atheist, or at least – please please – an agnostic. Having accessed secularism from the location of a casteist, patriarchal, and socially conservative Brahmanism, I was ignorant and arrogant enough to presume that religion and spirituality were essentially retrogressive. I bring up this bit of autobiography only to underscore the extent to which a particular version of secularism (a particular combination of elements or variables) had assumed universal normativity in my mind. Add to this the confidence that whatever problems the world might throw up, secularism and only secularism would save the day, and what you get is an official and dogmatic secularism with no room for "others" unless these "others" have already been diagnosed as potential patients of secularism.

Of course, as I start reading Connolly, it all makes sense. He is doing something that needs to be done quite urgently: opening up secularism to its own contradictions and inconsistencies and making it vulnerable to its own unreasonable genealogy. One of Connolly's main points is that the so-called break of secularism from the Judaeo-Christian tradition has been vastly exaggerated. What has happened is that many of the "essences" of that tradition have been thoroughly assimilated within secularism and in the process reconfigured as well. Thus, civilizationally, Judaeo-Christianity has been aligned (despite the separation of church and state) with the core values of secularism, whereas the "other" religions of the world remain marked as radically "alterior" to secularism. Just as Fanon makes the point that the anti-colonial struggles in the third world need to be as total and of the same scale as the colonialism that they seek to destroy (any thing less would be naive and shortsighted), Connolly observes that the historical mandate of secularism is to repeat, formally, the contours of the very structure that it seeks to replace.[64] To quote Connolly:

> The historical modus vivendi of secularism, while seeking to chasten religious dogmatism, embodies unacknowledged elements of immodesty in itself. The very intensity of the struggle it wages against religious intolerance may induce blind spots with respect to itself. I also wonder whether the time of the secular modus vivendi is drawing to a close. We may need to fashion modifications in secular practices today, modifications that both honor debts to it and support more religious and non-religious variety in public life than many traditional secularists and monotheists tend to appreciate.[65]

I particularly appreciate the casual but intensely polemical manner in which Connolly brings monotheists and traditional secularists within the same phrase. And I think he is right on. Both canonical secularists and monotheists are in pursuit of the One, with the secularist confident in her belief that her One is the very body of Reason itself (where in fulfillment of Hegelian historicism the contents of history have been purified and abstracted into the non-corporeal and formal body of Reason), and the monotheist taking the leap of faith and the path of revelation towards that One godhead. Whatever the thematic or "content" differences, there is an undeniable affinity, both morphological and polemical, between the two. As Connolly attempts to push secularism beyond its canonical closure, he makes a few diagnostic comments "from within the West" that are sharply covalent with the postcolonial critique of Occidental Reason. Connolly recognizes what I would call the "colonial moment within" when he observes how the discourse of secularism recuperates the contours of the very discourse that it is trying to destabilize. There is a clear parallel between Connolly's formulation and Partha Chatterjee's disjunctive reading of the relationship between epistemology and politics and between the problematic and the thematic of nationalism in the postcolonial context. In a sense then, derivativeness is not the mark of the colonized alone. It is being experienced in the Occident as well, however differentially. Connolly's symptomatic reading of the limitations of secularism (one could add nationalism and modernity) within the West lends itself to coalitional rearticulations with a number of third world disillusionments with the practice of secularism. These coalitional possibilities, across the asymmetry, need to be recognized and empowered right away if universality is to be renegotiated inclusively, relationally, and multilaterally.

It would be absurd to suggest that secularism is not a critique of religion or that it recuperates religious values. Rather, Judaeo-Christianity, in cultural and civilizational terms, has clinched a legitimate relationship with secular modernism, whereas the same claim cannot be made of Hinduism or Islam. To put it bluntly, in the context of the presidency of Bush Jr., the USA is indeed fast becoming a Christian nation-state. As Connolly argues, despite the break on certain levels and registers, there is a relationship of profound continuity between secular and Judaeo-Christian values.

Connolly's rhetoric, like that of Ashis Nandy, focuses on the affective phenomenology of "suffering," and it from that point of view that Connolly critiques the shortcomings of secularism. His objective, of course, is to push secularism beyond and perhaps even against itself. To sum up Connolly's case in a somewhat schematic fashion: (1) how is the being of secularism responsive to the processes of "becoming? (2) Is secularism capable of getting in touch with the affective–experiential side of existence? (3) How does secularism deal with the problem of alterity or (to change metaphors) with its *hors-texte*? In other words, how sensitively does it establish a differential relationship with itself? The point that Connolly makes again and again, with incremental strength and persuasiveness, as he elaborates "the politics of becoming," is that a number of areas of concern, constituencies, and interests are overlooked by secularism, and what is more, this oversight is intentional and ideological. How open is secularism really to hybridization, creolization, and to heterogenization? In touting secularism purely as an epistemology, "secular fundamentalists" make themselves oblivious of the state and governmental modes of apparatus that endow secularism with an absolute and non-negotiable sovereignty: the sovereignty of the modern citizen. The ongoing collusion or complicity between what Althusser called "the Ideological State apparatus" of modern citizenship and the epistemology of secularism is occluded from perception by the transparency of the entire project.

The modern world citizen is made to believe that "who she is" follows felicitously and non-coercively from the epistemology she believes in (i.e., her ontology and epistemology are reciprocal homes). However, what the process keeps from her is the understanding that she is being systematically interpellated to fit the pattern, even if it means excising dimensions of herself that do not harmonize with the politics of citizenship–sovereignty. As Connolly points out, there are all kinds of subterranean murmurs, groans, whispers, and complaints within secularism (secularism *sotto voce* with itself) that are pressing to be heard:

> The secular division of labor between "religious faith" and "secular argument," where faith and ritual are to be contained in a protected private preserve and rational argument is said to exhaust public life, suppresses complex registers of persuasion, judgment, and discourse operative in public life. Again, these registers continue to operate, even within secularism. But they do so largely below the threshold of appreciation by secularists. A cautious reconfiguration of secular conceptions of theory, thinking, discourse, subjectivity, and intersubjectivity is needed to come to terms more actively with these registers of being.[66]

I share with Connolly this nagging concern about the ideology of secularism: its imprimatur-like status, its official legitimacy to exhaust public life in its own name. There are two related points of focus here: the universalization of the sovereignty of secularism and the unheralded duplicities within secularism. Here (by way of exemplifying the latter concern) is a simple example taken from the news on September 26, 2002. Madeline Albright and Henry Kissinger, two former secretaries of state, are testifying to the Senate on matters concerning Iraq. As he welcomes and introduces the two former secretaries (they need no introduction), Senator Jesse Helmes congratulates and honors them both for the services they have rendered to the nation at the very highest levels, and adds parenthetically (but in effect, substantively) that no other naturalized citizen of the United States has demonstrated such patriotism, such loyalty to the US of A. Eerily (and I might add from my point of view, nauseatingly), Madeline Albright begins by commenting that though she was not fortunate enough to have been born an American citizen, she was lucky enough to be naturalized as an American, and then proceeds to eulogize the USA. If this had been a job interview, I think it would have been actionable for the interviewer to ask a question that required the candidate to divulge how they became a citizen – by birth or by naturalization. So secular citizenship, on the affective–visceral register, to use Connolly's phrasing, is genetic, biological, and filial, after all. I would prefer a situation where someone is denied citizenship outright rather than be considered in some insidiously tacit way a second-class citizen despite being a passport holding, tax-paying oath-taking individual. Within the secular citizenship of America, there is the "color" difference, the "ethnic" difference, and indeed the "genetic or natal" difference. And we thought that all these markers had been left behind in the name of secular belonging.[67]

Will Difference Become?

Connolly's project of pluralizing secularism is of great consequence to modern political thought. Unlike other thinkers who take pluralism for granted and laud it as such, Connolly in interested in the pluralization of pluralism.[68] But how does he theorize the relationship between a genuine pluralism and the politics of secularism? Is it conceivable, from Connolly's point of view, that in the project of pluralizing pluralism without bounds and without teleological recourse, that we might have to leave secularism behind and move in a post-secular direction? Underlying Connolly's project is the assumption (and I too operate on the assumption) that secular thought is the one and only horizon for the pluralization of pluralism. But isn't there a philosophical problem here? Once we call it secularist pluralism, as against Christian or Islamic pluralism, haven't we already centered pluralism on the axiology of secularism? In other words, hasn't the decentered spirit of pluralism already been compromised by its anchorage in secularism? Connolly is quite aware of this problem, but he does not give it enough attention. His strategy is to invoke an improved, more dialogic, and self-reflexive secularism, both as a process and as an ideological horizon. As canonical secular thought becomes more open and vulnerable to other registers of social being, it changes, transforms itself in response to those urgent calls, but in the end incrementalizes its authority as the only platform of progressive politicization. What if those other registers demanded the same privilege of hegemonic legitimacy?

Eventually in Connolly's discourse do not all progressive politics of the future get pre-named as versions of secularism, as instances of secularism's difference from itself? If that is the case, is there no outside, no *horstexte* to the grammatology of secularism, no forms of alterity that will not eventually be accommodated by secularism? Connolly's discourse is caught up in a desperate dilemma: the phenomenological all-inclusive embrace of multi-registered experience on the one hand, and the ideological valorization of such an embrace on the other. I pose these questions of Connolly's thought only because the generosity of his thinking invites such explorations. I cannot think of any other contemporary political philosopher who takes the kind of risks that Connolly takes: fearlessly invoking the politics of becoming – like Nietzsche and Deleuze – and remaining steadfastly committed to historically determinate transformations. Not many thinkers yoke themselves simultaneously but asynchronously to utopian as well as here-and-now imperatives, or dare to think the political with the ethical. I therefore suggest that Connolly's impassioned advocacy of secularism with a more protean and hybrid face has to be on a double register. It has to find a way to work on the contingent basis of secularism and at the same time surrender the authority of secularism to the flows of being, or the processes of becoming; that is, let the subject of knowledge be dissolved by the process of knowing.[69] Sure enough, Connolly's thought also has to face the challenge of deciding which processes of becoming are desirable, valuable, progressive, or "correct," and which are not. For surely, the politics of becoming cannot be undirected, or random, and aleatory? If that is the case, which "subject" will take charge and "in the name of what"? Is there an outside to Connolly's secularism, especially given the inter-historical and intra-historical incommensurabilities in the history of secularism? Is Connolly's project similar to the Derridean project of turning the pages of logocentrism "in a certain deconstructive way," without ever getting out of that text, or is he envisioning coevalness among different histories and experiences from a different ground?

William Connolly is a philosopher of the political, not a political philosopher. This is not a mere quibble, for a lot depends on the designation. A political philosopher philosophizes or theorizes politics from within political economy, whereas a philosopher of politics labors between two domains, two academic sovereignties. The sometimes delightful and the often frustrating relationship of incommensurability between philosophy and politics reached its climax with the advent of postmodernism, and to this day an essay by Nancy Fraser and Linda Nicholson on postmodern politics remains as valid as ever.[70] Either philosophy can be discarded as an untenable meta-ground, or it can be admitted in with profound cost to the practice of the political. Take, for example, the famous case of "binarity." I really don't think such a problem exists, pragmatically speaking, at the level of politics, or even if it does, it is not insoluble. For instance, often enough we in America bemoan the inadequacies of the two-party system. We have had diverse independent candidates such as Ross Perot and Ralph Nader, and there was Jesse Jackson's attempt to influence the Democratic Party from within by way of "the rainbow coalition." However, dissatisfaction with the two-party system is not immediately identified, rightly or wrongly, as a historical instantiation of the omni-historical phenomenon of binarity in Western thought. Within the discourse of philosophy it is a different story altogether. Binarity as such has a life of its own, as does logocentrism, and there is nothing that political praxis can do to escape the symptomatics of binarity. I am all for the deep-structure diagnosis of every palpable political problem or issue, but the challenge is how not to allow the deep diagnosis from paralyzing immediate and contextual action, or alienating praxis from its immediate historico-political configuration.

It was with this problem in mind that in a footnote to my essay on "Ethnic Identity and Poststructuralist Differance" I conjured up the following scenario.[71] There is a large crowd of people protesting against apartheid, and the city square is full of placards and signs that say "End Racism" and "Abolish Apartheid." But there is one other sign that reads "Abolish Binarity; End Logocentrism." What are these statements saying? There is a problem here with contextual readability. Surely it is understandable if most of the folks, except professors of poststructuralism, are in a state of mystification: Friend or Foe? Endorser or Heckler? A similar fate overtakes the history of the concept of representation. With the advent of postmodernism, representation "dies" philosophically or theoretically even as it continues to remain crucial – more crucial than ever before – at the level of politics. It is always easy to side with one or the other, but the really worthwhile task is to stay in the tension between the two and intervene through self-conscious praxis. All of Connolly's profound meditations on identity, difference, pluralism, and secularism are symptomatic of this uneasy disjunction. The philosophical subject and the political subject are caught up in a nameless relationship where neither can lead or follow.

To use the terms that I have been privileging all along, Connolly's thinking strives to maintain a credible tension between allegory and history. That Connolly names his passion as a passion for the politics of becoming and not the politics of secularism, or for that matter, the politics of the "becoming of secularism," establishes beyond the shadow of a doubt that he is inviting a conversation about the relationship of history to a radical ontology of change and transformation. Why else would he name his project namelessly? Is he more interested in the becoming of secularism, or in becoming as such, or to get fancy, "the becoming of becoming" without a titular subject? There is a complementary relationship between Spivak's poststructuralized practice of subalternity and Connolly's epistemologically informed advocacy of politics.

What happens to the "being" of a specific register or constituency in Connolly's politics of becoming is very similar to the fate of subaltern representation in Spivak's transactional theory.

Let us assume that Connolly is interested in the politics of becoming on a dual register. First, there is the concern *à la* Derrida, Spivak, and deconstruction, not to name the "becoming," but there is also the concern for representation, so that the register of suffering that is emerging differentially will be allowed its own temporality and duration. Now this "difference" is also politically coded and marked as "a difference from" the normative ontology.[72] This difference (let us say "ethnic difference") is indeed in a state of painful becoming and really wants "to be," and "be recognized." In this instance, where and how would Connolly's priorities play out? Would he arrest the hegemonic becoming of this particular form of difference in the name of a radical becoming? Would he insist that the arrival into being of that determinate form of difference be acknowledged only on condition that the same phenomenon also be understood as a contingent moment in the politics of becoming? The troubling hierarchical question for Connolly (as for Spivak as well as Gordimer) is how to tug at the allegorical register without pulling it as rank: how not to name in the spirit of allegory without claiming namelessness as a superior category. It would be much easier for someone like Gandhi, who is a passionately religious believer, to accept the allegorical as a transcendent *a priori* and derive politics from such a higher ground, but not for Connolly the secular anti-secular and postmodern thinker, who is negotiating with other registers without necessarily being a citizen of those registers, and without a belief in any sort of transcendent "ground" of being. Connolly's position is Kafkaesque rather than Kierkegardian in nature, in that it is a negotiation with allegory without the faith that has the capacity to embody the allegory meaningfully. It is a pseudo-allegory in search of transcendence.

Gandhi, for example, in his attempt to universalize a politics of empathy, or should I say, politicize empathy universally, could afford to rename the untouchable as Harijan on the axiomatic assumption that Hari referred to God, a Hindu God invoked as a non-denominational God. Hari is not a nonname: it is the ultimate Name in which all names find their meaning and purpose. But postmodern secularists do not have that comfort in the transcendent ontology of God. A post-Heideggerian political thinker cannot resort to the "ontico-ontological difference" except as a grounding gesture of groundlessness. There is no bridging that difference: no way to ontologize the contingency of the "gramme" into the "ousia" of presence, no way to bring about the coincidence of "the language of being" with "the being of language," and also no way to think of the "traces" of being except traces of a basic absence.[73] Within the stage of Connolly's politics of becoming, should the coming into its own of say, the "Arabic difference," (a) be necessarily dramatized on the theater of secular thought, (b) be construed as grist to the mill of allegorical becoming and thus be differentiated from its own "proper" ontology, and (c) be allowed to have its meaning in its own universe that is related to the world of secularism but is not appropriable by it? Whether one likes it or not, we are back to that intransigent tension between "who is saying" and "what is being said." I am indeed of the opinion that for the most part Connolly has done a remarkable job of aligning his phenomenological–empathic sensitivity to "affect" and "suffering" with the apparatus of representation necessary to put such impulses to political work. The only thing that is disappointing about the whole work is that he does not factor into his analysis that one macro-political index of difference: the East–West, first world–third world difference. If Connolly's advocacy of the politics of becoming is informed by an abiding solicitude for difference, then it is equally important for his thinking to examine how difference itself is different under different historico-theoretical circumstances. Beyond a cursory but significant discussion of Talal Asad's work, there is hardly any discussion of the colonial–modern genealogy of secularism.

Even if Connolly's objective is freeing the immanence of difference from the transcendent motivation of the dialectic, isn't his own project caught up recursively in a certain form of binarity: the being–becoming opposition? Isn't "becoming" as much and in much the same way haunted by ontology as "being," its binary counterpart? And if that is so, isn't "the politics of becoming" as much open to essentialization and hypostasis as the politics of being that it critiques? The difference of becoming itself cannot be a pure difference: it can only be a difference within the dialectic of binarity. Connolly is too complex and self-aware a thinker to be advocating "pure becoming" or a becoming that has no goals or direction. His thinking is symptomatic of a condition that it cannot escape: the incommensurability of the philosophical with the political. To put it somewhat crudely, politics cannot be thought through or theorized satisfactorily by philosophy, just as philosophy cannot instantiate its best utopian moments through politics. Ashis Nandy makes the comment (discussed in chapter 3) that utopian thoughts necessarily are characterized by the very flaws and contradictions of the historical moment from which they come. To apply that thought here to Connolly's work, the very longing for and the launching of a politics of becoming has to have for its starting point a determinate ontological site of "having become." The launching cannot be *ex nihilo*.

Unlike Michael Hardt and Antonio Negri, who in their book *Empire* champion the cause of immanence without really giving us sufficient reason for it, Connolly's passion for immanence, difference, and the history of the present is troubled and ambivalent. Though he certainly comes out as pro-difference when it comes to his vision and understanding of the world, he is unable to let go of the habit of the dialectic:

> I resist, then, the winter satisfaction of dialectical process without being able either to forgo its comforts at some moments or to disprove it definitively. Perhaps, even under conditions of good will, the entry of new identities into a cultural constellation, if and as they relieve palpable modes of suffering, often enough eventually engender in their turn a series of new surprises, including unexpected and poorly articulated modes of suffering. The publication of these obscure and unexpected injuries will, if we are lucky, become entangled in a new round in the politics of becoming. What if (a) the energy and suffering of embodied human beings provides a starting point from which becoming and critical responsiveness proceed and (b) no intrinsic pattern of identity/difference on the other side of suffering consolidates being as such? Would it not then be wise to maintain ethical tension between being and becoming, even to sanctify becoming so as to counter powerful tendencies normally in place to tilt ethico-political energies in the other direction?[74]

A few lines later Connolly remarks with succinct eloquence that a "dialectician is always poised in front of a final act always about to commence *or a dialectical reading of things cannot be vindicated.*"[75] Clearly, we are back to the immanence–transcendence stand-off as well as the presence–representation impasse. As Foucault puts it, albeit in a different but comparable context, in his unsparing critique of both phenomenologies – the Sartrean kind as well as the one preferred by Merleau-Ponty: "Either the cat whose good sense precedes the smile or the common sense of the smile that anticipates the cat. Either Sartre or Merleau-Ponty."[76] For Connolly, the jump into dialectical anticipation is both comforting and philosophically in bad faith, for the dialectic assumes a semantic horizon just out there, a horizon that cannot be exemplified by or instantiated in the present moment. To put a Hegelian phenomenological spin to it, the world-historical principle "in the name of which" the present moment is being read is itself alien to the present moment. It is in the name of the present moment, its experiential immanence ethically embodied as suffering, that Connolly's thinking thematizes the indifference of the dialectic to present history. The dialectic, for example, would seek to explain away eschatologically the suffering of hundreds of displaced and homeless villagers in the name of the new dam that will bring progress to the people. Connolly is distrustful of the *telos* of the dialectic that would legitimate secularism as both the horizon of being and as the unraveling of that horizon as process or becoming. Or as Nietzsche would have put it: Hegel as the body of history consummating himself with Hegel as the meaning of history.[77]

As moving and even perhaps magnificent as the paragraph from Connolly quoted above is, there are some distinct problems with his formulation. Even though he calls for a relationship of tension rather than an either/or (and I agree with him, whole heartedly and whole "headedly"), there is no mention of the tension between the ethical and the political. In the move of empathy and a non-judgmental ethical inclusiveness, the political is overlooked completely, and as a result there is no room in this model for talking about the causation of suffering by political practices of improper and illegitimate power. It is assumed automatically that the ethical register has already won its secession from politics. What is needed is not secession, but effective influence within the tension. The ethical functions beautifully, as beautifully as poignantly and ineffectually, in Connolly's fond wish and hope that "no intrinsic pattern of identity/difference on the *other side*[my emphasis] of suffering consolidates being as such." This is splendidly moving, much like some of the paradoxes in the Sermon on the Mount: "For blessed are the meek, for they shall inherit the earth." Without a doubt, much in the spirit of Spivak who would *not* want "the subaltern as perspective" to be eradicated by hegemonic success, Connolly, too, would want suffering, as register, *not* to be erased. What then is the "other" side: the binary opposite of suffering? The other side, in a world structured by dominance, in a world of the haves and the have-nots, could refer to the side that is not suffering and is perhaps responsible, consciously and unconsciously, for the suffering on this side. The suffering constituencies on this side, in a short-term sense, would want, to use Jim Morrison's words, to "break on through to the other side." No, but stop, but not really. For the other side stands for certain canonical and intrinsic ontological habits of identity and difference, and these habits are to be resisted. In no way should suffering as constituency, as against specific constituencies of suffering, be territorialized, in the name of enfranchisement, representation and hegemonization, back into the binary theatre of identity/difference. This is ethical utopianism at its very best, but where is the political pole of utopianism? So solicitous, indeed, is Connolly of the phenomenologies of emerging differences and their vulnerability to dialectic closure that he does not slow down in his ethical momentum to make room for the temporality of what I would call "political duration." How are these new forms to survive: where and within what political temporality or epistemic regime? Connolly, the postmodern philosopher of the politics of becoming, is not interested, and I use his word, in "consolidation" of any kind.

Whose consolidation and from whose or what point of view? Take, for example, the reality of emerging diasporas in the West: multiple and heterogeneous diasporas with different causations and motivations for international movement. There is clearly every reason for intellectuals and writers and thinkers and people at large to think of the diasporic condition namelessly and without consolidation as an open-ended ethical as well as epistemological possibility. But what about (and here I am not even talking about the extreme classed, gendered, and other differences within the diaspora that make it unrepresentable for other reasons) the mediation of the political that both thwarts and enables those ethical–epistemological dreams? What is a politics without consolidation, just as what is a politics without representation?

Here precisely is where I would have expected (along the lines of accountability I attempted to delineate in my discussion of Spivak) Connolly to have insisted on tension between the ethical and the political with the result that consolidation, just like representation, demands a "double thought." In other words, it is not enough to work merely with the tension between "being" and "becoming" without mapping that tension onto the tension between ethics and politics. Without the material and historically determinate mediation of the political (and that is always a drag, in that it drags the utopian–ethical down towards the ground), the very demands that Connolly is making of ethics remain impossible to fulfill, for lack of agency and direction. The emerging realities need to survive and they need to protect themselves through all kinds of subaltern bricolage even as they envision possibilities of a more radical or a second-order transformation. Part of the problem here with Connolly's discourse (and here one may see a similarity with Rosa Burger in *Burger's Daughter*) is its single-minded ethical articulation of suffering: not much on etiology, causation, history, the agent, the victim, and the relationship of the one to the other. The focus is on alleviation and not on issues of accountability, or even a contingent reversal of the power dynamic. The systemic, institutional, cultural, and national conditions of "stable being," under which suffering is relieved or new subjectivities are born, are not even brought into the picture. Ethics becomes pure allegory. Also missing is an account of the ethnicization, the minoritization, and the racialized genderization of difference in the secular modern national state. These are political conditions that need to be met with and negotiated by emerging subjectivities; and all of this happens not on the other side, but on this self-same side of lived experience.

I guess what I find missing in Connolly's rhetoric (a lack that is even more saddening because Connolly's ethical model is full of promise and rigorous hope) is the critical awareness of a constitutive double consciousness that will neither dwell acquiescingly in immanence nor resort to transcendence in violation of experience and the history of the present. The values that need to guide a contingent consolidation need to be produced from within the immanence of the present moment, but not necessarily in memorialization of that moment. If homosexuality, for example, is an emerging register of being that is being forced into the closet, then it has to come out of the closet both in a spirit of "self-consolidation" and in a spirit of defiance, questioning the very axiology that demands self-consolidation of an emerging homosexuality. It is not the one or the other, but both in double consciousness. I mean double consciousness here in a double sense: the hyphenation between the ethical and the political, as well as the hyphenation of an emerging subjectivity/constituency between "itself" and the dominant discourse or historiography. Double consciousness also involves the phenomenology as well as the ethics and the politics of "betweenness," which is both macro-political and micro-political, intra-historical and inter-historical. Connolly does not even attempt to go in that direction. For after all, what indeed would be the value of a purely ethical valorization of emerging values without the accompaniment of political legitimation? Of course, Connolly would point out right away, and rightly so, that the two are not the same, and perhaps the ethical register is the more worthwhile of the two. But that exactly is my point: it is precisely because ethics is so precious that it needs to be safeguarded not in isolation, but during a moment of tension with the political, when the latter is enough hegemony-oriented to repress or obviate the ethical altogether. When Connolly invokes the telling phrase "the politics of becoming," it is understood that it is the ethical that stands for the contingency of "becoming," whereas politics is still conceived in the old fashioned way, along paths of dominance and/or hegemony. But somewhere in his narrative, "politics" gets replaced by "becoming," and what we then get is "the becoming of becoming."

I would like to reiterate that it is precisely because I value and admire Connolly's intervention so much that I am taking the trouble of critiquing it in solidarity. The space that Connolly opens up is fraught with possibilities: all the more reason to proceed with great care and deliberation. Nothing to me is more persuasive or impressive than Connolly's engagement with "suffering." I see him engaged as a philosopher in the project of actualizing "suffering" as a staple and fundamental theme of all thought and thinking, without wanting in any way to "speak for" those who are suffering. Through philosophy, Connolly seeks a way out of an impoverished notion of "locationism" that dictates that a universal movement against suffering is not valid since not everybody suffers, or suffers in quite the same way. To mark knowledge or epistemology perennially with the register of suffering: that indeed is Connolly's objective. Mohandas Gandhi comes to mind here. One of his favorite bhajans in Gujarati runs thus: "Call him or her a Vaishnav [literally, one who follows Vishnu, one of the Hindu trinity of Brahma (Creator), Vishnu (Preserver), and Shiva (Destroyer)] who understands the pain of others or the other." The denominational Vaishnava is rendered anonymous by the definition. Gandhi's objective is also to mobilize an ethical–affective connection between those who suffer and those who understand the suffering of others. To a deeply ethical subject, suffering is that register that deconstructs the binarity of self and other.

One can indeed understand and recognize the pain and the suffering of the other and act on it as if it were one's own. It would be bizarre to imagine an ethical thinker saying something like "A good Samaritan is one who understands the pleasure of others." Though empathy as a channel is content- and value-neutral, it is only when it becomes a vehicle of universal suffering (remember Rosa Burger) that it takes on the ultimate test of ethics.

Connolly, in work after work, has raised these agonizing dilemmas passionately and perspectivally. And this particular work, in naming secularism as such as an episteme worthy of controversy, has already done a lot to concretize and historicize the Identity–Difference problematic. However, what is not at all clear to me is why Connolly does not go beyond the "West" in his delicate interrogation of secularism. Could it be that he doesn't want to be guilty of epistemic violence and invasive representation? But isn't secularism by definition a global–international phenomenon, propelled forward, among others, by the will of colonial modernity? Moreover, doesn't every normative mention of secularism point to the "other" who is anti-secular or deviantly secular and therefore politically roguish and ethically evil? Also, doesn't suffering as a theme overflow boundaries? If one were to situate Connolly's politics of becoming between "the West and the Rest," how would it unravel? How would one use the politics of becoming to understand the situation between Iraq and the United States? This is not an irrelevant question for Connolly, since he does (as indeed he should) connect secularism to the sovereignty of the nation-state, and the nation-state to a neo-Hegelian historicism. The politics of becoming, if it were to perform in remediation/rectification of the existing situation, would have to do so "in between" and relationally. Like the truths of E. M. Forster's *A Passage to India* and Joseph Conrad's *Heart of Darkness* (and in a different way, Amitav Ghosh's *The Shadow Lines*) that belong neither to the home country nor the colony, but to the space of dominant relationality where representation flounders in search of a legitimate perspective, so too should Connolly's telling insights have been made vulnerable to the space of the "between." As Gauri Viswanathan's recent work on "conversion" demonstrates, secularism was being forged in the colonies as well as in answer to the problems emerging in the mother country.[78] To adapt Rushdie somewhat: "What does secularism know about itself? It happened overseas."

Is There an Outside?

I would like to focus one last time on the directionality of "becoming" in Connolly's recommendations, and by way of exit, reiterate unevenness as an inescapable condition that has to be dealt with imaginatively so that uneven-ness may be made to work against itself, to the "good" of all concerned. How can Connolly's radicality as ethical theorist be transmitted to the realm of pol-itics? Is there room for agency? And are there ways of evaluating and predict-ing which flows and directions of becoming are worthwhile and which not? One can witness Hegel and Nietzsche in dire combat in Connolly's head. Nietzsche raises the kind of questions that are really worth asking, but alas, these questions have no answers, or the questions begin to serve as answers, in the name of open endedness. Hegel, on the other hand, is ready with answers, but they stop just short of the complexity of the questions. Sure enough, Nietzsche excoriates metaphysical thought for its sneaky anthro-pocentrism that attempts to "subjectify" the radical contingencies of process by subsuming them under an agent, a mythical subject in control. But this audacious move does not disarm the questions "becoming of what?" and "becoming in what direction?" A more productive way of understanding Nietzsche (both in the statement referred to above and in another equally famous assertion that "truth is nothing but a mobile army of anthropocentric metaphors") would be to read him as a powerful and ominous precursor to present day structuralists and poststructuralists who would rather see the subject, not as ontological through and through, but as an ontological effect produced by a highly interested and ideologically invested epistemology. But the subject effects have not been dismantled or disarmed. So it does become important to insert the subject effect back into the perennial syntax of becom-ing. Not so much "whose becoming" in a Hegelian or neo-Hegelian (the world spirit) sense, but rather the "becoming of what," and that is a very different question.

The other problem, rendered even more problematic when it is posed between two cultures or histories, is that of direction. How does any process of becoming in all its transitivity and immanence make a commitment to a particular direction? If the commitment to directionality is deemed unneces-sary, then how is one to differentiate the politics of immanent becoming from the politics of sheer contemporaneity, or the status quo? One has to take that critical step out of immanence to gesture in the direction of direction and to submit the politics of becoming to a symptomatic reading. One of the most endearing characteristics of Connolly's rhetoric throughout his book (endear-ing because it speaks for Connolly's unconditional honesty as an open-ended thinker) is that pause, that definitive hesitation, before he answers his own questions. It is as though he were succumbing to the answer not because it is the answer, but because he wishes it were the answer, but his ethical–epistemological integrity will not allow him the comfort of political closure. Thus, for example, we find him attracted by the dialectic and the solace it offers, but he cannot in all honesty accept that solace. In the ultimate analysis, he is indeed willing to accept in a neo-Hegelian spirit, somewhat uncritically and I think even dangerously, that "there is ethical value in treating the latest filling out of persons as approaching more closely to the highest standard of personhood."[79]

I think this is a sad and over-hasty concession to neo-Hegelianism. Whatever Connolly's personal reasons may be for this acceptance, the acceptance by itself falls well within the very historicism and unilinear developmentalism that he has been contesting all along. Here is the limitation to Connolly's thinking. He is still within the world of the One Reason and therefore, formally, he has no quarrels with the narratology of the coming-into-its-own of that One Reason. There is then a tacit capitulation to the "content" of the dialectic, even as there is resistance to the formal procedurality of the dialectic. How else can he be so confident about the ethical value of "the latest filling out of persons?" Is the latest embodiment of history then the best embodiment just by virtue of being the latest? And if so, then isn't such an evaluation hopelessly complicit with the rhetoric of developmentalism? Also, why and how does "personhood" become the exemplary bearer of historical progress? Personhood is typically invoked to secure the ethical (as against the political) and highlight the probity of the individual in opposition to the anonymity – as well as the corruptibility – of the collective. Not collectivities, ideologies, corporations, institutions, not macro-political formations such as colonialism, imperialism, Eurocentrism, etc. I am not implying that Connolly is not interested in a critique of macro-political formations and ideologies, but when it comes to a possible way out, it is the individual conceived of as the ethical agent who gets valorized. Suffering, too, becomes part of that register: that of individual–ethical subjectivity. I am not clear what Connolly means by "personhood," or to be more precise, in which ideological universe "personhood" is embedded. Would personhood stand for some kind of untrammeled subjectivity that is free to make choices in a spirit of ethical fullness and freedom? Or does he mean, given his self-confessed neo-Hegelianism, that the only thing that makes developmental historicism worthwhile is the objective of actualizing personhood progressively? Or could he be interpreted as saying that the platform or the conceptual register on which the world-historical spirit finds its true meaning is that of "personhood"? If that were the case, I would be genuinely concerned, for that would suggest by implication that the purpose of a neo-Hegelian historicism is the eventual sloughing off of the political and the communal/ideological/collective. All social, ideological, and political processes would then seem nothing but the unfortunately unavoidable means necessary to produce purer and purer and better and better forms of personhood. It is a bit unfortunate that Connolly does not unpack the notion of personhood more rigorously and circumstantially.

My question then for Connolly's project is this: why return to what seems like the status quo after all that radical interrogation of secularism? Neo-Hegelianism has to be negotiated with globally on a multilateral basis and not just from the confines of European becoming. How then does the European secular or post-secular subject understand and come to terms with the rise of Islamic fundamentalism or the dire "undemocratic" regime of Saddam Hussein, propped up just a few years ago by the USA in its attempt to contain an Iran-centered Islamic fundamentalism? (Even as I write there is news of the violent handling by police of anti-war protesters in Washington, DC, and Portland, ME, as part of the larger project of the "criminalization of dissent.") And, if one were to back-track some more, an Iranic fundamentalism that was an antithetical response to the Shah of Iran (the Pahlavi regime), who of course was endorsed and empowered by American foreign policy in the name of the democratization of the Middle East. And understand it must, if not for anything else, at least for reasons of geopolitical control and for the effective administration of its "oil rights," leave alone a dialogic mode of understanding the Middle East as part of a history where the West is imbricated, primarily in a mode of complicity. To apply Connolly's neo-Hegelianism here, is the "being" of Saddam Hussein or the relentless persecution of Palestinians by the State of Israel part of the latest chapter in history? The problem with Hegel is that he cannot be invoked except world-historically. Not personhood here, but a different kind of happening that is "the latest filling out" of world-historical political reality. Once Hegel is in the discourse, Connolly's discourse is in trouble.

The project of making secularism vulnerable to its many "others and out-sides" is now suddenly pulled back, thanks to Hegel, to the phenomenology of world history. Secularism is back in the saddle as the avant-garde horseman of all history. And here is how neo-Hegelianism misrecognizes Connolly's precious project. If it is indeed a project of "the politics of becoming" on behalf of the world and world history, Connolly is constrained to explain such large global situations as the USA's war on Iraq and terrorism in general. The scope and reach of the crisis of Enlightenment reason and "Western secularism" cannot be conveniently deglobalized or contained manageably within national or privatized ethical boundaries. Indeed, secular reason, renamed as "the politics of becoming," should have something to say to Saddam Hussein at his most despotic, something other than "Capitulate absolutely, without conditions." My objective in saying this is not to exonerate Saddam Hussein or to contain his dictatorship within his national boundaries, but to foster an atmosphere where critical positions either on Iraq and the USA or on Western-style democratic secularism and non-Western "fundamentalisms" and dictatorships do not get forced into the binary trap of the Bush formula: "Either you are with us, or you are against us." It should be possible to think both against the arrogance of colonial modernity and against non-Western dictatorships on a third and different register, a register that is transcendent of the Us/Them structure.

If the purpose of the critique of secularism is to enfranchise hitherto "dissed" registers of experience, it must also be acknowledged that these registers are not all lodged within one evolving neo-Hegelian historicism, but in many possible historicisms. Lurking even within the most open and generous "politics of becoming" is a tacit ideology of a "world-historical phenomenology," and this world, despite the phenomenology, is very much structured in dominance – so much structured in dominance, indeed, that even experiences as basically human as "suffering" and "dying" are being coded in national terms before they are valorized. To put it simply, in a possible war against Iraq, a war initiated by the USA, the USA is concerned only about the loss of American lives and "sufferings" marked with the stars and stripes. Pointing this out functions as a double gesture. Nothing could be more valuable, more radical, more risky than the emphasis on suffering in ethical terms; by the same token, nothing is more suspect, more open to cooptation, and more vulnerable to liberal–humanist recuperation than a unidimensional focus on suffering. It does matter: which instrument of torture, which specific abuse of power, which regime is holding the whip – all the difference between an ethical allegory of the human condition, and the condition of ethical allegory in human history.

Allegory, History, Theory

This chapter (indeed, this entire book) is premised on the reality of the unevenness that structures the relationship between "worlds within the same world," and for that matter between history and allegory. We have all seen during the last twenty years, in response to the ascendancy of theory, either in the name of postmodernism or poststructuralism, that voices have emerged in defense of history and of material circumstantiality. These voices are best expressed through the slogan raised by Fredric Jameson, "Always historicize."[80] Though this exhortation is an appropriate polemical rejoinder to the high-flying indifference of theory to lived realities, it simplifies the epistemological conditions of both theory and history. Here, in the context of my engagement in this chapter, I will say something about theory. In a certain sense, theory should indeed overlook history and "imagine" beyond, across, and against the actualities of history. I am reminded here of that wonderfully triangulated argument that Philip Sidney makes in his essay on poetry when he compares the legitimacies of Poesie, History, and Philosophy.[81] He is of course also interested in a polemics of pedagogy, and his intention, as a neo-Aristotelian, is to demonstrate that not only is Poesie the best domain of worthwhile knowledge, but also that it is the best medium through which pedagogy can be performed. Sidney dismisses history as being too close to, repetitive of, and justificatory of reality. Philosophy, on the other hand, is too ideal, too abstract, and too difficult to be available for historical exemplification and instantiation. How then to bridge the distance between "what is" and "what should be?" Of course, through literature, that golden mean between the far from desirable real and the impossible and incredible ideal, that cannot be tested for veracity for it does not profess to tell the truth. It is hilarious, for example, how Sidney, through strategic rhetorical reading, coopts Plato into the side of the poets. To Sidney, the ethics of Poesie is best safeguarded by according to it a different kind of generic accountability. Theory, too, as an intended fiction, has the obligation to overlook history in certain ways, rather than remain trapped by history that has hardened into historicism, developmentalism, empiricism, and a unilinear eschatologism. My objective is to align theory with the counter-memory of Foucault that is not reducible to the binary simplicity of forgetting versus remembering.

No one in their right minds, except the foreign policy experts that run the USA, would argue in favor of forgetting history. The contestation is not over history, but over the constructed historicity of history; and if that is the case, the call "Always historicize" needs to be re-understood.[82] Both "always" and "historicize" need to be "de-axiomatized," and by that I mean both terms need to be interrogated contingently. The term "always" has to be dangled, abyssally as it were, between the two semantic poles of its meaning: on the one hand, "always" as a transcendent temporal horizon that functions as an *a priori* that makes sense of history even though history is nothing but a series of "contemporaneities"; and on the other hand, "always" as an impossibility forever stranded in the random logic of serialization: a succession of "immanent nows" that are resistant to temporal totalization either of the ideological or the procedural/formal kind. Similarly, "historicizing" is not a transparent project that speaks in the name of reality. The project of making sense of history critically is much more than the obvious call to historicize. Between the putative objectivity of "history" and the ideological mobilization of history in the name of a heterogeneity of "the present," there is so much slippage, so much polemical and partisan oversimplification and instrumentalization; and the formula

"Always historicize" is too pious and too sanctimonious to do justice to the duplicities and deliberate misrecognitions that constitute historicity.[83]

Let us face it: there is no consensus as to what it means "to historicize," except as a rallying cry to stem certain forms of irresponsible avant-gardism. No category has come under greater deconstructive pressure than "history," and the pressure is coming from the subalterns themselves and not just from metropolitan theorists. If the concern is how to honor the problematics of history and not just to pay homage to the natural rectitude of history, then history needs to be addressed both as a problem and as the source of the answer to the problem. The objective is not just how to conserve and return to history whatever is its due, but also to escape, forget, and go beyond history in search of other and different possibilities. The Joycean sense of the nightmare of history, the Marxian desire to liberate humanity of the shackles of history, and the Nietzschean advocacy of forgetting in the name of creativity have to be thought through together with the imperative to reclaim histories, to produce a different history by rubbing dominant history against the grain, and the ethical impulse to let no moment die in the name of progress, victory, and evolution.[84] There are ways in which "the elsewhere" that history looks for as the possible topos of its utopian realization has to be produced as a function of a rigorous suspension of the historical, so that possibilities occluded by history could be made visible to a speculative theory. Of course, it goes without saying that this rigor works in both directions, since history needs to perennially call the bluff of theory, particularly when the latter begins to suspend representation and history merely as a game and as a theoretical end in itself.

I realize that the very idea of the suspension of representation and history sounds "postal" and apocalyptic in the most banal way possible. I am not talking about the end of history, whatever that may mean, or about a facile aestheticization of the political. My claim is very simple: history as it is is impoverished, is crying out for multiple, heterogeneous, and undreamt of historiographies, and for scenarios, locations, sites, and venues that do not exist except in the utopian imagination. For these sites and possibilities to be imagined both ethically and politically, history needs to be invested in on a double register: realized circumstantially and thus conserved (what is good in it) and de-realized and de-referentialized in a spirit of critical utopianism. It is only when referentiality is suspended in a spirit of critique that certain flows and realities become visible: phenomena that remain hidden when the momentum of the representational apparatus is continuously on. This suspension of referentiality is not automatic, nor is it purely formal or figural. There is agency behind it, and there are ways of differentiating between those occasions when the dominant discourse cries "time out," and when subaltern constituencies make the same cry. Thus, when referentiality stands still, as in the case of Rosa

Burger's hallucinatory moment, it is possible to spell out the politics of the moment. The "time out" is called by a member of the dominant group so that she may break her filiation with that group, and if that moment of suspension had not taken place, Rosa Burger would have been unable to align ethics with politics, theory with praxis.[85] Her ethical vision, like those of Connolly, Nandy, and Spivak, makes us see possibilities and realities that are lost in the all-too visible present–historical world. And this is the work that theory should dedicate itself to in an uneven world: bear witness, and see in ways disallowed by the forms and regimes of present history. One of the taboos, of course, is to acknowledge and reflect on unevenness, leave alone think transformatively beyond and in remediation of the unevenness.

In such a condition, it becomes necessary, to borrow from Derrida, to think "thought itself" intransitively and self-reflexively without allowing this meta-theoretical activity to degenerate into mere procedurality. I have been arguing all along, both in the context of the politics of location and that of subject positionality, that theoretical and meta-theoretical investigations ought not to be the special preserve of developed metropolitan constituencies. There is much at stake here for all constituencies: in particular, for subaltern discourses that are necessarily dependent on the apparatus of representation but are by no means exhaustible by it. Too often it is conceded that meta-theoretical and second-order deconstructive investigations into the nature of reality and representation are the sanctioned domain of the avant-garde. In this scheme of values, subaltern realities are expected to accept the blessing of representation (a blessing that they gain for themselves by learning to use the master's tool in their own agential interests) and never raise representation as such as a problem or a crisis. That job is better left to postmodernity and poststructuralism, which are advanced enough to undertake such avant-garde experimentation. It is not up to the lowly subaltern to raise the epistemological condition or the theoretical condition until after it has negotiated successfully with the historical, the political, and the economic phases. By the time this is all done – sort of – and subaltern discourse is prepared to make its own theoretical/epistemological contribution, the game of epistemology has moved on elsewhere in fulfillment of its internal momentum that cannot by definition be in sync with the subaltern chronotope. Such a ghettoization of subaltern discourses is as much to be resisted as the dangers of metropolitan seduction.

As for subject positionality, knowledge purists and identity purists need to understand that it is just not possible either to quarantine "who one is" from contamination by "where one thinks," or to sanitize "where one is" against the need to know "who one is." The dialogue between ontology and epistemology needs to go on without assurances or guarantees, but with the critical awareness that this dialogue too, like all other dialogues, is structured in dominance, enabled in unevenness. "Where one thinks" is neither a matter of absolute choice nor a non-constitutive secondary instrument that receives its mandate from "who one is." I am not arguing for a changeling or metamorphic reality where one sloughs off one identity for another, but rather (and here I follow Edward Said) for an active and rich space of "the between" responsive, not to the binary politics of identity–difference and self–other, but to possibilities of perennially shifting coalitions. The only way to offer resistance and break down asymmetry and unevenness in the long run is through the rigorous cultivation of common grounds, dreams, and possibilities that run counter to existing arrangements and regimes. In such a project the category of "where one thinks" has an important role to play. When "where one thinks" is mobilized in opposition to "where one is supposed to think," a space of critical relationality opens up that is capable of holding its own against the restrictive demands of "both culture and system."[86]

As the protagonist (who has never been to London) in Amitav Ghosh's *The Shadow Lines* remarks to Ila (who has lived in London): "I could not persuade her that a place does not merely exist, that it has to be invented in one's imagination; that her practical, bustling London was no less invented than mine, neither more nor less true, only very far apart."[87] Both Londons are imagined (i.e., they are not ontologically given), but imagined perspectivally and "with precision." It is in the course of the dialogue between your London and my London that the historicity of London and of British colonialism begins to unfold both locally and globally and as a site of coeval historical negotiation. It is in the same spirit of asymmetrical dialogue that Tridib tells his English lover, May, that the Victoria Memorial, the very presence of which in the heart of Calcutta disgusts and nauseates her, is part of his history as well, but not in the same way. Amitav Ghosh makes a valiant and an almost quixotic (I am using the adjective here positively and affirmatively to suggest the range of utopian longing in the novel) attempt to bring together or bring into mutual focus the motif of the window and that of the mirror. The window looks outward, whereas the mirror reflects oneself back to oneself in alienation as well as recognition, as recognition through alienation. Could the window be made to function as the mirror (and vice versa) to help humanity go beyond centuries of colonialist anthropology, as well as the reverse anthropologies to come in the name of subaltern/postcolonial hegemony? In a radically re-remembered and re-coordinated world that promises emerging recognitions and affiliations hitherto considered unacceptable, is it possible to see oneself through the window and the other in the mirror – imagine the world with such affective precision and cognitive generosity across the shadow lines of nationalisms and nation-states that divide, and divide again, and again, all in the name of dominant Reason? If coming and going, and home and away, nationalism and diaspora, are constantly dialogized in Ghosh's novel (so much, indeed, that often all we are left with is the figurality of the movement itself and not the solidity of either the diaspora or the nation), it is only in the utopian hope that such movement will serve to loosen up the fixity of positions hardened beyond persuasion and rendered impermeable by the state to populist impulses. Like Nandy, Ghosh also insists that it is only by going through the shadow lines of existing regimes in a certain way, and not by avoiding them, that the peoples of the world can get beyond the sovereignty of those lines. In other words, it is only through a critical engagement with the history of the present that any utopian vision can be inaugurated.

In all the contestations, necessary of course, about who can speak for whom and from what positions of expertise or experiential organicity, it must not be forgotten that the obstacle to be dismantled is unevenness in every form and manifestation. If the objective is not to remain captive as symptoms of the unevenness, but to generate a move beyond it, then clearly, the polemical positions that need to be held should be mobile enough to transcend the rigidities imposed by the unevenness. The resident and the diasporic, the proper and the improper, the inside and the outside, professional formations and grassroots projects, need to dream up an emergent cartography of daring ethico-political directions. And in this task of critical–utopian imagining, it seems to me that poststructuralism and postcoloniality have a valuable role to play: in principle, in history, and in theory.

Notes

Chapter 1 Postmodernism and the Rest of the World

1 For a thorough analysis of the impact of "capital" on the time-space of global culture, see Karl Marx, *Grundrisse: Foundations of the Critique of Political Economy*, trans. Martin Nicolaus (New York: Random House, 1973). Also see Ranajit Guha, "Dominance without Hegemony and its Historiography," in *Subaltern Studies, Vol. 6: Writings on South Asian History and Society*, ed. Guha (Delhi: Oxford University Press, 1989), pp. 210–309, for a sensitive analysis of selected formulations from *Grundrisse*.

2 The category of "process without Subject or goals" is elaborated by the French structuralist–Marxist Louis Althusser, who inflects the Leninist-Marxist concept of "the motor of history" through the discourse of structuralism. See Louis Althusser, *Essays on Ideology*, trans. Ben Brewster (London: Verso, 1984). My point is that while on the one hand NAFTA would seem to have inaugurated the seamless transnational mobility of "capital," the Zapatistas in Mexico were involved in a very different relationship with Mexican nationalism. For more on the Zapatista insurgence and the deleterious effects of NAFTA on the Zapatistas, see Alexander Cockburn, "Beat the Devil," in *The Nation*, March 28, 1994. Similarly, just when national borders are sought to be erased through economic transactions, Europe and the USA are engaged in controversies about such things as whether American whisky has the right to call itself "Scotch," and whether "Bourbon" is a proper name for liquor produced in France.

3 Walt Whitman uses the term "Nation of nations" to signify America as a mosaic formation in search of effective cultural unification.

4 For a useful typology of a variety of nationalisms, see Ernest Gellner, *Nations and Nationalism* (Oxford: Blackwell, 1983).

5 Samir Amin has theorized the notion of "unequal development" memorably, and the work of geographer Neil Smith constitutes "unevenness" as an unavoidable

category in the study of global systems. See Samir Amin, *Eurocentrism* (New York: Monthly Review Press, 1989).

6   Jean François Lyotard, *The Postmodern Condition*, trans. Geoff Bennington and Brian Massumi (Minneapolis: University of Minnesota Press, 1984).

7   Jürgen Habermas, for one, would argue that modernity has been an incomplete project, and that postmodernity is but a telling symptom of that incompletion. See Jürgen Habermas, "Modernity – an Incomplete Project" in *The Anti-Aesthetic: Essays on Postmodern Culture*, ed. Hal Foster (Port Townsend, WA: Bay Press, 1983), p. 315. For different positions on the modernist–postmodernist debate see also the contributions of Frederic Jameson, *Postmodernism, or The Cultural Logic of Late Capitalism* (Durham, NC: Duke University Press, 1991); Nancy Fraser, *Unruly Practices: Power, Discourse and Gender in Contemporary Social Theory* (Minneapolis: University of Minnesota Press, 1989), and *Justice Interruptus: Critical Reflections on the Post-socialist Condition* (New York: Routledge, 1997); Linda Hutcheon, *A Poetics of Postmodernism: History, Theory, Fiction* (New York: Routledge, 1988); and Andreas Huyssen, "Mapping the Postmodern," in *New German Critique* 33, (1984), p. 552.

8   The difference between "dominating" and "dominated" knowledges has been developed by a number of South Asian scholars. For a spirited, antagonistic engagement with the secularist episteme, see Ashis Nandy, ed., *Science, Hegemony, and Violence: A Requiem for Modernity* (Tokyo: UN University; Delhi: Oxford University Press, 1990).

9   For a careful differentiation of the "post," see Anthony Appiah, "Is the 'Post' in Postcoloniality the Same as the 'Post' in Postmodernism?" in *Critical Inquiry* 17 (1991), pp. 336–57.

10 In general, it has become customary to separate out two kinds of postmodernism: the postmodernism of play and pleasure, and a more serious postmodernism interested in oppositionality and resistance. But here, too, the privileged site has been "epistemology."

11 For an enabling articulation of universalism that functions as a critique both of Eurocentrism and Marxism, see Samir Amin, *Eurocentrism*.

12 Conrad, as an author canonized by modernism, is an interesting example of narrative practice that fails in the presence of the other. Whereas Chinua Achebe would attribute to *Heart of Darkness* a conscious fear and hatred of the "unknowability" of Africa, Edward Said gives more credence to the ambivalence in Conrad's narrative, even as he reads the text symptomatically in the context of Eurocentrism and colonialism. See Conrad, *Heart of Darkness* (Oxford: Oxford University Press 1984). See also Chinua Achebe, *Things Fall Apart* (London: Heinemann, 1958).

13 For a particularly mechanical and uninspiring application of poststructuralist self-reflexivity to third world feminism, see Julie Stephens, "Feminist Fictions, A Critique of the Category, 'Non-Western Woman in Feminist Writings on India,'" in *Subaltern Studies, Vol. 6: Writings on South Asian History and Society*, ed. Ranajit Guha (Delhi: Oxford University Press, 1989), pp. 92–125. See also Susie Tharu, "Response to Julie Stephens," in the same volume, pp. 126–31.

14 See Edward W. Said's essay on Camus' Algerian politics, "Narrative, Geography, and Interpretation," in *New Left Review*, 180 (1990), pp. 81–107. See also his *Culture and Imperialism* (New York: Alfred Knopf, 1993) for further discussions of overlapping territories and relationships between the center and the periphery.

15 See the collection of essays, *Postmodernism/Jameson/Critique*, ed. Douglas Kellner (Washington, DC: Maisonneuve Press, 1989), for more on the nature of the "critique" as a form of knowledge.

16 "Where does the critique come from?" is a pertinent question that is raised and discussed by Ranajit Guha in his essay, "Dominance without Hegemony and its Historiography," in *Subaltern Studies, Vol. 6: Writings on South Asian History and Society*, ed. Guha (Delhi: Oxford University Press, 1989), pp. 210–309.

17 I would refer here to the work of Raymond Williams, to whom alternatives for change were more important than mere systems-building or a deterministic celebration of technology. See his *Politics of Modernism* (London: Verso, 1989).

18 See Ella Shohat, "Notes on the 'Post-Colonial,'" in *Social Text* 31/32 (1992), pp. 99–113. See also my essays, "Ethnic Identity and Poststructuralist Difference," in *Cultural Critique* (spring 1987), and "Postcoloniality and the Boundaries of Identity," in *Callaloo*, special issue on "Post-Colonial Discourse," ed. Tejumola Olaniyan (fall 1993), p. 164.

19 The notion of "decapitation" is discussed at length by Jacques Derrida in *Dissemination* as he analyses the nature of "entitlement" and "disentitlement" in the context of Mallarmé's poetry. Jacques Derrida, *Dissemination*, trans. Barbara Johnson (Chicago, IL: University of Chicago Press, 1981). For a discussion of the decapitation of history by theory, see my essay, "The Changing Subject and the Politics of Theory," in *differences*, 2.2 (1990), pp. 126–52, and in *Diasporic Mediations: Between Home and Location* (Minneapolis: University of Minnesota Press, 1996).

20 This flying away from history could also be read as postmodernism's rejection of a Marxian dialectic.

21 Jean Baudrillard's treatment of America, for example, is virtual and not historical.

22 See Raymond Williams' posthumously published *Politics of Modernism* for a critique of such a hypostasis of theory. See also Tony Pinckney's introduction to that volume.

23 For a wide-ranging discussion of Western guilt in the context of global ecology and the Earth Summit held in Rio de Janeiro, June 1992, see Akhil Gupta, "Peasants and Global Environmentalism: Safeguarding the Future of 'Our World' or Initiating a New Form of Governmentality," part of a forthcoming book and a talk presented at the Agrarian Studies Seminar (Yale University, March 25, 1994). See also Edward W. Said, "Intellectuals in a Postcolonial World," in *Salmagundi*, (spring/summer 1986), pp. 70–1, for an insightful exhortation to go beyond the politics of blame and guilt.

24 I refer here to Jean François Lyotard and Jean-Loup Thébaud, *Just Gaming*, trans. Wlad Godzich (Minneapolis: University of Minnesota Press, 1985).

25   African-American intellectuals like Cornel West and bell hooks have eloquently articulated the "postmodern difference within" the first world. See the interview with Cornel West in *Universal Abandon: The Politics of Postmodernism*, ed. Andrew Ross (Minneapolis: University of Minnesota Press, 1988), pp. 268–86.

26   For a polemical discussion of "hybridity," see my "Postcoloniality and the Boundaries of Identity," p. 164.

27   Nadine Gordimer thinks through this issue of conscience in the context of "white relevance" in post-apartheid South Africa in her collection of essays, *The Essential Gesture: Writing, Politics and Places* (New York: Alfred Knopf, 1988). See also Stephen Clingman's introduction to that volume, p. 115.

28   See Gayatri Chakravorty Spivak, "Can the Subaltern Speak?" in *Marxism and the Interpretation of Culture*, ed. Cary Nelson and Lawrence Grossberg (Urbana: University of Illinois Press, 1988), pp. 271–313. See also my essay, "Towards an Effective Intellectual," in *Intellectuals: Aesthetics/Politics/Academics*, ed. Bruce Robbins (Minneapolis: University of Minnesota Press, 1990), and in *Diasporic Mediations: Between Home and Location* (Minneapolis: University of Minnesota Press, 1996.)

29   By "feminization" I mean the ethico-political authority of feminism which functions both as a "special interest" and as a general perspective with the capacity to influence the overall scheme of things. For a brilliant argument that advocates the generalization of feminist historiography, see Kumkum Sangari and Sudesh Vaid's introduction to *Recasting Women: Essays in Indian Colonial History* (New Brunswick, NJ: Rutgers University Press, 1989), p. 126.

30   See Gayatri Chakravorty Spivak's essay, "Feminism and Critical Theory," in *In Other Worlds: Essays in Cultural Politics* (London: Methuen, 1987) pp. 77–92 and 277–80, for a provocative conjunctural articulation of feminist theoretical agendas.

31   See the special issues of *Social Text* 31/32 (1992) and *Callaloo* (fall 1993) on postcoloniality for discussions of the "post." See also Aijaz Ahmad's *In Theory* (London: Verso, 1992), and Arif Dirlik's essay, "The Postcolonial Aura: Third World Criticism in the Age of Global Capitalism," in *Critical Inquiry*, 20 (2) (1994), pp. 328–56.

32   See the collection *Feminism/Postmodernism*, ed. Linda Nicholson (New York: Routledge, 1990), and Nancy Fraser's *Unruly Practices*.

33   See Edward W. Said's *The World, The Text, The Critic* (Cambridge, MA: Harvard University Press, 1983) for a sustained advocacy on behalf of "worldliness."

34   See *Third World Women and the Politics of Feminism*, ed. Chandra Mohanty, Ann Russo, and Lourdes Torres (Bloomington: Indiana University Press, 1991); *Feminist Genealogies, Colonial Legacies, Democratic Futures*, ed. Chandra Mohanty and M. Jacqui Alexander (New York: Routledge, 1997); *This Bridge Called My Back: Writings by Radical Women of Color*, ed. Gloria Anzaldua and Cherry Moraga (New York: Kitchen Table/Women of Color Press, 1983).

35   Both Chandra Talpade Mohanty and Lata Mani in their work have consistently addressed the problematics as well as the potentialities of "location." See Mohanty, Russo, and Torres, *Third World Women and the Politics of Feminism*, and Lata Mani, "Multiple Mediations: Feminist Scholarship in the Age of Multinational Reception," in *Inscriptions* 5 (1989), p. 123.

36   Gayatri Chakravorty Spivak has undertaken in quite a pervasive manner this
      project of the epistemological critique of identity as such, in conjunction with a
      strategic practice of essentialism for certain political ends. See Gayatri Chakravorty
      Spivak, *The Postcolonial Critic* (New York: Routledge, 1990).
37   See the work of Peggy Kamuf, Naomi Schor, and others in this regard.
38   I refer here to Michel Foucault's essay "Nietzsche, Genealogy, History," in *Language,
      Countermemory, Practice*, trans. Donald F. Bouchard and Shery Simon (Ithaca, NY:
      Cornell University Press, 1977), pp. 139–64, where he reads Nietzsche radically in
      the name of "present history."
39   See Jacques Derrida, "Structure, Sign, and Play in the Human Sciences," in *Writing
      and Difference*, trans. Alan Bass (Chicago, IL: University of Chicago Press, 1978),
      pp. 278–93, 339.
40   Gilles Deleuze and Félix Guattari's *Anti-Oedipus: Capitalism and Schizophrenia*,
      trans. Robert Hurley, Mark Seem, and Helen R. Lane (New York: Richard Seaver
      Press, 1977), is written in the vein of flows and energies. See also Foucault's intro-
      duction to that volume. Also refer to Gilles Deleuze and Michel Foucault's *The
      Foucault Phenomenon: The Problematics of Style*, trans. Sean Hand (Minneapolis:
      University of Minnesota Press, 1986), and Paul Bove's foreword to that volume,
      pp. vii–xl.
41   In spite of all this brave "border busting" and the travel of commodities, we are
      witnessing virulent forms of racism and xenophobia in the West when it comes to
      the migration or movement of people from the underdeveloped to the developed
      world. Even in the area of economics and trade, Western governments are con-
      stantly following an "industrial policy" though their laissez-faire chauvinism will
      not let them identify their practices as policy. See Arjun Appadurai, "Patriotism
      and Its Futures," in *Public Culture* 5 (3) (1993), pp. 411–25, and Bruce Babbitt,
      "Free Trade and Environmental Isolationism," in *New Perspectives Quarterly* 9 (3)
      (1992), pp. 35–7.
42   See Anuradha Dinghwaney Needham, "Inhabiting the Metropole: C. L. R. James
      and the Postcolonial Intellectual of the African Diaspora," in *Diaspora* 2 (3) (1993),
      pp. 281–303. For a more exhaustive treatment of this theme, see Edward W. Said,
      Culture and Imperialism (New York: Alfred Knopf, 1993), and Aijaz Ahmad's
      chapter on Said in *In Theory* where Ahmad, in my reading, thoroughly misreads
      the nature of Said's critical agency, and constitutes "metropolitan ambivalence" as
      a cardinal sin against the third world.
43   See Slavoj Žižek's *Enjoy Your Symptom: Jacques Lacan in Hollywood and Out* (New
      York: Routledge, 1992). See also the interview with Žižek in *Found Object*, 2 (1993),
      pp. 93–110.
44   See Gayatri Chakravorty Spivak, *The Postcolonial Critic*. See also Satya P. Mohanty's
      essay on Toni Morrison's *Beloved* and the issue of identity politics, "The Epistemic
      Status of Cultural Identity: On *Beloved* and the Postcolonial Condition," in
      Cultural Critique 24 (spring 1993), pp. 41–80.
45   See Michel Foucault, "Theatrum Philosophicum," in *Language, Countermemory,
      Practice*.

46   Chinua Achebe, in his celebrated essay on Conrad's *Heart of Darkness*, makes the point that even when Marlow grants humanity to the African, the African is always perceived as a junior. See Achebe, *Things Fall Apart.*

47   In modernist work after modernist work, Africa becomes the backdrop for the working out of the European psyche, and in a real way the "forwardness" as well as the complexity of the psychological enterprise is posited on the simple backwardness of Africa. For a critical reading of modernity in terms of gender, see Alice Jardine, *Gynesis: Configurations of Woman and Modernity* (Ithaca, NY: Cornell University Press, 1986).

48   Gauri Viswanathan's *The Masks of Conquest* (New York: Columbia University Press, 1989), as well as her essay "Raymond Williams and British Colonialism: The Limits of Metropolitan Cultural Theory," demonstrates this thesis with clarity. See *Views from the Border Country: Raymond Williams and Cultural Politics*, ed. Dennis L. Dworkin and Leslie H. Roman (New York: Routledge, 1993), pp. 217–30.

49   The point to be made here is that the axiomatic force of binarity has been coextensive with the authority of anthropological thought.

50   See *The Invention of Tradition*, ed. Terence Ranger and Eric Hobsbawm (Cambridge: Cambridge University Press, 1983).

51   Dipesh Chakrabarty's essays in *Representations* and *Public Culture* take up the question of "who is speaking for the Indian past," as well as the native's obsession with colonialist historiography. See "Postcoloniality and the Artifice of History: Who Speaks for 'Indian' Pasts?" in *Representations*, 37 (winter 1992), p. 125, and "The Death of History? Historical Consciousness and the Culture of Late Capitalism," in *Public Culture* 4 (2) (1992), pp. 47–65.

52   The vicious development of Hindutva in India today is a conscious political practice to "other" the Muslim and secure for Hindutva the legitimacy of nationalism. Madhu Kishwar and others have been compelled to question such an ideological fixing of the meaning of Hinduism and in the process call the bluff of the Hindu zealots.

53   Here again, Jameson's work has been crucial for, more than most other Marxists, he has accepted the cultural logic of postmodernism without at the same time relinquishing the ethico-political mandate of Marxian thought. See Jameson's *Postmodernism, or The Cultural Logic of Late Capitalism.*

54   Much of this problem with narrative can be subsumed under the general rubric "legitimation crisis." Lyotard's *Postmodern Condition* discusses at some length the relationship between narrative and the epistemic authority of knowledge.

55   For a postmodern interrogation of the aprioristic status of "value," see Donald Barthelme's *The Dead Father* (New York: Farrar, Straus, and Giroux, 1975).

56   Philosophical discussions of *En-Soi* and *Pour-Soi* have been fundamental to Western thought. See in particular Jean-Paul Sartre's elaboration of these concepts in his *Being and Nothingness*, trans. Hazel E. Barnes (New York: Philosophical Library, 1956).

57   One of the most poignant delineations of this invisibility of the subaltern self has been Ralph Ellison's *Invisible Man* (New York: Random House, 1952). Fyodor

Dostoevsky's *Notes from Underground*, trans. Mirra Ginsberg (New York: Bantam Books, 1974), is a powerful forerunner.

58 Gayatri Spivak's distinction between the two meanings of "representation" in her essay "Can the Subaltern Speak?" (pp. 271–313) has been most illuminating.

59 Michael Ryan's *Marxism and Deconstruction: A Critical Articulation* (Ithaca, NY: Cornell University Press, 1982) faces the same problem of assigning priorities. Are Marxism and deconstruction coordinated in an equal relationship, or is deconstruction to be instrumentalized in the service of Marxism?

60 I refer here to Anthony Appiah's essay, "Is the 'Post' in Postcoloniality the Same as the 'Post' in Postmodernism?" *Critical Inquiry* 17 (winter 1991), pp. 336–57.

61 See Homi K. Bhabha, "Dissemination, Time, Narrative, and the Margins of the Modern Nation," in *Nation and Narration*, ed. Bhabha (London: Routledge, 1990), pp. 291–322.

62 See Benedict Anderson, *Imagined Communities: Reflections on the Origins and Spread of Nationalism* (London: Verso, 1991).

63 See my "Postcoloniality and the Boundaries of Identity."

64 The Lacanian algebra completely preempts the specificity of a historically located semantics.

65 See Partha Chatterjee's *Nationalist Thought and the Colonial World: A Derivative Discourse?* (London: Zed Books, 1986) for a lucid discussion of the East–West divide via nationalism. See also his later work, *The Nation and Its Fragments* (Princeton, NJ: Princeton University Press, 1993).

66 One of the characters in Salman Rushdie's *Satanic Verses* (New York: Viking, 1988) expresses this idea succinctly: "What do the English know of their history? It happened overseas."

67 See Homi K. Bhabha, *The Location of Culture* (New York: Routledge, 1994).

68 Audre Lorde develops and points out the limitations of this strategy of using the master's weapons to destroy the master's house.

69 The term "politics of location" goes back to Adrienne Rich's essay, "Notes Toward a Politics of Location," in *Rich, Blood, Bread and Poetry: Selected Prose 1979–1985* (New York: Norton, 1986).

70 Lata Mani, "Multiple Mediations: Feminist Scholarship in the Age of Multinational Reception," in *Inscriptions*, special edition on "Traveling etc.," ed. Vivek Dhareshwar and James Clifford, 5 (1989), p. 123.

71 I am using the term "totality" to reinvigorate it as a Marxian concept to question the immanence of the "fragment" and its autonomy. See *Aesthetics and Politics*, ed. Ronald Taylor (London: New Left Books, 1977), with an afterword by Frederic Jameson.

72 The notion of "ethnoscape" is developed persuasively by Arjun Appadurai in "Disjuncture and Difference in the Global Cultural Economy," in *Public Culture* 2 (2) (spring 1990), p. 124.

73 See my "Postcoloniality and the Boundaries of Identity."

74 See Homi K. Bhabha, "Interrogating Identity: The Postcolonial Prerogative," in *The Anatomy of Racism*, ed. D. T. Goldberg (Minneapolis: University of Minnesota Press, 1990), pp. 183–209.

75 For a compelling elaboration of "double-coding," see Kumkum Sangari, "The Politics of the Possible," in *The Nature and Context of Minority Discourse*, ed. David Lloyd and Abdul Jan Mohamed (Oxford: Oxford University Press, 1990).

76 See Spivak's *In Other Worlds*, and her *Outside in the Teaching Machine* (New York: Routledge, 1993).

77 I would like to make an analogous connection between the question of language and the question of knowledge. We must not forget that Volosinov/Bakhtin emphasized the reality that language itself is the contested terrain and not a mere non-ideological vehicle of meaning.

78 See Edward Said, "Third World Intellectuals and Metropolitan Culture."

79 The "beyond" is to be conceived as a proactive seeking out of alternative knowledges, value systems, and worldviews.

80 See also the work of theorists such as Vandana Shiva, *Staying Alive: Women, Ecology and Development* (Delhi: Kali for Women, 1988); Ashis Nandy, ed., *Science, Hegemony, and Violence: A Requiem for Modernity* (Tokyo: UN University; Delhi: Oxford University Press, 1990); and Alok Yadav, "Nationalism and Contemporaneity: Political Economy of a Discourse," in *Cultural Critique*, 26 (1993–94), pp. 191–229. For a hopeful and populist take on nationalism, see David Lloyd, *Anomalous States: Irish Writing and the Post-Colonial Moment* (Durham, NC: Duke University Press, 1993).

81 Madhu Kishwar, "Why I Do Not Call Myself A Feminist," *Manushi* 62 (1990), p. 28.

82 See the *Inscriptions* 6 (1992) special issue on "Orientalism and Cultural Differences," ed. Mahmut Mutman and Meyda Yegenoglu. In particular, see the essay by Françoise Lionnet.

83 One of the most influential books in this area is Edward Soja's *Postmodern Geographies* (London: Verso, 1989). Equally illuminating is David Harvey's *Condition of Postmodernity* (Oxford: Blackwell, 1989).

84 It is to Michel Foucault that we owe this notion of "heterotopia." See Michel Foucault, "Heterotopias," in *Diacritics* (spring 1986), p. 22–7.

85 Amitav Ghosh, *The Shadow Lines* (London: Bloomsbury, 1988).

86 A. K. Ramanujan has identified and analyzed the mirror–window dyadic function in Tamil poetry. See the introduction to *Folktales from India*, ed. Ramanujan (India: Viking, Penguin, 1993), pp. xiii–xxxii.

87 In this context I would like to make a qualitative distinction between the need – a postcolonial one – for transcendence as delineated by Ghosh through the character of Tridib in *The Shadow Lines*, and the colonialist cartography of Conrad.

88 The French feminists (Hélène Cixous and Catherine Clement in particular) have worked on strategies to empower the Imaginary against the Symbolic. See their *Newly Born Woman*, trans. Betsy Wing (Minneapolis: University of Minnesota

Press, 1986). Deleuze and Guattari have critiqued Freud and "the Oedipus" along similar lines in *Anti-Oedipus*. See also Franz Kafka's *Letter to His Father* for a poignant rendition of an incurably Oedipalized condition that has no direct access to the Mother.

89 I owe the insight that the "postmodern" should be "post-Western" to an essay on Du Bois that I refereed anonymously.

90 Amin, *Eurocentrism*, p. 152.

91 The controversy over *Miss Saigon* is a case in point. See Yoko Yoshikawa, "The Heat is On Miss Saigon Coalition: Organizing Across Race and Sexuality," in *The State of Asian America: Activism and Resistance in the 1990s*, ed. Karin Aguilar San Juan (Boston, MA: South End Press, 1994), pp. 275–94.

Chapter 2 The Use and Abuse of Multiculturalism

1 In many ways, Ralph Ellison's critique of "monopolated whiteness" in *Invisible Man* (New York: Random House, 1952) still remains valid in the context of assimilation and integration. See also W. E. B. Du Bois' *The Souls of Black Folk* (New York: Penguin Books, 1996) for a profoundly diagnostic reading of African-American "double consciousness." Ali Behdad's essay, "INS and Outs: Producing Delinquency at the Border," *AZTLAN: A Journal of Chicano Studies*, 23, 1 (spring 1998), pp. 103–14, goes a long way in illuminating how deep rooted the notion of the "other" is in notions of American citizenship and sovereignty.

2 Among the many collections that have been published on the topic of multiculturalism, *Multiculturalism: A Critical Reader*, edited by David Theo Goldberg (Oxford: Blackwell, 1994), is remarkable for its range of positions. For a more recent intervention on the drama of multiculturalism as it unfolds in England, see Brian Barry, "The Muddles of Multiculturalism," *New Left Review*, 8 March/April (2001), pp. 49–71.

3 Jacques Derrida makes this crucial distinction between "centered play" and "the center in play" in his celebrated essay "Structure, Sign, and Play in the Human Sciences," in *Writing and Difference*, trans. Alan Bass (Chicago, IL: University of Chicago Press, 1978).

4 Johannes Fabian develops the notion of "coevalness" in his work, *Time and the Other: How Anthropology Makes its Object* (New York: Columbia University Press, 1983). See also Satya Mohanty's ongoing work, which seeks to find post-positivist ways of talking about one history in terms of another.

5 There has been no greater or more complex advocate of "the big O" than Jacques Lacan, whose work has constantly underscored the transcendent importance of "the Other who knows no other."

6 Though Žižek's work in general focuses on the importance of the category of "universality," I refer here in particular to his book *The Ticklish Subject* (London: Verso, 1999). Equally relevant here is William Connolly's work on secularism and the ethos of pluralism.

7   For more on the relationship between ontological stability or the depth of being
    and loss of sovereignty through the process of mirroring, see Michel Foucault's
    The Order of Things: An Archaeology of the Human Sciences, trans. Alan Sheridan
    (New York: Vintage, 1973), in particular, the section on "the analytic of finitude."
8   The works of Emmanuel Levinas and Edward Said, each in their own way, high-
    light the tensions between ethical and political notions of accountability. See also
    Adrienne Rich, Simon Critchley, and Alenka Zupancic.
9   This inviolable space of the Lacanian Real has been ably theorized by Žižek. See
    also the contributions of Chantal Mouffe and Ernesto Laclau, who attempt to co-
    ordinate a critical space between Marxism and psychoanalysis.
10 William Julius Wilson's work focuses on justice and Lani Guinier's sophisticated
    critique of a winner-take-all democracy cost her her nomination by President
    Clinton.
11 Jacques Derrida deals with the notion of "the parergon" in *The Truth of Painting*,
    trans. Geoff Bennington and Ian McLeod (Chicago, IL: University of Chicago
    Press, 1987), and thematizes the relationship between the frame and what is in the
    frame.
12 Judith Butler's work on hate speech is particularly remarkable for the manner in
    which it instrumentalizes poststructuralist theory for a political cause. See also
    David Scott's discussion of Orlando Patterson's theorization of the relationship of
    freedom to slavery in chapter 3 of his book *Refashioning Futures: Criticism after
    Postcoloniality* (Princeton, NJ: Princeton University Press, 1999).
13 William Connolly's *Why I am not a Secularist* (Minneapolis: University of
    Minnesota Press, 1999) explores the politics of becoming by way of Nietzsche
    and argues how a normative secularism preempts and colonizes possibilities of
    becoming.
14 See the dialogue between Michel Foucault and Noam Chomsky in *Reflexive Water:
    The Basic Concerns of Mankind*, ed. Fons Elders (London: Souvenir, 1974), where
    the two philosophers, while they concur on what is to be done, differ radically
    when it comes to accounting for the nature of concepts such as justice, freedom,
    human nature, etc.
15 This is a notion rigorously developed by Foucault in *The Order of Things*.
16 Chantal Mouffe's *The Democratic Paradox* (London: Verso, 2000) differentiates
    agonism from antagonism.
17 Terry Eagleton's essay in *Nationalism, Colonialism, and Literature*, ed. Terry
    Eagleton, Fredric Jameson, and Edward W. Said (Minneapolis: University of
    Minnesota Press, 1990), makes the powerful argument that the objective of revo-
    lutionary movements should be to diagnose and understand oppression in all its
    specificity, such as women's oppression and class oppression, but goes on to argue
    that the purpose of such an understanding is not to perpetuate the hegemony of
    these categories. These categories are meant to be transcended in the name of a
    full and indivisible humanity.
18 There is a poignant scene in Nadine Gordimer's *Burger's Daughter* (Har-
    mondsworth: Penguin Books, 1979) in which a donkey is mercilessly flayed by an

African. Gordimer's portrayal is simultaneously allegorical and historical: historical to the extent that there is a determinate agent of oppression, and allegorical to
the extent that the reality of the whip transcends, namelessly as it were, the determinacy of historical agency towards an omni-historical horizon.

19 See Judith Butler's discussion of the slave–master relationship in Hegel in *The
Psychic Life of Power: Theories in Subjection* (Stanford, CA: Stanford University
Press, 1997).

20 Pheng Cheah's recent work on the spectrality of nationalism, by way of Derrida,
focuses on the nature and the production of the collective subject.

21 See Edward W. Said, *The World, the Text, the Critic* (Cambridge, MA: Harvard
University Press, 1983), especially the chapters "Secular Criticism" and "Criticism
between Culture and System."

22 See Derrida's discussion of the double session in *Dissemination*, trans. Barbara
Johnson (Chicago, IL: University of Chicago Press, 1981).

23 Charles Taylor, "The Politics of Recognition," in *Multiculturalism: A Critical Reader*,
ed. David Theo Goldberg (Oxford: Blackwell, 1994), pp. 75–106.

24 See the collection of essays *Cosmopolitics*, ed. Bruce Robbins and Pheng Cheah
(Minneapolis: University of Minnesota Press, 1998).

25 Taylor, "The Politics of Recognition," p. 75.

26 I refer here to Partha Chatterjee's brilliant articulation of nationalism in the third
world in his *Nationalist Thought and the Colonial Word: A Derivative Discourse?*
(London: Zed Books, 1986).

27 See Etienne Balibar and Immanuel Wallerstein's *Race, Nation, Class: Ambiguous
Identities* (London: Verso, 1991), a book that is a philosophical and theoretical
demystification of the claims of nationalism.

28 The movie *Being John Malkovich* (1999) is a hilarious and though-provoking look
into the ontological as well as the performative nature of what it means "to be"
anybody.

29 Charles Taylor, "The Politics of Recognition," in *Multiculturalism: A Critical Reader*,
ed. David Theo Goldberg (Oxford: Blackwell, 1994), p. 83.

30 Paul Bove makes a similar point in his critique of Charles Taylor's egregious mis-
recognition of Foucault's politics – a misrecognition that has everything to do with
Taylor's philosophical humanism that disavows its political and ideological
"unconscious." See Bove's foreword to Gilles Deleuze and Michel Foucault's *The
Foucault Phenomenon: The Problematics of Style*, trans. Sean Hand (Minneapolis:
University of Minnesota Press, 1986), pp. vii–xl.

31 Nancy Fraser, *Justice Interreptus: Critical Reflections on the "Post-socialist"
Condition* (New York: Routledge, 1997).

32 This is the point Chinua Achebe makes in his response to Conrad: Conrad may
well have problematized the Eurocentric narrative from within, but this does not
prevent his narrative from inferiorizing and/or infantilizing the African point of
view. Europe does not need to school itself in Africa, whereas Africa has to follow
in European footsteps. The same point was made by Jayakanthan, the preeminent
contemporary Tamil novelist. When he asked if he had read Sartre, he retorted

instantly, "Has Sartre read me?" Dipesh Chakrabarty theorizes this issue brilliantly in his book, *Provincializing Europe: Postcolonial Thought and Historical Difference* (Princeton, NJ: Princeton University Press, 2000).

33 Kumkum Sangari's essay "Politics of the Possible," in *The Nature and Context of Minority Discourse*, ed. David Lloyd and Abdul Jan Mohamed (Oxford: Oxford University Press, 1990), parses the double-coding that characterizes a number of postcolonial novels that straddle East and West.

34 See Anthony Appiah, "Is the 'Post' in Postcoloniality the same as the 'Post' in Postmodernism?" *Critical Inquiry* 17 (1991), pp. 336–57.

35 Charles Taylor in the *Multiculturalism Reader*, p. 98.

36 T. S. Eliot's essay "Tradition and the Individual Talent," in *Critical Theory Since Plato*, ed. Hazard Adams (New York: Harcourt Brace, 1991), takes up the problem of what it means to honor a contemporary work in the name of a tradition. To Eliot, the present work by itself is incapable of creating standards for evaluation: it is the tradition that makes valorization possible. The real question in the constitution of tradition is that of perspective: is tradition a way of aligning what is contemporary with the canonical, or is tradition-building another name for problematizing the past from the point of view of the present? In Gadamerian terms, how is the fusion of horizons between past and present to be attempted and realized?

37 See my essay "Aesthetic Truth: Production or 'Letting Be,'" in *Maps and Mirrors: Topologies of Art and Politics*, ed. Steve Martinot (Chicago, IL: Northwestern University Press, 2001), pp. 304–18. See also Dipesh Chakrabarty, *Provincializing Europe*, especially the introduction, pp. 4–23.

38 See Akhil Gupta, *Postcolonial Developments* (Durham, NC: Duke University Press, 1998).

39 See Thomas Keenan, *Fables of Responsibility: Aberrations and Predicaments in Ethics and Politics* (Stanford, CA: Stanford University Press, 1997).

Chapter 3 Globalization, Desire, and the Politics of Representation

1 Fredric Jameson, "Notes on Globalization as a Philosophical Issue," in *The Cultures of Globalization*, ed. Fredric Jameson and Masao Miyoshi (Durham, NC: Duke University Press, 1998), p. 54.

2 For a rigorous analysis of the relationship between nationalism and super nationalism, see Etienne Balibar and Immanuel Wallerstein, *Race, Nation, Class: Ambiguous Identities* (London: Verso, 1991).

3 Noam Chomsky, "Free Trade and Free Market: Pretense and Practice," in *The Cultures of Globalization*, ed. Fredric Jameson and Masao Miyoshi (Durham, NC: Duke University Press, 1998), p. 361.

4 See Akhil Gupta, *Postcolonial Developments: Agriculture in the Making of Modern India* (Durham, NC: Duke University Press, 1998), for more on the genealogy of "underdevelopment" as it is used to essentialize "indigenous" modes of production.

5 See Praul Bidwai and Achin Vinaik, *New Nukes: India, Pakistan, and Global Disarmament* (Northampton, MA: Interlink Books, 2000).

6 See, in particular, *New Left Review* 238 (1999) and *The Nation*, January 31, 2000; April 24, 2000; May 8, 2000.

7 It is of course impossible to use the phrase "derivative discourse" without immediately acknowledging Partha Chatterjee's ground-breaking work, *Nationalist Thought and the Colonial World: A Derivative Discourse?* (Tokyo: UN University, 1986).

8 For a succinct and insightful diagnosis of the pitfalls of postcolonial historiography, see Dipesh Chakrabarty, "Postcoloniality and the Artifice of History: Who Speaks for 'Indian' Pasts?" in *Representations* 37 (winter 1992), pp. 1–26. Also, see his book, *Provincializing Europe: Postcolonial Thought and Historical Difference* (Princeton, NJ: Princeton University Press, 2000).

9 For a postcolonial critique of postmodernity, see chapter 1 of this volume, also published in *The Pre-Occupation of Postcolonial Studies*, ed. Fawzia Afzal-Khan and Kalpana Seshadri-Crooks (Durham, NC: Duke University Press, 2000), pp. 37–70.

10 Slavoj Žižek has been relentless in his insistence on the importance of the big O in the project of reconceptualizing universalism. See, in particular, *The Ticklish Subject* (London: Verso, 1999), and "Cyberspace, or, How to Traverse the Fantasy in the Age of the Retreat of the Big Other," in *Public Culture*, 10 (3) (spring 1998), pp. 483–513.

11 See "Talking 'Anarchy' with Chomsky," in *The Nation*, April 24, 2000, pp. 28–30.

12 See Ralph Ellison, *Invisible Man* (New York: Random House, 1952), p. 7.

13 See Nestor Garcia Canclini, *Hybrid Cultures: Strategies for Entering and Leaving Modernity*, trans. Christopher L. Chiappati and Silvia L. Lopez (Minneapolis: University of Minnesota Press, 1995).

14 See Edward W. Said, "Traveling Theory," in *The World, the Text, the Critic* (Cambridge, MA: Harvard University Press, 1983). For an articulation of "contrapuntal" reading strategies, see Said's *Culture and Imperialism* (New York: Alfred Knopf, 1993).

15 For a brilliant co-articulation of the metropolitan with the postcolonial, see Gayatri Chakravorty Spivak, "Reading *The Satanic Verses*," in *Outside in the Teaching Machine* (New York: Routledge, 1993), pp. 217–41.

16 Ashis Nandy, "Towards a Third World Utopia," in *Traditions, Tyranny, and Utopias: Essays in the Politics of Awareness* (Oxford: Oxford University Press, 1992), p. 21.

17 Ibid: p. 21.

18 Ibid.

19 For a similar appeal to the ethico-political from the standpoint of economics, see Amartya Sen, *Development as Freedom* (New York: Alfred Knopf, 1999).

20 For a passionate and eloquent appeal against the winner-take-all model, see Lani Guinier, *The Tyranny of the Majority* (New York: Free Press, 1994).

21 For more on the relationship of self-centered to other-oriented imaginings, see T. N. Madan, *Pathways: Approaches to the Study of Society in India* (Oxford: Oxford University Press, 1994).

22   For more on exotopy, see Mikhail Bakhtin, *The Dialogic Imagination*, trans. Caryl Emerson and Michael Holquist (Austin: University of Texas Press, 1981).

23   Slavoj Žižek and Judith Butler, along Hegelian–Lacanian lines, have discussed the master–slave relationship throughout their writings.

24   See Veena Das, "Subaltern as Perspective," in *Subaltern Studies, Vol. 6: Writings on South Asian History and Society*, ed. Ranajit Guha (Delhi: Oxford University Press, 1989), pp. 310–24.

25   For passionate and theoretically astute elaborations of borderly existential phenomenologies, see Gloria Anzaldua, *Borderlands/La Frontera: The New Mestiza* (San Francisco, CA: Aunt Lute, 1987), and Trinh T. Minhh-ha, *Woman, Native, Other* (Bloomington: Indiana University Press, 1989).

26   Ashis Nandy, *Traditions, Tyranny, and Utopias* (Oxford: Oxford University Press, 1992), p. 22.

27   Theorists such as William Connolly and Giorgio Agamben, each in his own way, have been attempting in their work to articulate a transformative praxis between pure form and/or procedurality and the determinacy of specific ideological contents.

28   Amitav Ghosh, *The Shadow Lines* (New York: Viking Penguin, 1988), p. 29.

29   Ibid: p. 3.

30   I refer here of course to "filiation" and "affiliation" as developed by Edward Said in his essay "Secular Criticism" in *The World, the Text, the Critic* (Cambridge, MA: Harvard University Press, 1983).

31   Rustom Bharucha's *In the Name of the Secular: Contemporary Cultural Activism* (Oxford: Oxford University Press, 1998) takes up the concept of *sarva dharma sama bhava* and provides a useful analysis of the relationship of humanity to itself through denominational variants.

32   For more on the colonialist gaze in the context of colonial female sexuality, see Meyda Yegenoglu, *Colonial Fantasies: Towards a Feminist Reading of Orientalism* (Cambridge: Cambridge University Press, 1998).

33   For a provocative reading of the relationship of the "agonistic" to the "antagonistic" in the context of modern democracy, see Chantal Mouffe, *The Democratic Paradox* (London: Verso, 2000). See also Judith Butler, Ernesto Laclau, and Slavoj Žižek, *Contingency, Hegemony, Universality: Contemporary Dialogues on the Left* (London: Verso, 2000).

34   For more on the nature of the ethical in the context of Lacan and Kant, see Alenka Zupancic, *Ethics of the Real: Kant, Lacan* (London: Verso, 2000). See also Simon Critchley, *Ethics, Politics, Subjectivity* (London: Verso, 1999).

35   I refer here to bell hooks' essay, "Eating the Other," in *Black Looks: Race and Representation* (Boston, MA: South End Press, 1992), pp. 21–39.

36   This entire register of the big O is of course the profound effect of Lacan's thought on the contemporary project of ethicizing the political.

37   For more on the joys and perils of recognition, see chapter 2 of this volume, where I discuss in great length the contributions of Charles Taylor and Nancy Fraser, among others, to the politics of multiculturalism.

38   For more on the epistemological relationship between poststructuralism and
     postcoloniality/subalternity, see Gayatri Chakravorty Spivak, "Subaltern Studies:
     Deconstructing Historiography," in *In Other Worlds: Essays in Cultural Politics*
     (London: Methuen, 1987), pp. 197–221, 299–301. See also John Beverley,
     Subalternity and Representation: Arguments in Cultural Theory (Durham, NC:
     Duke University Press, 1999).

Chapter 4 Derivative Discourses and the Problem of Signification

1   Amitav Ghosh, *The Shadow Lines* (Delhi: Ravi Dayal Publishers, 1988).
2   I am reminded here of the movie *Hiroshima, Mon Amour* (1959), scripted by
    Marguerite Duras, where the theme is also that of love between two people: one
    French, and the other Japanese.
3   The reference here is to Antonio Gramsci, who insists that an inventory
    needs to be made of the many traces of the past so that the present may be
    understood.
4   Without a doubt, the reference here is to the category of "double consciousness"
    as articulated by Du Bois in *The Souls of Black Folk* (New York: Pengiun Books,
    1996). For an interesting application of Du Bois to the South Asian context, see
    Vijay Prashad, *The Karma of Brown Folk* (Minneapolis: University of Minnesota
    Press, 2000).
5   The idea of "traveling theory" was initiated by Edward Said in his essay of the same
    title, initially published in *Raritan* 1 (3) (winter 1982), pp. 41–67, and republished
    as a chapter in his book, *The World, the Text, the Critic* (Cambridge, MA: Harvard
    University Press, 1983).
6   Paul Gilroy's *The Black Atlantic* (Cambridge, MA: Harvard University Press, 1992)
    is a persuasive historical–theoretical rendition of the double-conscious African-
    American condition *vis-à-vis* modernity.
7   Edward W. Said, "Intellectuals in a Post-colonial World," *Salmagundi* 70–1
    (spring/summer 1986), pp. 44–81.
8   See Jacques Derrida, *Negotiations: Interventions and Interviews*, trans. Elizabeth
    Rottenberg (Stanford, CA: Stanford University Press, 2002), pp. 11–40.
9   Edward W. Said, *Culture and Imperialism* (New York: Alfred Knopf, 1993).
10 I am reminded here of Amitav Ghosh's crisp and persuasive rejection of the very
    category of "Commonwealth Literature" for the simple reason that the kind of
    world where this category made sense does not exist any more.
11 For more on Eurocentrism, post-Eurocentrism, and their relationship to global-
    ization, see Arif Dirlik, "Globalization as the End and the Beginning of History,"
    in *Rethinking Marxism* 12 (4) (winter 2000), and R. Radhakrishnan, "We are the
    World, but Who are We, and How do We Know?" forthcoming in *Rethinking
    Marxism* (spring 2003).
12 The "voyage within" is a concept that Edward Said develops in *Culture and
    Imperialism*.

13 Ernst Renan's essay "What is a Nation?" in *Nation and Narration*, ed. Homi K. Bhabha (London: Routledge, 1990) makes conceptual connections between the making of a nation and willed patterns of remembering and forgetting.

14 For more on this, see chapter 2, this volume.

15 See *Cosmopolitics*, ed. Pheng Cheah and Bruce Robbins (Minneapolis: University of Minnesota Press, 1998), Tim Brennan, *At Home in the World: Cosmopolitanism Now* (Cambridge, MA: Harvard University Press, 1997), Rob Nixon, *London Calling: V. S. Naipaul, Postcolonial Mandarin* (New York: Oxford University Press, 1992), and R. Radhakrishnan, "Towards an Eccentric Cosmopolitanism," in *Positions* 3.3 (1995), pp. 814–21.

16 See Partha Chatterjee, "Nationalism as a Problem in the History of Ideas," in his *Nationalist Thought and the Colonial World* (Minneapolis: University of Minnesota Press, 1993).

17 See R. Radhakrishnan, *Diasporic Mediations: Between Home and Location* (Minneapolis: University of Minnesota Press, 1996).

18 David Harvey, among others such as Neil Smith, Edward Soja, and Henri LeFebvre, has been particularly insightful in the way he has combined questions of phenomenology, history, and lived experience with postmodern notions of epistemic spatiality.

19 Ghosh, *The Shadow Lines*, p. 21.

20 For more on "imagining with precision," see chapter 3, this volume.

21 Walter Mignolo, *Local Histories/Global Designs: Coloniality, Subaltern Knowledges and Border Thinking* (Princeton, NJ: Princeton University Press, 2000), part two, "I Am Where I Think," p. 89.

22 Salman Rushdie, *The Satanic Verses* (New York: Viking/Penguin, 1988).

23 Judith Butler, among others such as Žižek, has intervened powerfully in unpacking the master–slave dialectic. See, in particular, *The Psychic Life of Power* (Stanford, CA: Stanford University Press, 1997).

24 See Ashis Nandy, "Notes Towards a Third World Utopia," in *Traditions, Tyranny, and Utopias* (Delhi: Oxford University Press, 1992).

25 The concept of the *addas* as social space is developed brilliantly by Dipesh Chakrabarty in *Provincializing Europe: Postcolonial Thought and Historical Difference* (Princeton, NJ: Princeton University Press, 2000).

26 See Chakrabarty's *Provincializing Europe*.

27 Jacques Derrida's *Dissemination*, trans. Barbara Johnson (Chicago, IL: University of Chicago Press, 1981), deals with the theme of the materiality of writing and the valorization of writing by the king who himself cannot write.

28 Partha Chatterjee, *Nationalist Thought and the Colonial World* (Minneapolis: University of Minnesota Press, 1993).

29 See Ngugi wa Thiong'O, *Decolonizing the Mind* (London: James Curry, 1986).

30 Ngugi's novel *A Grain of Wheat* (London: Heinemann, 1986) is a memorable depiction of the poisoned moment of independence: both liberation and mourning.

31 Homi Bhabha has been quite brilliant in the way he has developed notions of pedagogical authority and the performative in the shaping of national consciousness. See his essay, "Dissemination: Time, Narrative, and the Margins of the Modern Nation," in *Nation and Narration*, ed. Bhabha (New York: Routledge, 1990).

32 Gayatri Chakravorty Spivak, "Deconstructing Historiography," in her book, *In Other Worlds* (London: Methuen, 1987).

33 Gayatri Chakravorty Spivak, "Can the Subaltern Speak?" in *Marxism and the Interpretation of Culture*, ed. Cary Nelson and Lawrence Grossberg (Urbana: University of Illinois Press, 1988).

34 See R. Radhakrishnan, "Towards an Effective Intellectual: Foucault or Gramsci?" in *Diasporic Mediations* (Minneapolis: University of Minnesota Press, 1996).

35 Frantz Fanon's statement occurs in *Black Skin, White Masks*, trans. Charles Markmann (New York: Grove Press, 1967), p. 31. For more on a poststructuralist elaboration of Fanon, see Homi Bhabha's essay on Fanon, "Interrogating Identity: Frantz Fanon and the Postcolonial Prerogative," in *The Location of Culture* (New York: Routledge, 1994). See also Neil Lazarus, *Nationalism and Cultural Practice in the Postcolonial World* (New York: Cambridge University Press, 1999), for a vigorous disagreement with Bhabha's rendition of Fanon. See also Ibish Hussein's doctoral thesis on "The Ethical Dilemmas of the Postcolonial Intellectual," Department of Comparative Literature, University of Massachusetts, Amherst, 2001.

36 Du Bois in *The Souls of Black Folk* makes the famous declaration that Europe, too, is part of his intellectual–aesthetic formation.

37 Ghosh, *The Shadow Lines*, p. 29.

38 Jacques Derrida, *Monolingualism of the Other: or, Prosthesis of Origin*, trans. Patrick Mensah (Stanford, CA: Stanford University Press, 1998), p. 7. For an interesting use of Derrida's formulation in the context of Indian nationalism and secularism, see Satish Kolluri's doctoral dissertation, Department of Communication Studies, University of Massachusetts, Amherst, 2001.

Chapter 5 Theory in an Uneven World

1 Adrienne Rich, "Notes Towards a Politics of Location," in *Rich, Blood, Bread and Poetry: Selected Prose 1979–1985* (New York: Norton, 1986).

2 See *Feminism and Postmodernism*, ed. Nancy Fraser and Linda Nicholson (New York: Routledge, 1990). See also *Feminism as Critique*, ed. Seyla Benhabib and Drucilla Cornell (Minneapolis: University of Minnesota Press, 1987).

3 *This Bridge Called My Back: Writings by Radical Women of Color*, ed. Gloria Anzaldua and Cherry Moraga (New York: Kitchen Table/Women of Color Press, 1983), and *Third World Women and the Politics of Feminism*, ed. Chandra Mohanty, Ann Russo, and Lourdes Torres (Bloomington: Indiana University Press, 1991), are two of the finest collections of essays to have raised the issue of the difference of color within Western feminism.

4   For more on the ongoing debates about the intersections of gender, sexuality, and the national state, see *Nation and Narration*, ed. Homi K. Bhabha (London: Routledge, 1990), *Nationalisms and Sexualities*, ed. Andrew Parker, Mary Russo et al. (New York: Routledge, 1991), *Scattered Hegemonies: Postmodernity and Transnational Feminist Practices*, ed. Caren Kaplan and Inderpal Grewal (Minneapolis: University of Minnesota Press, 1994), and *Feminist Genealogies, Colonial Legacies, Democratic Futures*, ed. Chandra Mohanty and M. Jacqui Alexander (New York: Routledge, 1997).

5   I refer here of course to Audre Lorde's famous formulation of the strategy of "using the master's tools to dismantle the master's house."

6   Nadine Gordimer, *Burger's Daughter* (Harmondsworth: Penguin Books, 1979). Some of the important critics who have contributed richly to the growing body of scholarship on Nadine Gordimer are Stephen Clingman, Elizabeth Meese, and Abdul JanMohamed. For a critical exchange on *Burger's Daughter*, see the essays by Elizabeth Meese and R. Radhakrishnan in *Feminism and Institutions: Dialogues on Feminist Theory*, ed. Linda Kauffman (Oxford: Blackwell, 1989).

7   It is impossible to mention "embodiment" without reference to the works of Michel Foucault and Donna Haraway.

8   The strategy of "rubbing history against the grain" as the hallmark of historical materialism was developed by Walter Benjamin.

9   This critical distinction is made by Edward Said in his critical essay on Michel Foucault in *The Foucault Reader*, ed. David Couzens Hoy (Oxford: Blackwell, 1986).

10   It is not coincidental that Gordimer has Rosa Burger menstruating as she comes out of prison, and commenting within herself on the process of menstruation as something that turns her inside out, even as she faces the larger political situation "without." Several feminist critics have found Gordimer wanting in her advocacy of a gendered feminist politics of resistance.

11   Much has been written about allegory. Of particular importance is Paul de Man's distinction between allegory and symbolism, both in his *Blindness and Insight* (Minneapolis: University of Minnesota Press, 1983) and *Allegories of Reading* (New Haven, CT: Yale University Press, 1979). In the context of postcolonial nationalism, see Aijaz Ahmad's critique, in his book *In Theory* (London: Verso, 1992), of Fredric Jameson's allegorical endorsement of third world nationalisms.

12   Hélène Cixous for one has called a certain "male-dominant" tendency to idealize critical negativity as nothing more than "building a monument to the lack," in a psychoanalytic sense. Lacanian feminists, however, would refute such a characterization.

13   The term "coevalness" comes from Johannes Fabian's work, *Time and the Other: How Anthropology Makes its Object* (New York: Columbia University Press, 1983) and the "chronotope" goes back to Mikhail Bakhtin.

14   The intersection of history and psychoanalysis marks the relationship of the empirical here and now to the elsewhereness of psychoanalytic thought and diagnostic insight.

15 See Nadine Gordimer, *The Essential Gesture: Writing, Politics and Places* (New York: Alfred Knopf, 1988).

16 Dominick LaCapra's work on "empathy" goes much farther than liberal–humanist notions that keep empathy captive to the histrionics of the dominant historiography.

17 The predicate of the animal or the inhuman has been a consistent theme of Coetzee's work, in particular *Disgrace* (New York: Viking, 1999).

18 Nadine Gordimer, *Burger's Daughter*, p. 208.

19 See Fredric Jameson, *The Political Unconscious: Narrative as a Socially Symbolic Act* (Ithaca, NY: Cornell University Press, 1981).

20 For a phenomenological understanding of the nature of perception and visuality, see Maurice Merleau-Ponty, *The Visible and the Invisible*, ed Claude LeFort, trans. Alphonso Lingis (Evanston, IL: Northwestern University Press, 1968).

21 Lacanian theorists, in particular Slavoj Žižek, have been attempting to reformulate the category of "the universal" by way of reviving the authority of the big O in the context of the historical relationships among historical selves and others.

22 It is Michel Foucault who enables this entire politics of discourse, both by way of his "analytic of finitude" in *The Order of Things: An Archaeology of the Human Sciences*, trans. Alan Sheridan (New York: Vintage, 1973), and the category of the subject position as articulated in *The Archaeology of Knowledge*, trans. Alan Sheridan (London: Tavistock, 1972).

23 For more on this Mobius strip-like figurality in the context of diasporic subjectivity, see R. Radhakrishnan, *Diasporic Mediations: Between Home and Location* (Minneapolis: University of Minnesota Press, 1996), in particular the introduction.

24 The worlding of the world is developed phenomenologically by Martin Heidegger in the context of the "earth–world" relationship in his essay, "The Origin of a Work of Art." Spivak develops the same problematic in the context of the third world. The significant question is this: is the third "world" different in any way?

25 Aijaz Ahmad, in an egregiously erroneous and unself-reflexive reading, takes Said to task for his critical ambivalence and eclectic critical practices. See Ahmad, *In Theory*.

26 The famous/notorious statement by Derrida in *Of Grammatology* that there is "nothing outside the text" continues to cause fraught debates about the "being of textuality" and the "textuality of being," rather reminiscent of a similar debate about the "language of being" and the "being of language" in the context of Martin Heidegger.

27 Immanuel Kant theorizes the category of "purposeless purposiveness" as an aesthetic category. We could perhaps also think of the old man in Hemingway's *Old Man and the Sea* as embodying and exemplifying the same principle, as he does his task ethically and aesthetically, even though deprived of public kudos.

28 For more on this, see *Orientations: Mapping Studies in the Asian Diaspora*, ed. Kandice Chuh and Karen Shimakawa (Durham, NC: Duke University Press, 2001), in particular the essays by Dipesh Chakrabarty and R. Radhakrishnan.

29 See W. E. B. Du Bois, *The Souls of Black Folk* (New York: Pengiun Books, 1996), and Paul Gilroy's *The Black Atlantic* (Cambridge, MA: Harvard University Press, 1992) for the advantages and disadvantages of double consciousness.

30 Samir Amin and Neil Smith, among others, have focused on "unevenness" as a geopolitical structure.

31 Judith Butler's *Gender Trouble: Feminism and the Subversion of Identity* (New York: Routledge, 1990) remains a classic in this field.

32 See Edward W. Said, "Secular Criticism," in *The World, the Text, the Critic* (Cambridge, MA: Harvard University Press, 1983), and *Beginnings: Intention and Method* (New York: Basic Books, 1975). Also see the work of critics like Mahmud Mutman and Aamir Mufti, who have further unpacked Said's notion of the secular.

33 For a fascinating discussion of Said as a "border intellectual," see Abdul JanMohamed's essay in *Edward Said: A Critical Reader*, ed. Michael Sprinker (Cambridge, MA: Harvard University Press, 1993).

34 See Edward Said's autobiography, *Out of Place: A Memoir* (New York: Alfred Knopf, 1999).

35 For a provocatively ground-breaking reading of the genealogy of reason in the historical context of colonial modernity, see "Nationalism as a Problem," in Partha Chatterjee's *Nationalist Thought and the Colonial World: A Derivative Discourse?* (Minneapolis: University of Minnesota Press, 1993).

36 Among recent postcolonial interrogations of Enlightenment Reason, Dipesh Chakrabarty's *Provincializing Europe: Postcolonial Thought and Historical Difference* (Princeton, NJ: Princeton University Press, 2000) and *Habitations of Modernity: Essays in the Wake of Subaltern Studies* (Chicago, IL: University of Chicago Press, 2002), and Gayatri Chakravorty Spivak's *The Postcolonial Critique of Reason: Toward a History of the Vanising Moment* (Cambridge, MA: Harvard University Press, 1999), are outstanding in their range and critical acumen.

37 Jean-Luc Nancy, Philippe Lacou-Labarthe, and Iris Marion Young have made memorable contributions to the "reasonable possibility" of community. There, behind it all, of course, is Foucault's understanding of the constructedness of madness: a construction undertaken by Reason as it delivers its monologue on "madness."

38 Rustom Bharucha, *In the Name of the Secular: Contemporary Cultural Activism in India* (Delhi: Oxford University Press, 1998), p. 16.

39 There is always the treacherous ambiguity of the algebraic nature of the pronoun that both invites and derails nominalization. Thus, in the story of Ulysses and Polyphemus, Ulysses gets away with his blinding of the mighty Cyclops by virtue of his name, "Noman." The Cyclops really believes that "Noman" has blinded him, and hence his situation is beyond redress, for no man is accountable for the deed. But this same logic of the indeterminate pronoun can take a different direction, as in the American policy against terrorism. It is precisely because *no one* or *no ones* have been identified as the perpetrators of the deed, the paranoid might of the USA can write itself a *carte blanche* that authorizes attack on one and all: just about everybody. The superpower, in a unipolar world, is able to get away with an

all-out war on unnamed opponents in the name of a global and generalized war on terrorism as such.

40   Foucault's essay on "Governmentality" makes the point that the state both collectivizes and individuates at the same time, thus rendering "subjection" unrescuable from the iron grid of official binarity.

41   See Gauri Viswanathan's *The Masks of Conquest* (New York: Columbia University Press, 1989) and *Outside the Fold: Conversion, Modernity and Belief* (Princeton, NJ: Princeton University Press, 1998).

42   Rudolf Carnap, among the positivists, was the fiercest of them all in his polemical "witch hunt" of all forms of fuzzy and existential thinking.

43   Jacques Derrida, "Structure, Sign, and Play in the Human Sciences," in *Writing and Difference*, trans. Alan Bass (Chicago, IL: University of Chicago Press, 1978).

44   *Suya Dharisanam*, in Jayakanthan Sirukathaigal, *The Short Stories of Jayakanthan* (India: National Book Trust, 1973), pp. 101–19.

45   Madhu Kishwar, in essays such as "Why I Do Not Call Myself A Feminist," *Manushi* 62 (1990), pp. 2–8, has been consistently posing the question of "which Tradition," "which Hinduism."

46   For a deconstructive elaboration of the pharmakon, see Jacques Derrida, *Dissemination*, trans. Barbara Johnson (Chicago, IL: University of Chicago Press, 1981).

47   S. Shankar, in an essay on the cultural politics of translation, "Midnight's Orphans, or A Postcolonialism Worth Its Name" forthcoming in *Cultural Critique*, offers a stimulating non-Western version of postcoloniality.

48   Gayatri Chakravorty Spivak, "Can the Subaltern Speak?' in *Marxism and the Interpretation of Culture*, ed. Cary Nelson and Lawrence Grossberg (Urbana: University of Illinois Press, 1988), pp. 271–313, and "Deconstructing Historiography," in *In Other Worlds: Essays in Cultural Politics* (London: Methuen, 1987).

49   For more on this issue of representation, see R. Radhakrishnan, "Towards an Effective Intellectual: Foucault or Gramsci?" in *Diasporic Mediations* (Minneapolis: University of Minnesota Press, 1996).

50   Antonio Gramsci, *Selections from the Prison Notebooks*, ed. and trans. Quintin Hoare and Geoffrey Nowell Smith (New York: International Publishers, 1971).

51   For an affective and critical account of the psychic and psychological effects of colonialism, see Ashis Nandy, *The Intimate Enemy* (Delhi: Oxford University Press, 1983), and Ngugi wa Thiong'O, *Decolonizing the Mind* (London: James Curry, 1986).

52   Gayatri Chakravorty Spivak, *The Postcolonial Critic* (New York: Routledge, 1990).

53   See Veena Das, "The Subaltern as Perspective," in *Subaltern Studies, Vol. 11*, ed. Ranajit Guha (Delhi: Oxford University Press, 1989).

54   See Lani Guinier, *The Tyranny of the Majority* (New York: Free Press, 1994).

55   For a poignant fictional account of how the "morning after" decolonization could degenerate into the "mourning after," see Ngugi wa Thiong'O, *A Grain of Wheat* (London: Heinemann, 1986).

56   The disagreement between Sartre and Camus, both in the context of communism after Stalin, and the realities of French colonialism, still remains a classic. Camus'

prioritization of his mother's safety, in the name of the ethical, trivializes the macro-political significance of colonialism. It is not coincidental that until the end Camus, unlike Sartre, never supported Algerian independence. See also Edward Said's critical reading of Camus in *Culture and Imperialism* (New York: Alfred Knopf, 1993). In a related manner, Emmamuel Levinas' absolute ethical sensibility essentializes itself as a "first philosophy" that does very little to influence his outrageously Zionist position on the Palestinian issue.

57 William Connolly, *Why I am not a Secularist* (Minneapolis: University of Minnesota Press, 1999).

58 See Ashis Nandy, *The Savage Freud and Other Essays on Possible and Retrievable Selves* (Princeton, NJ: Princeton University Press, 1995).

59 Connolly, *Why I am not a Secularist*, p. 3.

60 Michel Foucault, *Madness and Civilization: A History of Insanity in the Age of Reason*, trans. Richard Howard (New York: Vintage, 1973).

61 Dipesh Chakrabarty, *Provincializing Europe*.

62 Walter Benjamin, "The Task of the Translator," in *Illuminations*, trans. Harry Zohn (New York: Schocken, 1968), pp. 69–82.

63 All the socially revolutionary movements in Tamil Nadu, like the Dravida Kazhakam (DK) and its offshoot, Dravida Munnetrakkazhakam (DMK), were all atheistic in nature.

64 See Frantz Fanon on nationalist consciousness in *The Wretched of the Earth*, trans. Constance Farrington (New York: Grove Press, 1968).

65 Connolly, *Why I am not a Secularist*, p. 4.

66 Ibid: p. 20.

67 I cannot think of a more profound or more incisive theoretical–ideological critique of nationalism than Etienne Balibar and Immanuel Wallerstein's *Race, Nation, Class: Ambiguous Identities* (London: Verso, 1991).

68 See William Connolly, *The Ethos of Pluralization* (Minneapolis: University of Minnesota Press, 1995).

69 The distinction between the Being and the "being of Being" of course goes back to Martin Heidegger and the concept of the "ontico-ontological difference." For powerful and politically revolutionary articulations of Heidegger, see the works of William V. Spanos, in particular *America's Shadow: An Anatomy of Empire* (Minneapolis: University of Minnesota Press, 2000).

70 See the essay by Fraser and Nicholson in *Feminism and Postmodernism*, ed. Fraser and Nicholson.

71 R. Radhakrishnan, "Ethnic Identity and Poststructuralist Difference," in *Diasporic Mediations: Between Home and Location* (Minneapolis: University of Minnesota Press, 1996).

72 In his appreciative critique of Deleuze, Michel Foucault makes the point that within the dialectic regime of thought, "difference as such" is constrained to finds its meaning as "difference from" and "difference within" the regnant taxonomic imperatives. See Foucault, "Theatrum Philosophicum," in *Language, Counter-Memory, Practice: Selected Essays and Interviews*, trans. Donald F. Bouchard and Sherry Simon (Ithaca, NY: Cornell University Press, 1977), pp. 165–96.

73 I refer here to Martin Heidegger's attempt, particularly in his later work, to authenticate the supplementarity of language in the name of being. For a powerful reading both of the extraordinary freedom as well as the limitations of Heidegger's destruction of metaphysics and ontotheology, see Jacques Derrida, "Ousia and Gramme," in *The Margins of Philosophy*, trans. Alan Bass (Chicago, IL: University of Chicago Press, 1982).

74 Connolly, *Why I am not a Secularist*, pp. 70–1. See also Michael Hardt and Antonio Negri, *Empire* (Cambridge, MA: Harvard University Press, 2000).

75 Ibid: p. 71.

76 Michel Foucault, "Theatrum Philosophicum," p. 175.

77 See Friedrich Nietzsche, *The Use and Abuse of History*, trans. Adrian Collins (Indianapolis, IN: Bobbs-Merrill, 1949).

78 See Gauri Viswanathan, *Outside the Fold*.

79 Connolly, *Why I am not a Secularist*, p. 70.

80 On the question of history and its relationship to subaltern theory, see R. Radhakrishnan, "Why History, and Why Now?" in *Interventions*, Fall 2003.

81 Philip Sidney, *A Defence of Poetry*, ed. J. A. Van Dorsten (Oxford: Oxford University Press, 1973).

82 David Scott's book, *Refashioning Futures: Criticism after Postcoloniality* (Princeton, NJ: Princeton University Press, 1999) is an inspiring attempt to rethink history in response to subaltern and postcolonial experiences. Even as he pays critical attention to the concept of "usable pasts," Scott has the intellectual courage and integrity to problematize "history as such" from a subaltern perspective.

83 For more on this theme of "history as a problem," see R. Radhakrishnan, "Why History, Why Now?" forthcoming in *Interventions*, Fall 2003.

84 Among the many memorable texts that deal with revisionism and the reclaiming of history, I would like to single out Toni Morrison's *Beloved* and Adrienne Rich's poem "Diving into the Wreck" for the exquisite manner in which they combine memory and counter-memory, the pain of the political and the pleasure of the aesthetic.

85 Rosa Burger, when she returns to South Africa after her apolitical sojourn in Europe, is able to align her politics with her ethics in the context of the struggle against apartheid. She goes to jail again, without privilege, as herself and not as Lionel Burger's daughter. See Stephen Clingman's admirable biography of Bram Fischer, *Bram Fischer: Afrikaner Revolutionary* (Amherst: University of Massachusetts Press, 1998), the historical person who provided the fictional basis for the character, Lionel Burger.

86 Edward W. Said, "Criticism between Culture and System," in *The World, the Text, the Critic*.

87 Amitav Ghosh, *The Shadow Lines* (New York: Viking Penguin, 1988), p. 21.

Index